Garfield
BLOTS OUT THE SUN

BY JIM DAVIS

Ballantine Books • **New York**

A Ballantine Books Trade Paperback Original

Published in the United States by Ballantine Books, an imprint of The Random House Publishing Group,
a division of Random House, Inc., New York.

BALLANTINE and colophon are registered trademarks of Random House, Inc.

ISBN 978-0-345-46615-0

Printed in the United States of America

www.ballantinebooks.com

9 8 7 6 5 4

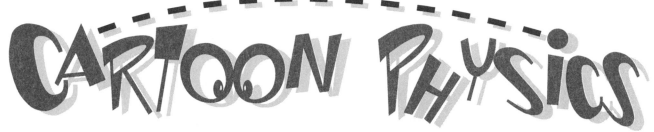

CARTOON PHYSICS

Forget the law of gravity! Cartoons follow the law of laughter. Here's Garfield's goofy guide to this silly science.

Fig. 1

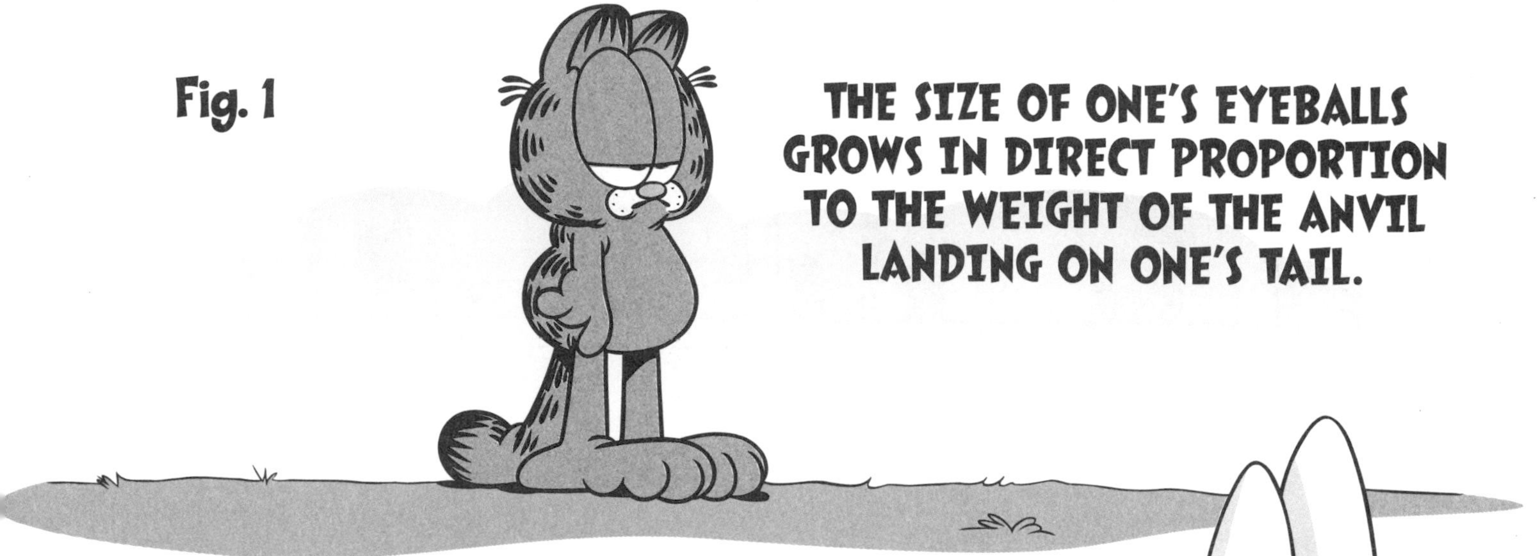

THE SIZE OF ONE'S EYEBALLS GROWS IN DIRECT PROPORTION TO THE WEIGHT OF THE ANVIL LANDING ON ONE'S TAIL.

Fig. 2

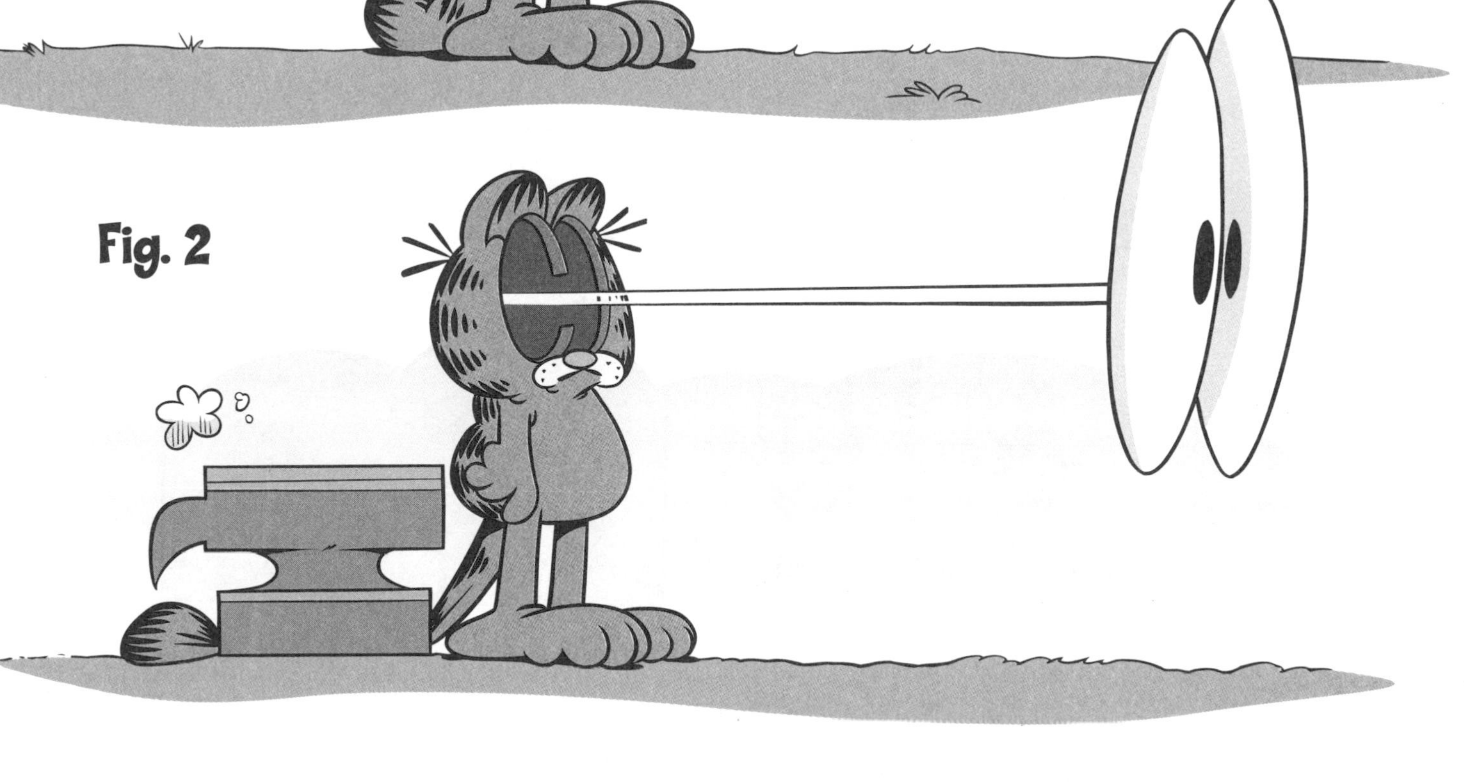

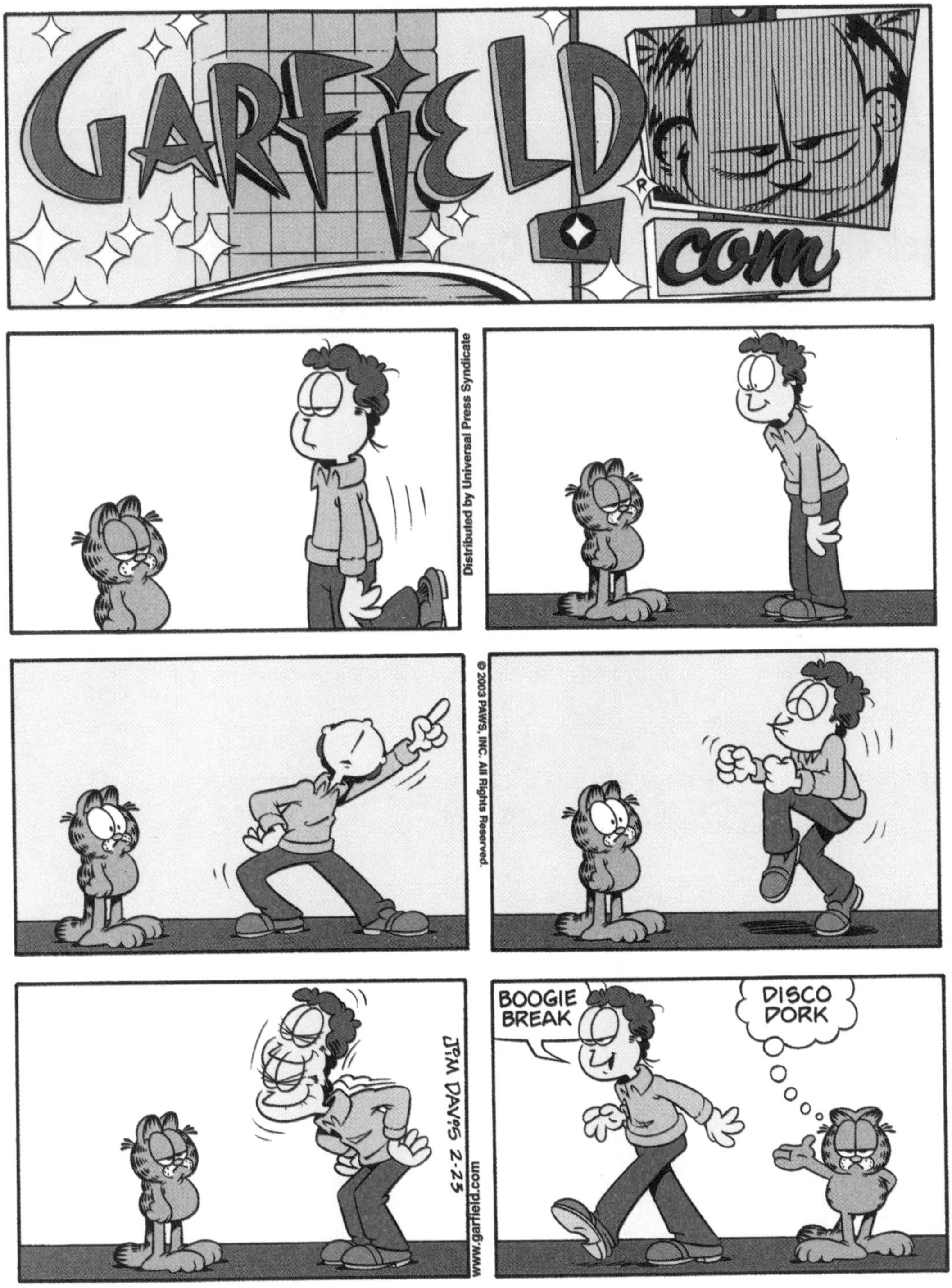
GARFIELD
.com
Distributed by Universal Press Syndicate
© 2003 PAWS, INC. All Rights Reserved.
JIM DAVIS 2-23
www.garfield.com
BOOGIE BREAK
DISCO DORK

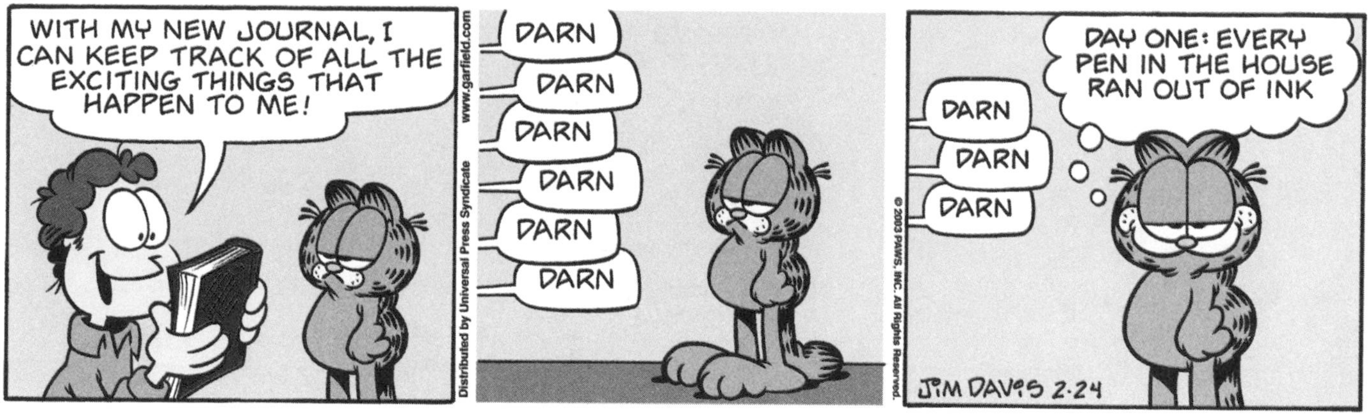
WITH MY NEW JOURNAL, I CAN KEEP TRACK OF ALL THE EXCITING THINGS THAT HAPPEN TO ME!
Distributed by Universal Press Syndicate www.garfield.com
DARN
DARN
DARN
DARN
DARN
DARN
© 2003 PAWS, INC. All Rights Reserved.
DARN
DARN
DARN
DAY ONE: EVERY PEN IN THE HOUSE RAN OUT OF INK
JIM DAVIS 2-24

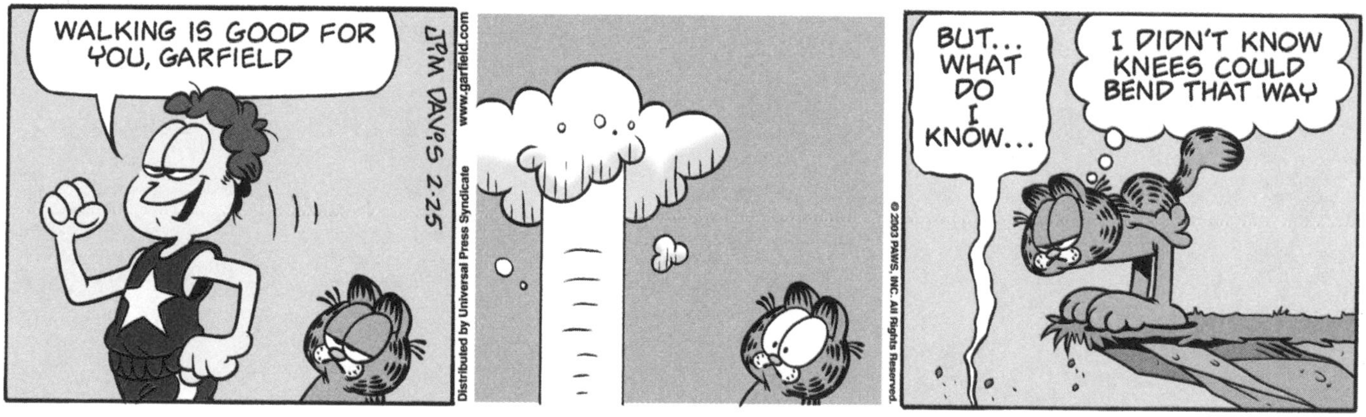
WALKING IS GOOD FOR YOU, GARFIELD
JIM DAVIS 2-25
Distributed by Universal Press Syndicate www.garfield.com
© 2003 PAWS, INC. All Rights Reserved.
BUT... WHAT DO I KNOW...
I DIDN'T KNOW KNEES COULD BEND THAT WAY

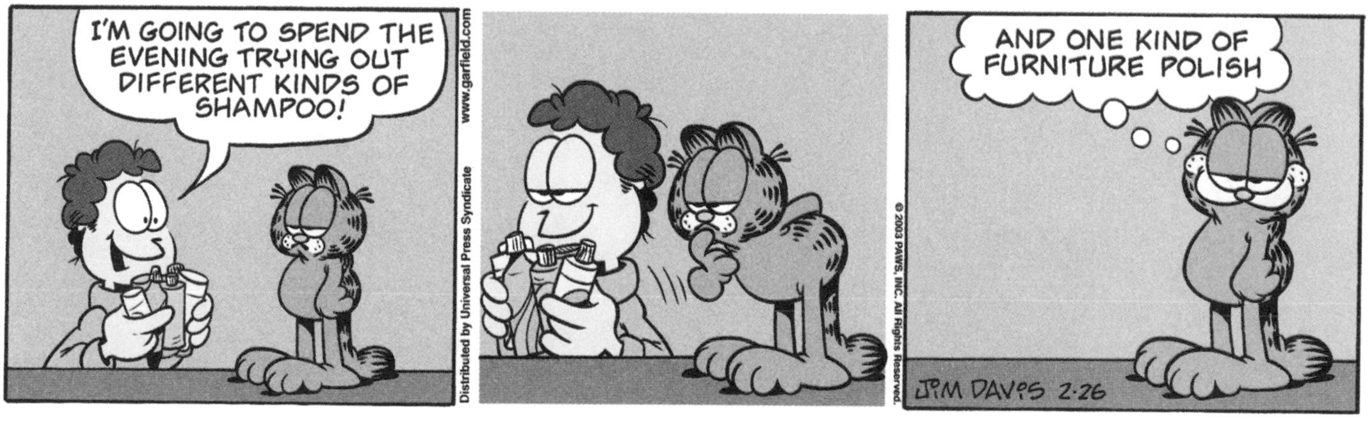
I'M GOING TO SPEND THE EVENING TRYING OUT DIFFERENT KINDS OF SHAMPOO!
Distributed by Universal Press Syndicate www.garfield.com
© 2003 PAWS, INC. All Rights Reserved.
AND ONE KIND OF FURNITURE POLISH
JIM DAVIS 2-26

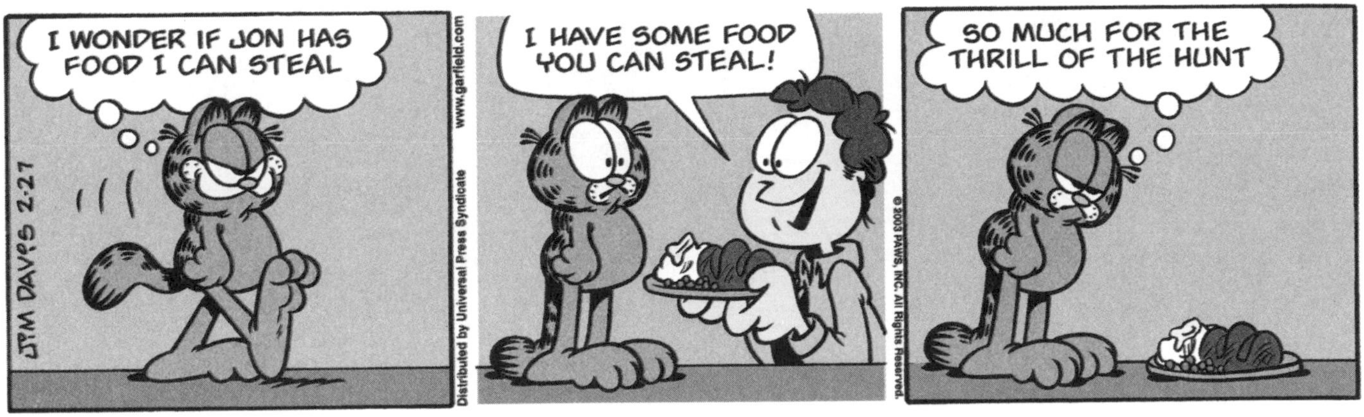
I WONDER IF JON HAS FOOD I CAN STEAL
JIM DAVIS 2-27
Distributed by Universal Press Syndicate www.garfield.com
I HAVE SOME FOOD YOU CAN STEAL!
© 2003 PAWS, INC. All Rights Reserved.
SO MUCH FOR THE THRILL OF THE HUNT

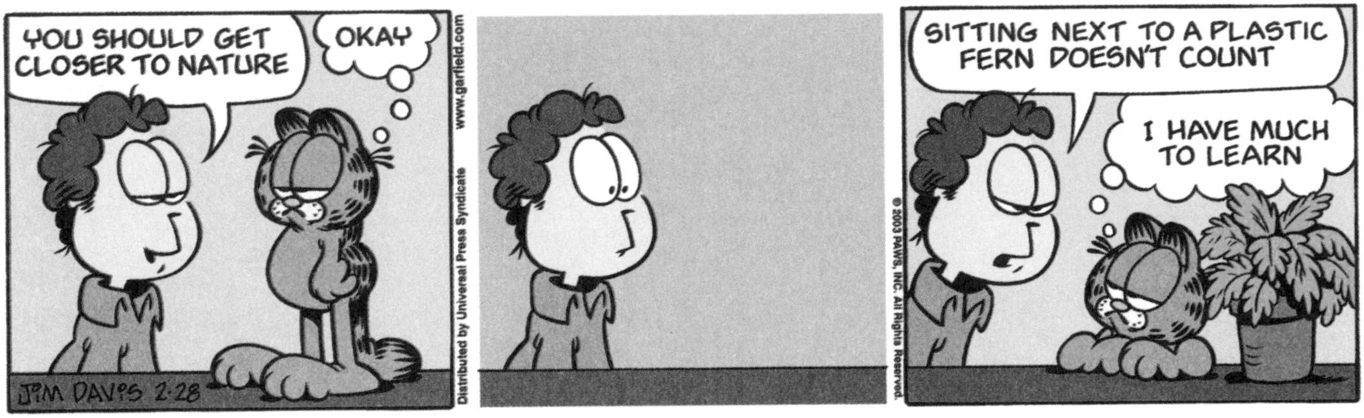
YOU SHOULD GET CLOSER TO NATURE
OKAY
JIM DAVIS 2-28
Distributed by Universal Press Syndicate www.garfield.com
© 2003 PAWS, INC. All Rights Reserved.
SITTING NEXT TO A PLASTIC FERN DOESN'T COUNT
I HAVE MUCH TO LEARN

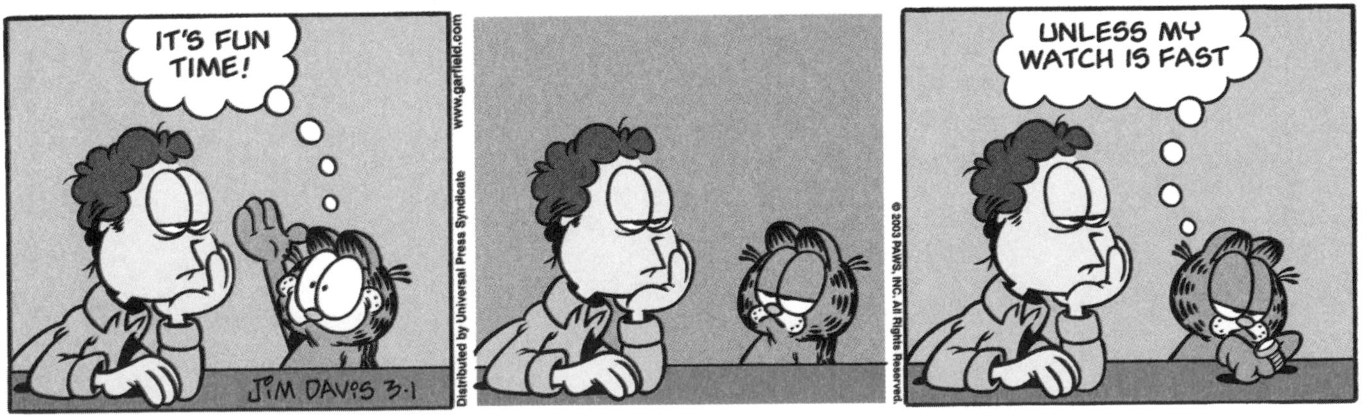
IT'S FUN TIME!
JIM DAVIS 3-1
Distributed by Universal Press Syndicate www.garfield.com
© 2003 PAWS, INC. All Rights Reserved.
UNLESS MY WATCH IS FAST

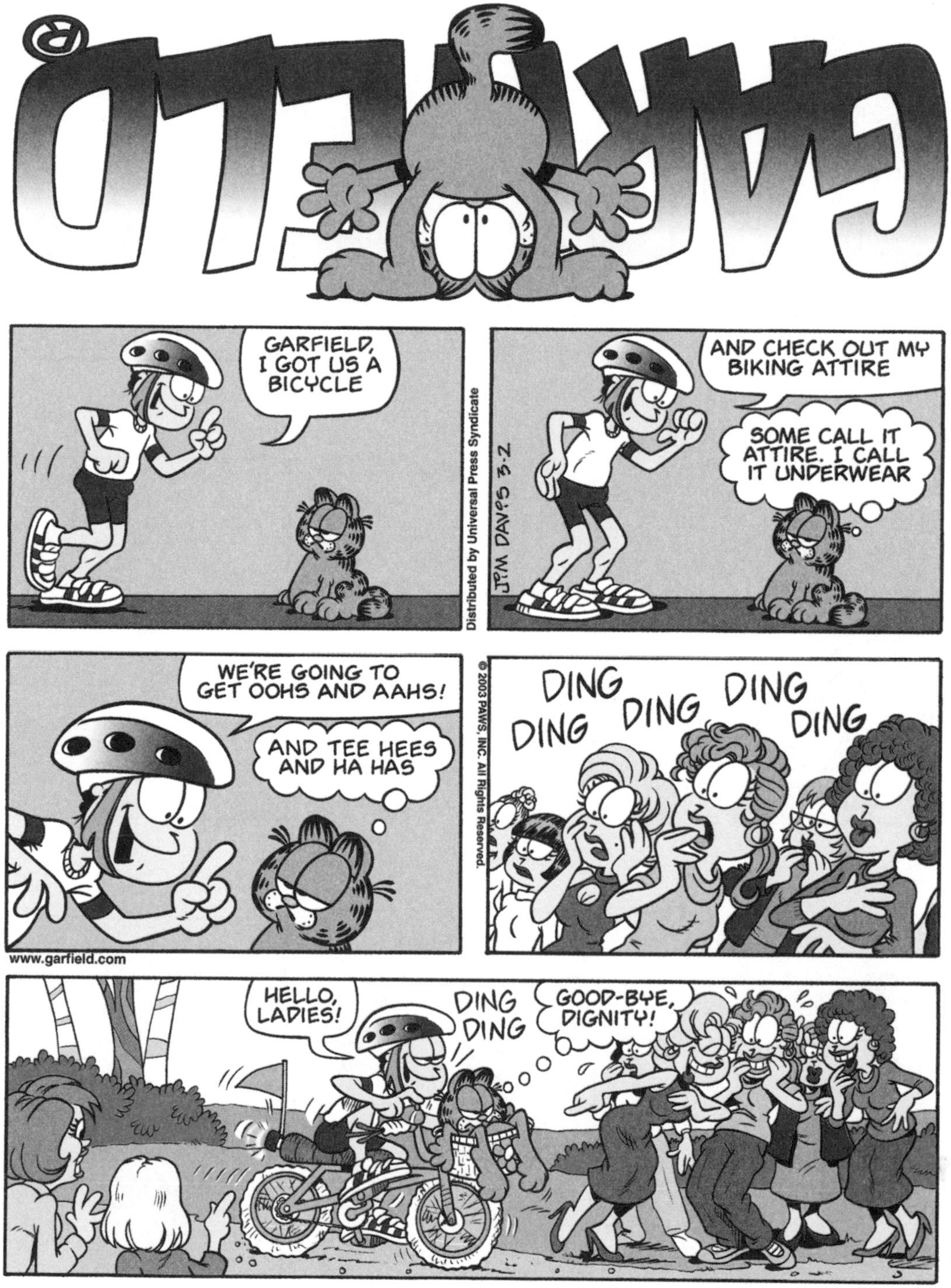
GARFIELD
GARFIELD, I GOT US A BICYCLE
Distributed by Universal Press Syndicate
JIM DAVIS 3-2
AND CHECK OUT MY BIKING ATTIRE
SOME CALL IT ATTIRE. I CALL IT UNDERWEAR
WE'RE GOING TO GET OOHS AND AAHS!
AND TEE HEES AND HA HAS
© 2003 PAWS, INC. All Rights Reserved.
www.garfield.com
DING DING DING DING DING DING
HELLO, LADIES!
DING DING
GOOD-BYE, DIGNITY!

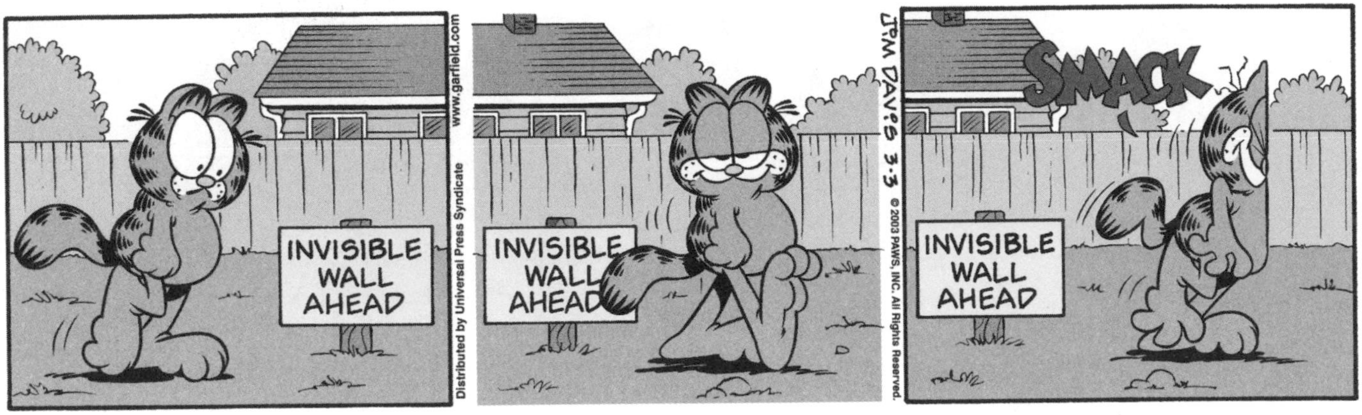
INVISIBLE WALL AHEAD
www.garfield.com
Distributed by Universal Press Syndicate
INVISIBLE WALL AHEAD
JIM DAVIS 3-3
© 2003 PAWS, INC. All Rights Reserved.
SMACK
INVISIBLE WALL AHEAD

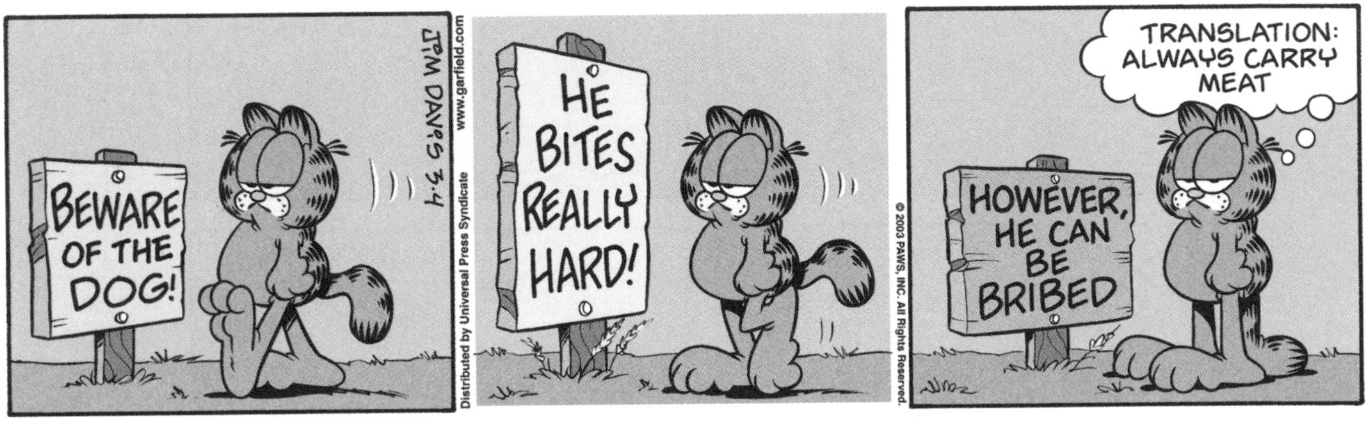
BEWARE OF THE DOG!
JIM DAVIS 3-4
www.garfield.com
Distributed by Universal Press Syndicate
HE BITES REALLY HARD!
© 2003 PAWS, INC. All Rights Reserved.
TRANSLATION: ALWAYS CARRY MEAT
HOWEVER, HE CAN BE BRIBED

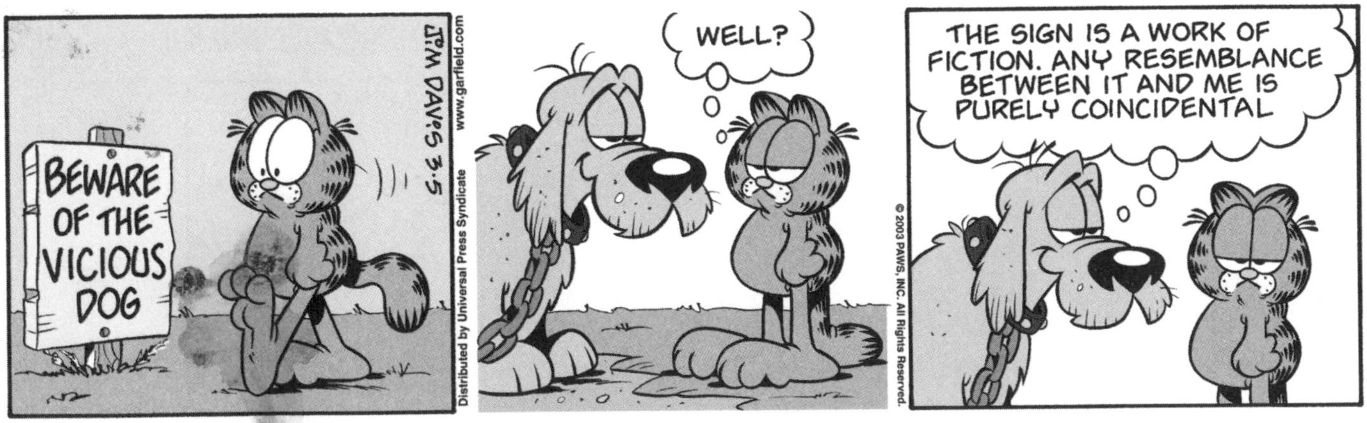
BEWARE OF THE VICIOUS DOG
JIM DAVIS 3-5
www.garfield.com
Distributed by Universal Press Syndicate
WELL?
© 2003 PAWS, INC. All Rights Reserved.
THE SIGN IS A WORK OF FICTION. ANY RESEMBLANCE BETWEEN IT AND ME IS PURELY COINCIDENTAL

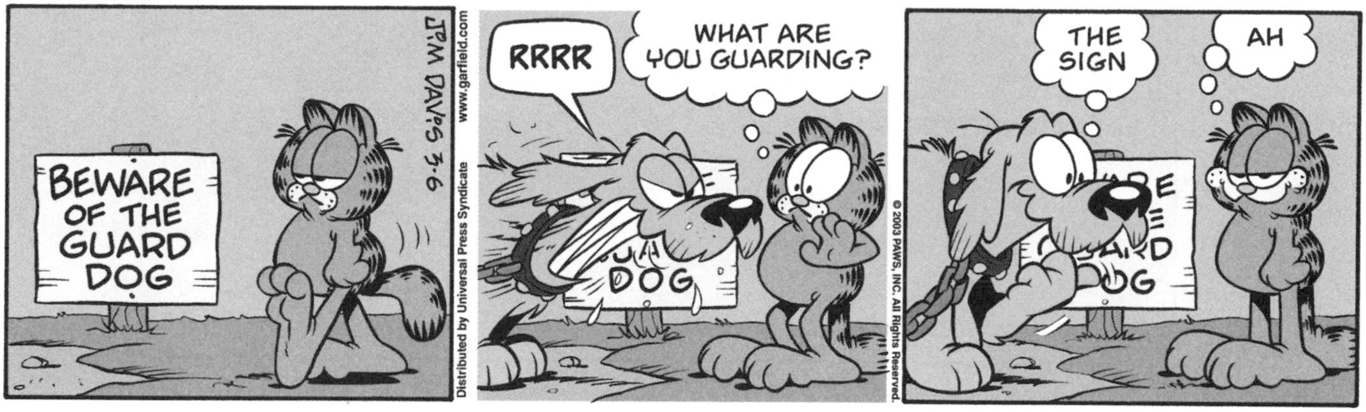
BEWARE OF THE GUARD DOG
JIM DAVIS 3-6
www.garfield.com
Distributed by Universal Press Syndicate
RRRR
WHAT ARE YOU GUARDING?
© 2003 PAWS, INC. All Rights Reserved.
THE SIGN
AH

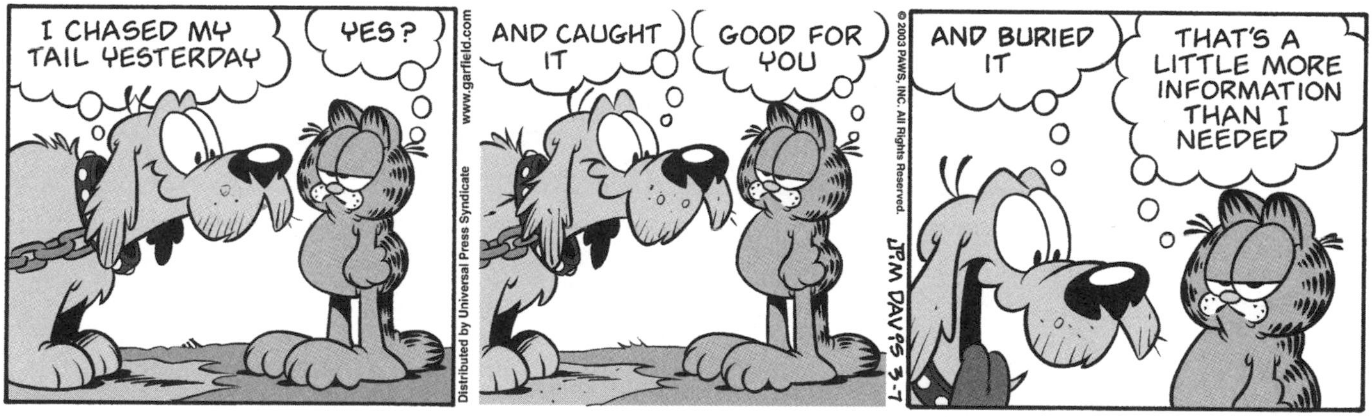
I CHASED MY TAIL YESTERDAY
YES?
www.garfield.com
Distributed by Universal Press Syndicate
AND CAUGHT IT
GOOD FOR YOU
© 2003 PAWS, INC. All Rights Reserved.
JIM DAVIS 3-7
AND BURIED IT
THAT'S A LITTLE MORE INFORMATION THAN I NEEDED

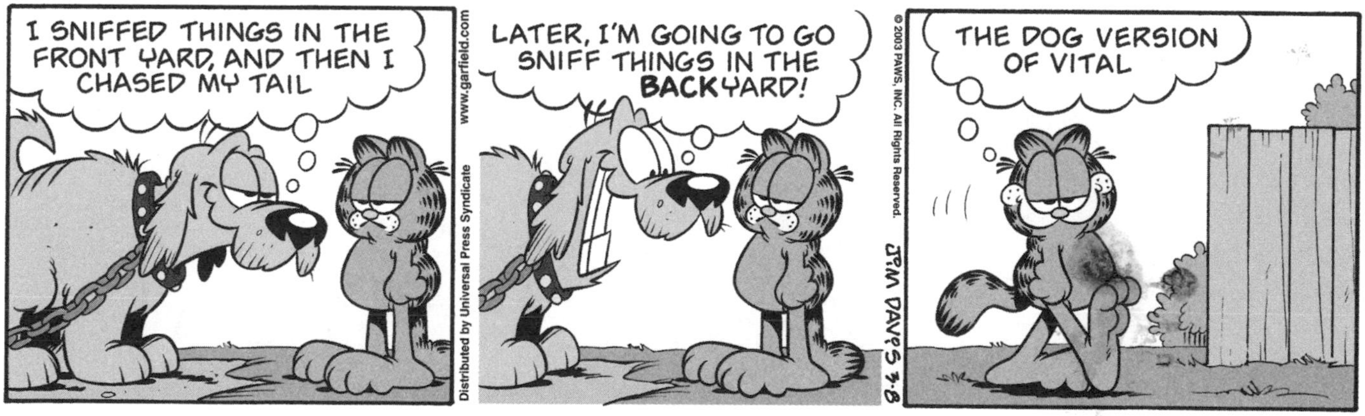
I SNIFFED THINGS IN THE FRONT YARD, AND THEN I CHASED MY TAIL
www.garfield.com
Distributed by Universal Press Syndicate
LATER, I'M GOING TO GO SNIFF THINGS IN THE BACKYARD!
© 2003 PAWS, INC. All Rights Reserved.
JIM DAVIS 3-8
THE DOG VERSION OF VITAL

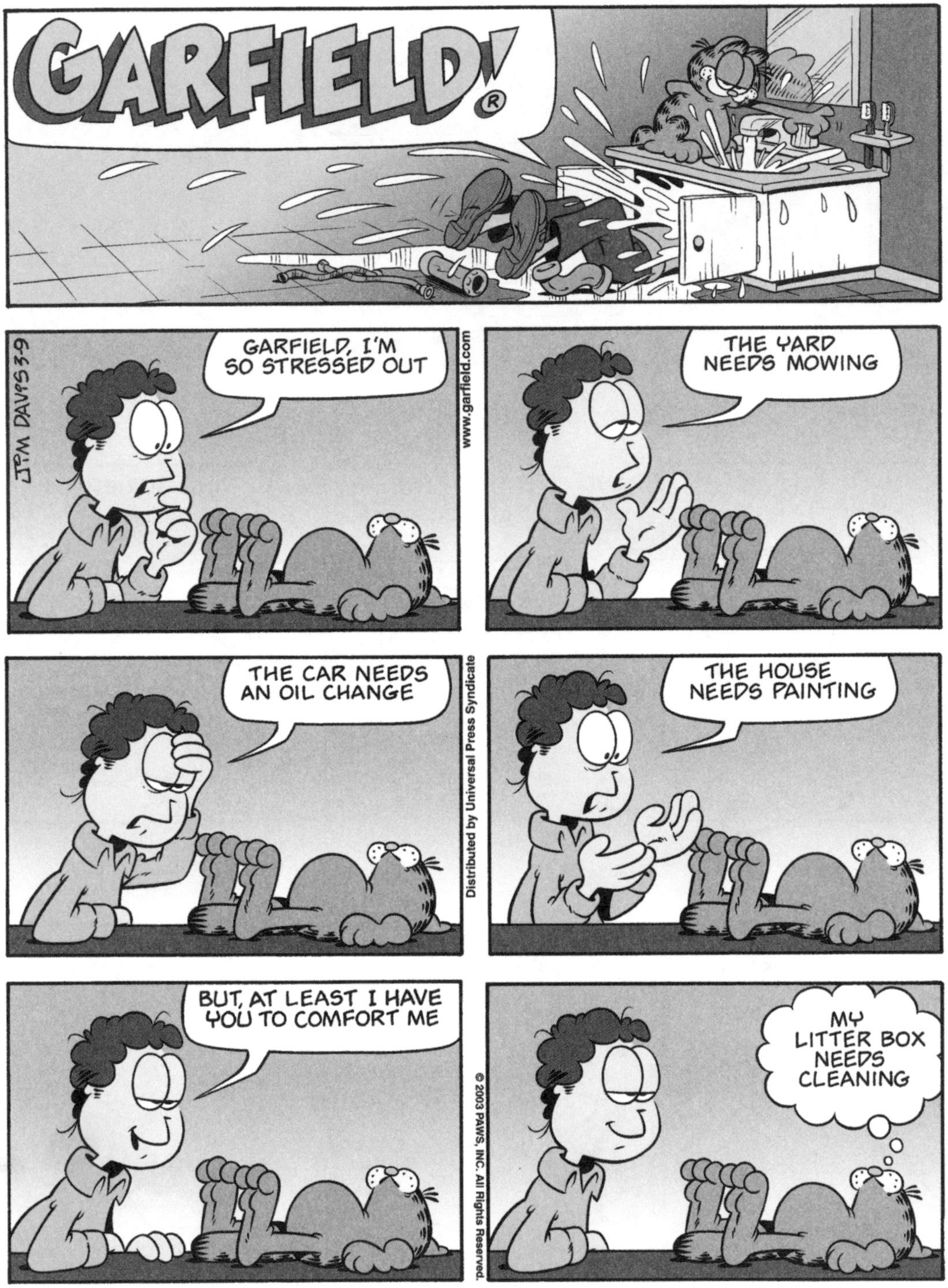
GARFIELD!®
JIM DAVIS 3-9
www.garfield.com
GARFIELD, I'M SO STRESSED OUT
THE YARD NEEDS MOWING
THE CAR NEEDS AN OIL CHANGE
THE HOUSE NEEDS PAINTING
Distributed by Universal Press Syndicate
BUT, AT LEAST I HAVE YOU TO COMFORT ME
MY LITTER BOX NEEDS CLEANING
© 2003 PAWS, INC. All Rights Reserved.

HARD WORK IS ITS OWN REWARD!
OKAY, OKAY! GIMME THE PUNCH LINE!
www.garfield.com
Distributed by Universal Press Syndicate
JIM DAVIS 3-10
© 2003 PAWS, INC. All Rights Reserved.

I'M THINKING OF BURPING
BURP
I BURPED
YOU DON'T HAVE A LOT GOING ON, DO YOU, GARFIELD?
www.garfield.com
Distributed by Universal Press Syndicate
© 2003 PAWS, INC. All Rights Reserved.
JIM DAVIS 3-11

I'M GOING TO SPEND THE DAY DOING NOTHING
COUGH
AMATEUR
www.garfield.com
Distributed by Universal Press Syndicate
JIM DAVIS 3-12
© 2003 PAWS, INC. All Rights Reserved.

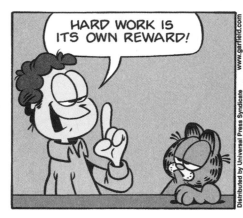

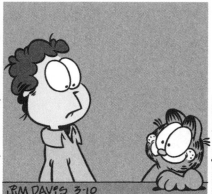

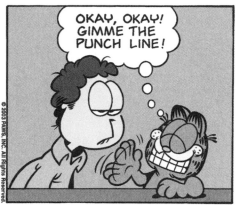

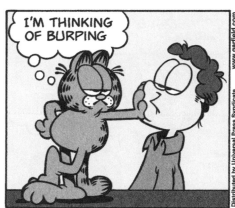

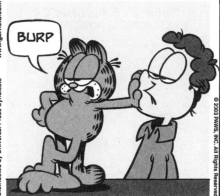

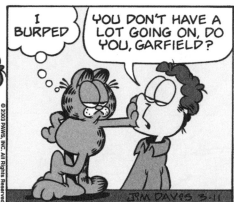

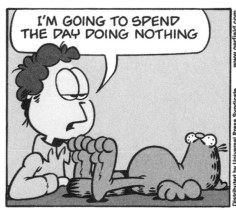

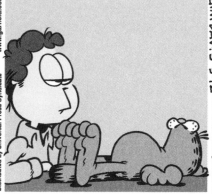

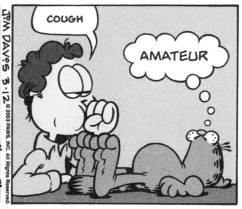

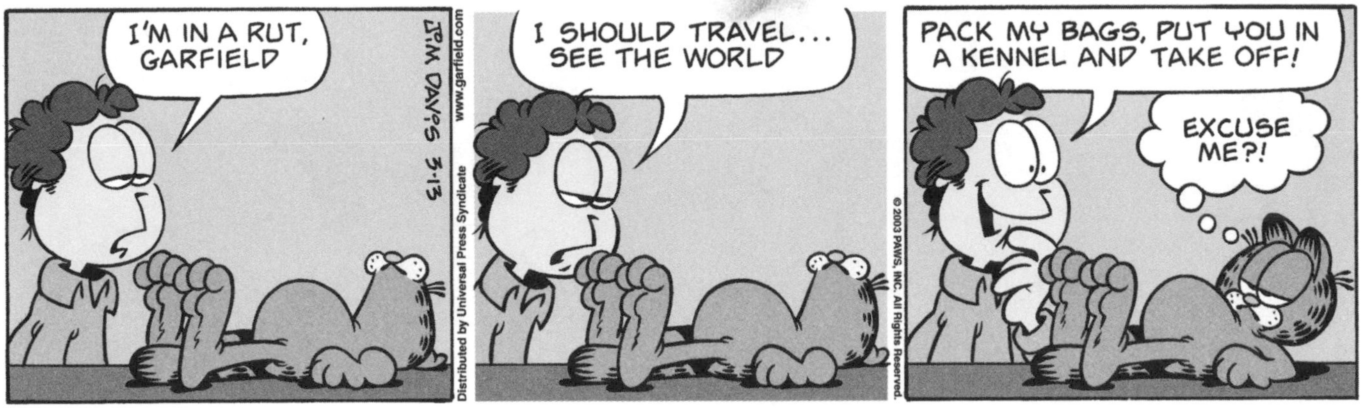
I'M IN A RUT, GARFIELD
JIM DAVIS 3-13
www.garfield.com
Distributed by Universal Press Syndicate
I SHOULD TRAVEL... SEE THE WORLD
© 2003 PAWS, INC. All Rights Reserved.
PACK MY BAGS, PUT YOU IN A KENNEL AND TAKE OFF!
EXCUSE ME?!

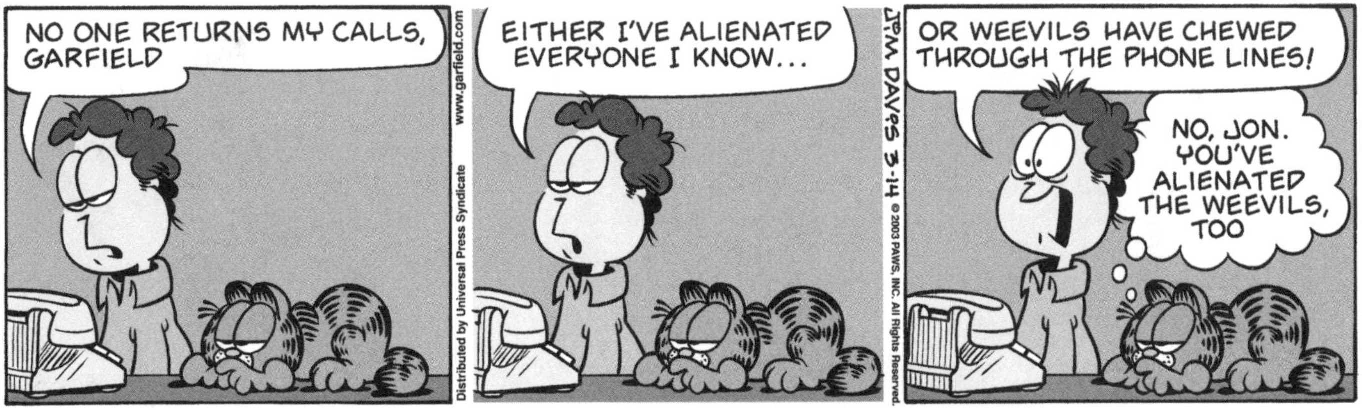
NO ONE RETURNS MY CALLS, GARFIELD
www.garfield.com
Distributed by Universal Press Syndicate
EITHER I'VE ALIENATED EVERYONE I KNOW...
JIM DAVIS 3-14
© 2003 PAWS, INC. All Rights Reserved.
OR WEEVILS HAVE CHEWED THROUGH THE PHONE LINES!
NO, JON. YOU'VE ALIENATED THE WEEVILS, TOO

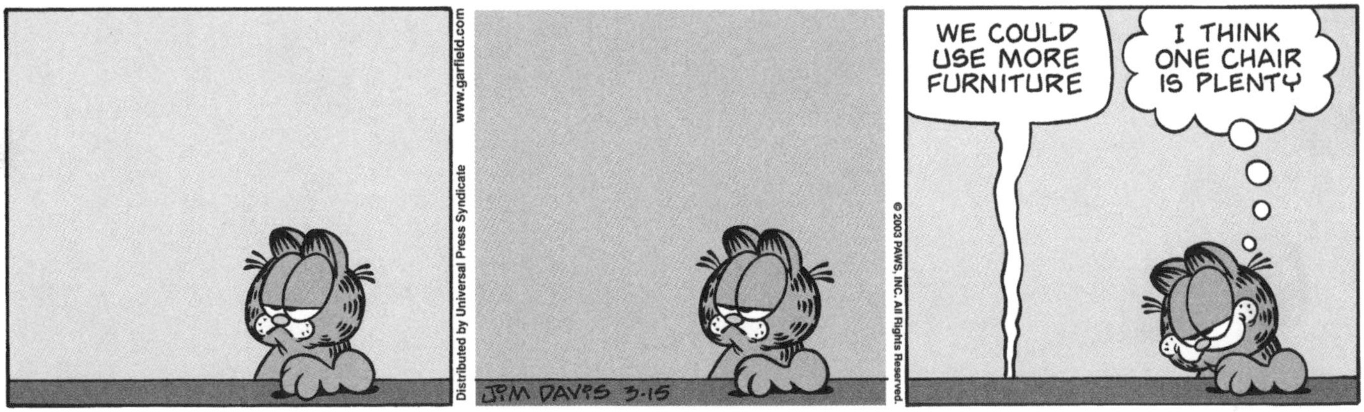
www.garfield.com
Distributed by Universal Press Syndicate
JIM DAVIS 3-15
© 2003 PAWS, INC. All Rights Reserved.
WE COULD USE MORE FURNITURE
I THINK ONE CHAIR IS PLENTY

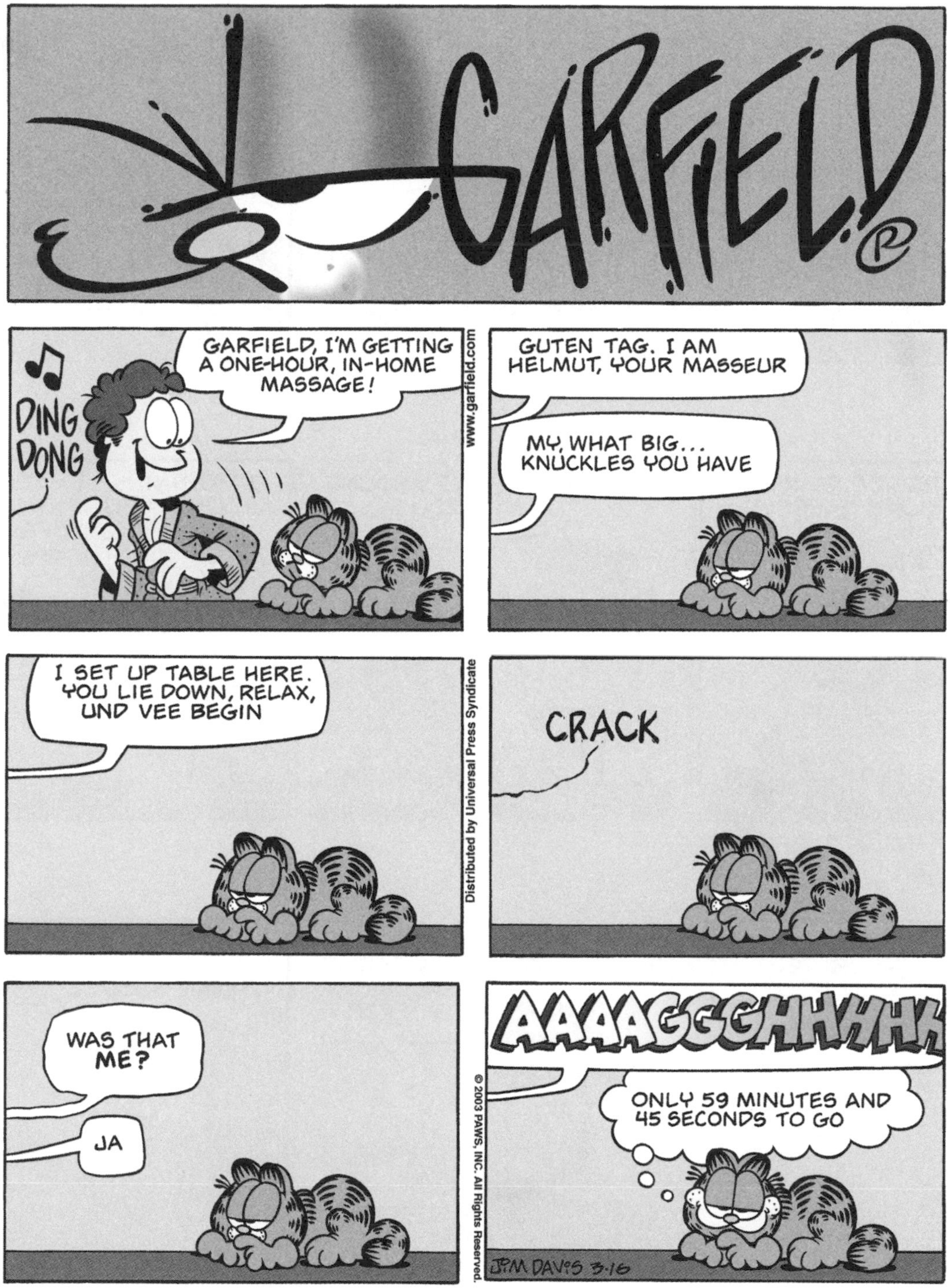
GARFIELD®
DING DONG
GARFIELD, I'M GETTING A ONE-HOUR, IN-HOME MASSAGE!
www.garfield.com
GUTEN TAG. I AM HELMUT, YOUR MASSEUR
MY, WHAT BIG... KNUCKLES YOU HAVE
I SET UP TABLE HERE. YOU LIE DOWN, RELAX, UND VEE BEGIN
Distributed by Universal Press Syndicate
CRACK
WAS THAT ME?
JA
© 2003 PAWS, INC. All Rights Reserved.
AAAAGGGHHHHH
ONLY 59 MINUTES AND 45 SECONDS TO GO
JIM DAVIS 3-16

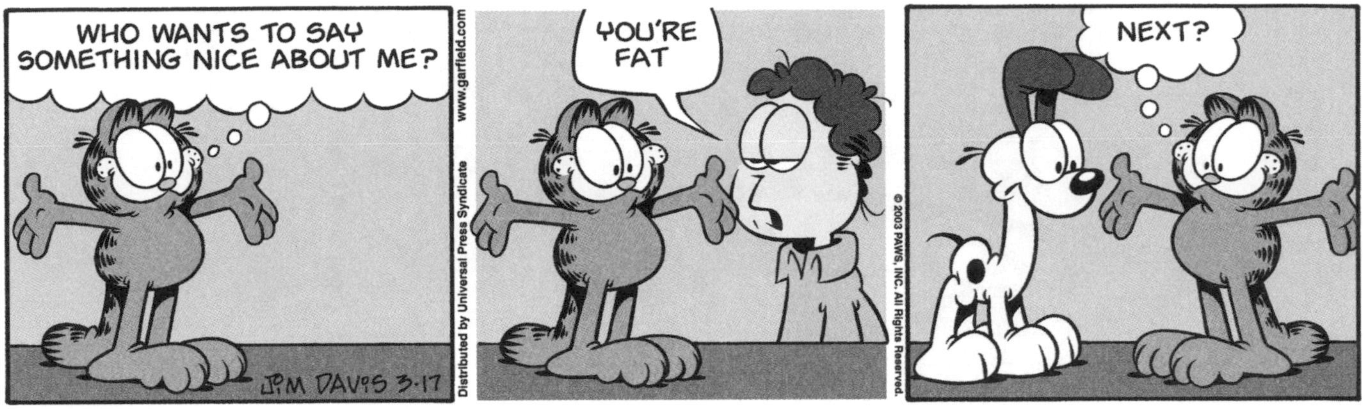
WHO WANTS TO SAY SOMETHING NICE ABOUT ME?
JIM DAVIS 3-17
www.garfield.com
Distributed by Universal Press Syndicate
YOU'RE FAT
© 2003 PAWS, INC. All Rights Reserved.
NEXT?

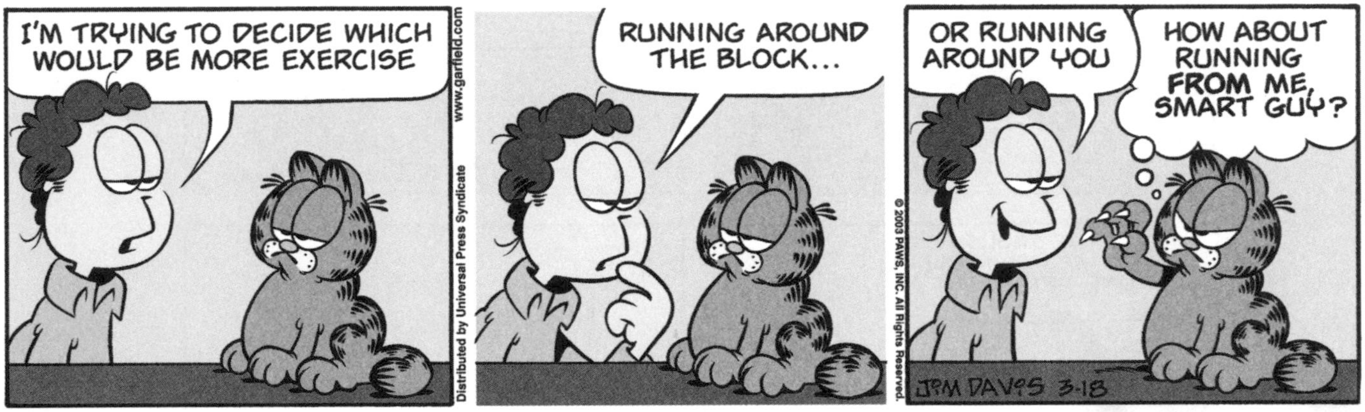
I'M TRYING TO DECIDE WHICH WOULD BE MORE EXERCISE
www.garfield.com
Distributed by Universal Press Syndicate
RUNNING AROUND THE BLOCK...
© 2003 PAWS, INC. All Rights Reserved.
OR RUNNING AROUND YOU
HOW ABOUT RUNNING **FROM** ME, SMART GUY?
JIM DAVIS 3-18

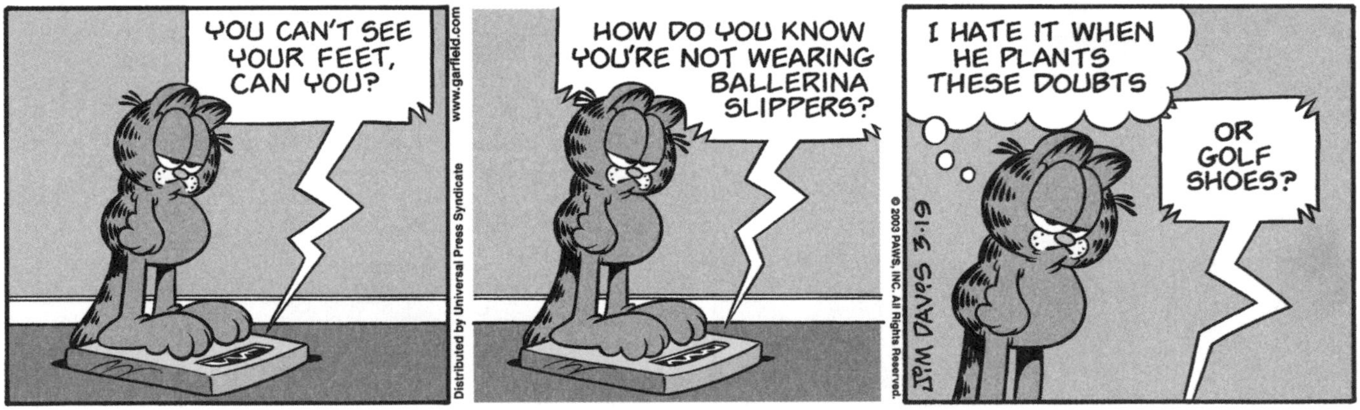
YOU CAN'T SEE YOUR FEET, CAN YOU?
www.garfield.com
Distributed by Universal Press Syndicate
HOW DO YOU KNOW YOU'RE NOT WEARING BALLERINA SLIPPERS?
© 2003 PAWS, INC. All Rights Reserved.
JIM DAVIS 3-19
I HATE IT WHEN HE PLANTS THESE DOUBTS
OR GOLF SHOES?

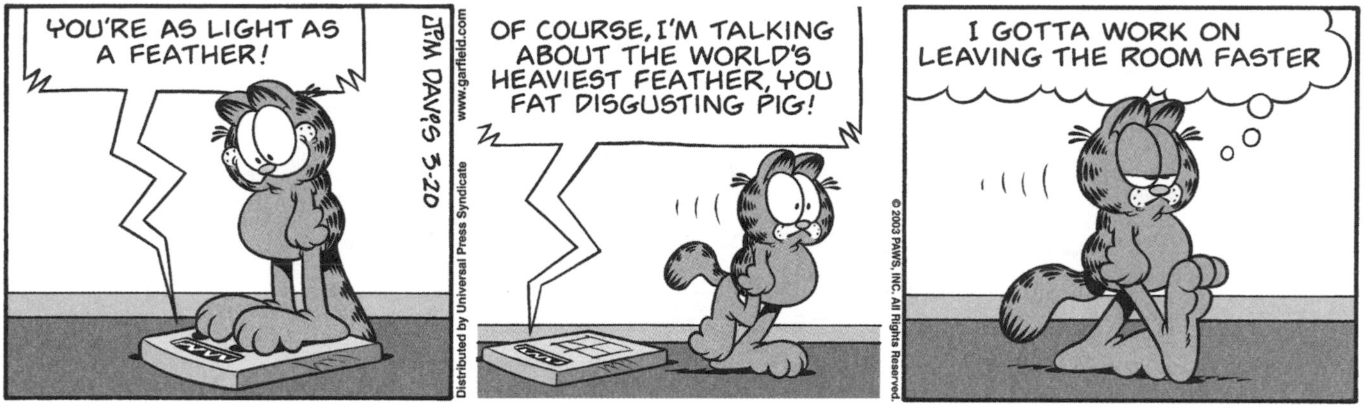
YOU'RE AS LIGHT AS A FEATHER!
JIM DAVIS 3-20
www.garfield.com
Distributed by Universal Press Syndicate
OF COURSE, I'M TALKING ABOUT THE WORLD'S HEAVIEST FEATHER, YOU FAT DISGUSTING PIG!
© 2003 PAWS, INC. All Rights Reserved.
I GOTTA WORK ON LEAVING THE ROOM FASTER

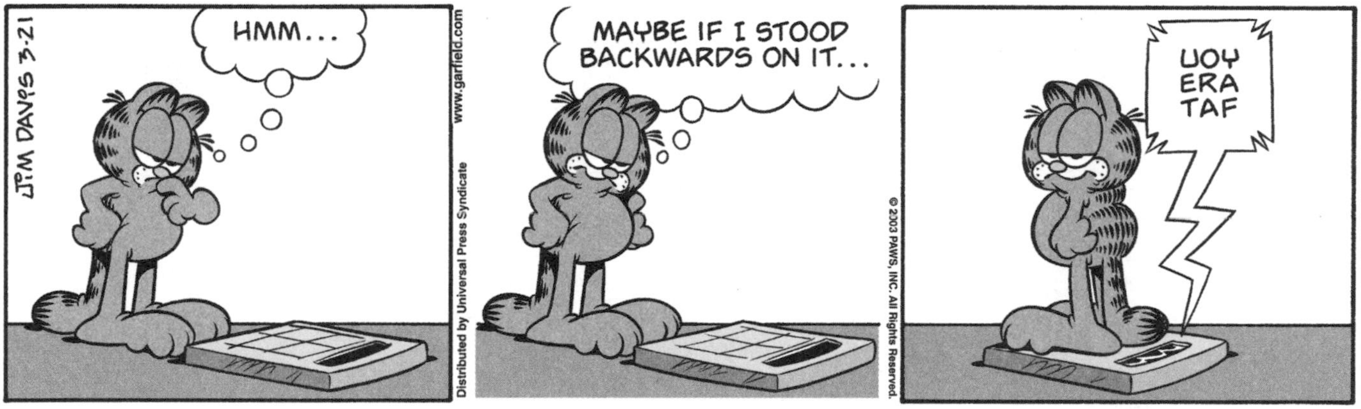
JIM DAVIS 3-21
HMM...
www.garfield.com
Distributed by Universal Press Syndicate
MAYBE IF I STOOD BACKWARDS ON IT...
© 2003 PAWS, INC. All Rights Reserved.
UOY ERA TAF

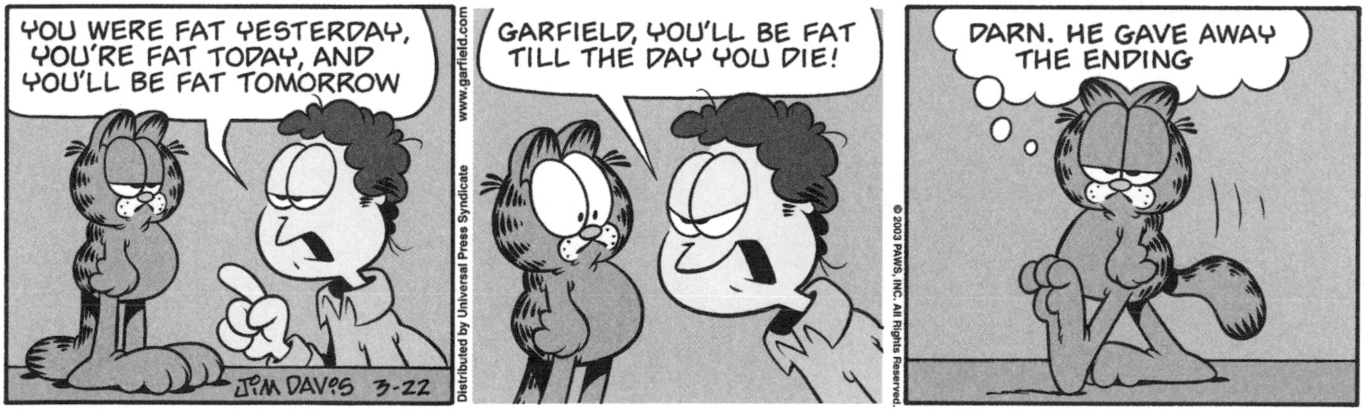
YOU WERE FAT YESTERDAY, YOU'RE FAT TODAY, AND YOU'LL BE FAT TOMORROW
JIM DAVIS 3-22
www.garfield.com
Distributed by Universal Press Syndicate
GARFIELD, YOU'LL BE FAT TILL THE DAY YOU DIE!
© 2003 PAWS, INC. All Rights Reserved.
DARN. HE GAVE AWAY THE ENDING

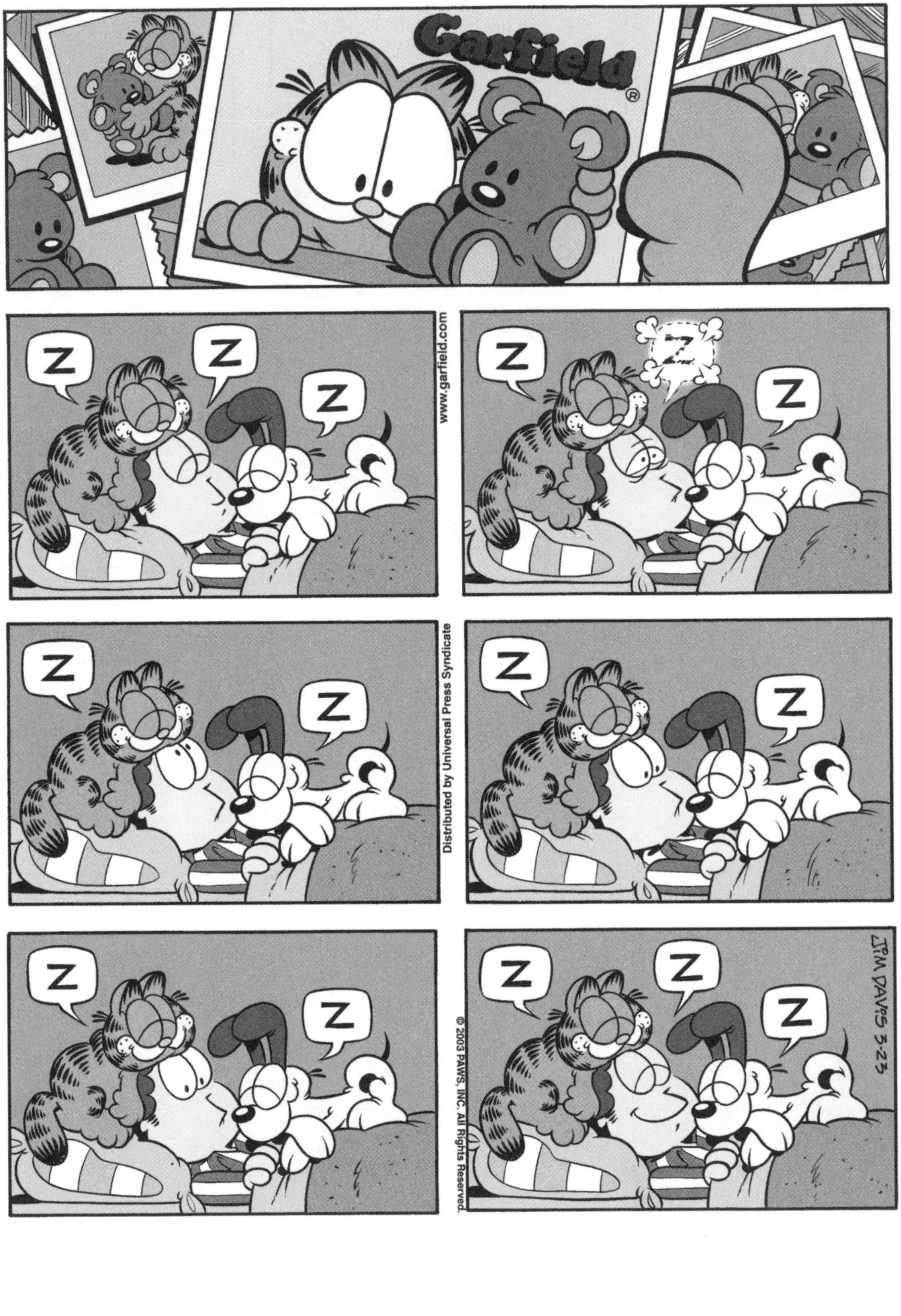
Garfield®
Z
Z
Z
www.garfield.com
Z
Z
Z
Z
Distributed by Universal Press Syndicate
Z
Z
Z
Z
Z
Z
© 2003 PAWS, INC. All Rights Reserved.
JIM DAVIS 3-23
Z
Z
Z

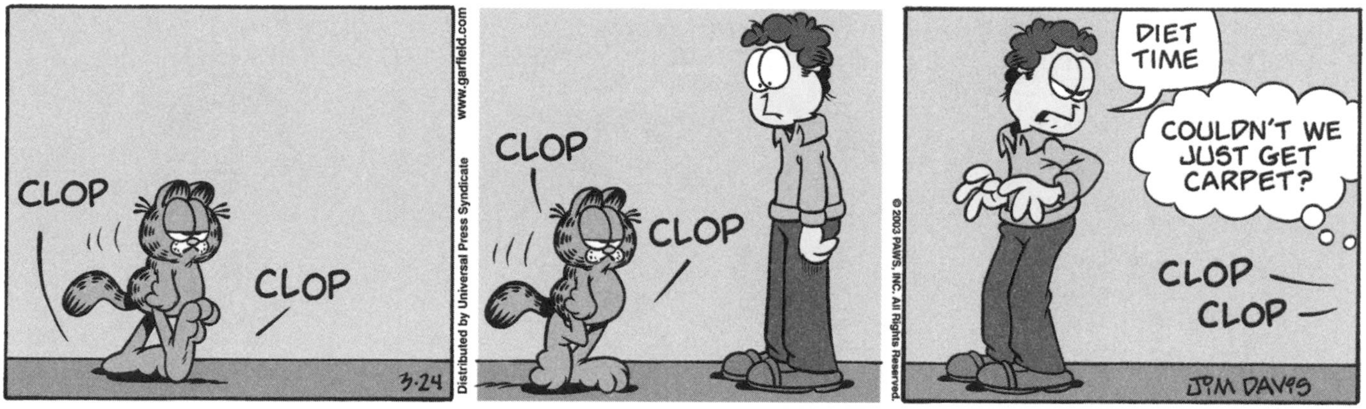
CLOP
CLOP
3-24
www.garfield.com
Distributed by Universal Press Syndicate
CLOP
CLOP
© 2003 PAWS, INC. All Rights Reserved.
DIET TIME
COULDN'T WE JUST GET CARPET?
CLOP
CLOP
JIM DAVIS

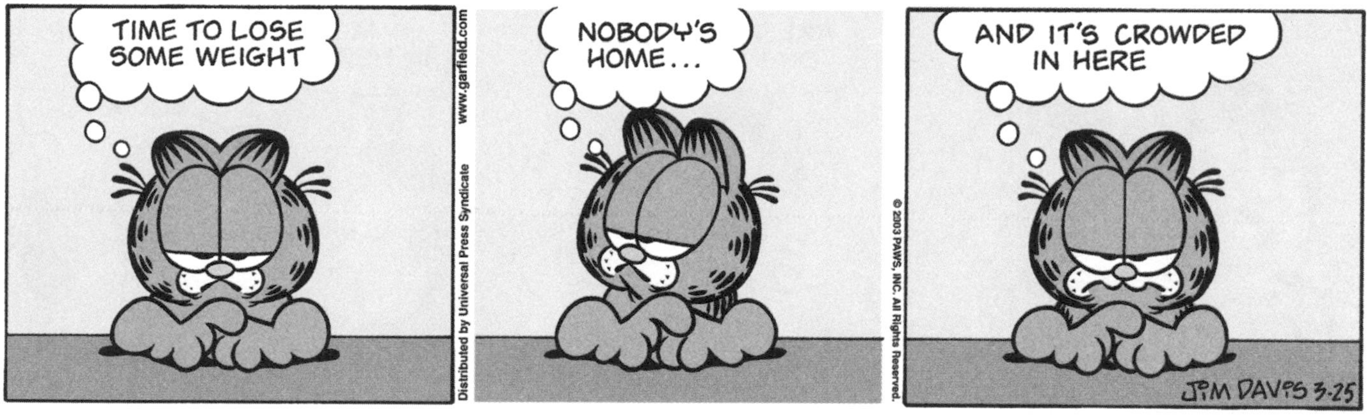
TIME TO LOSE SOME WEIGHT
www.garfield.com
Distributed by Universal Press Syndicate
NOBODY'S HOME...
© 2003 PAWS, INC. All Rights Reserved.
AND IT'S CROWDED IN HERE
JIM DAVIS 3-25

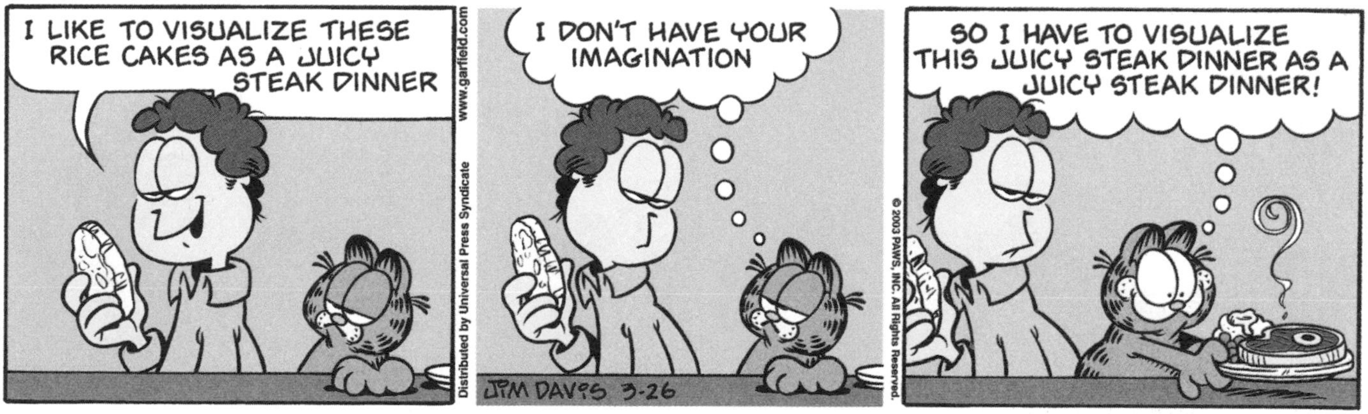
I LIKE TO VISUALIZE THESE RICE CAKES AS A JUICY STEAK DINNER
www.garfield.com
Distributed by Universal Press Syndicate
I DON'T HAVE YOUR IMAGINATION
JIM DAVIS 3-26
© 2003 PAWS, INC. All Rights Reserved.
SO I HAVE TO VISUALIZE THIS JUICY STEAK DINNER AS A JUICY STEAK DINNER!

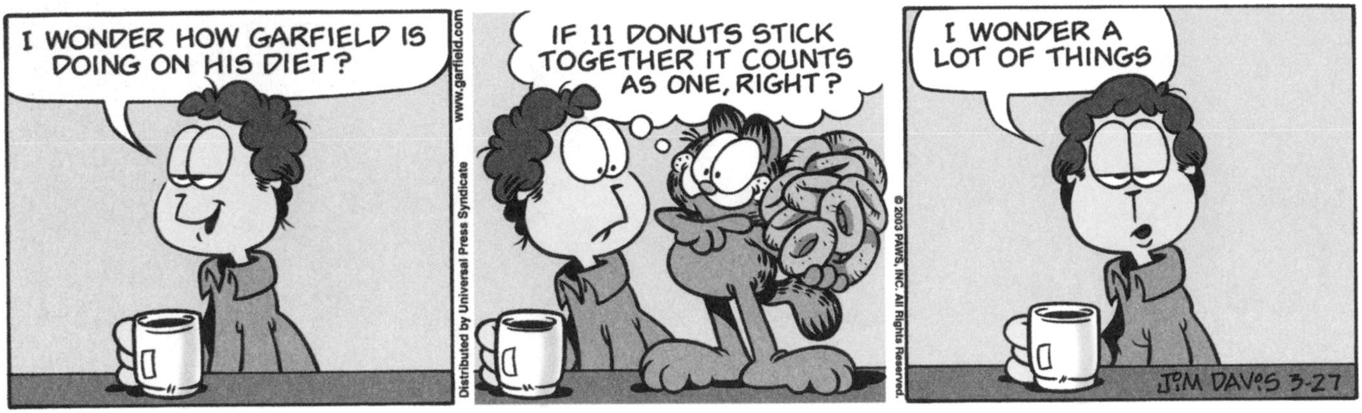
I WONDER HOW GARFIELD IS DOING ON HIS DIET?
IF 11 DONUTS STICK TOGETHER IT COUNTS AS ONE, RIGHT?
I WONDER A LOT OF THINGS
JIM DAVIS 3-27
Distributed by Universal Press Syndicate www.garfield.com
© 2003 PAWS, INC. All Rights Reserved.

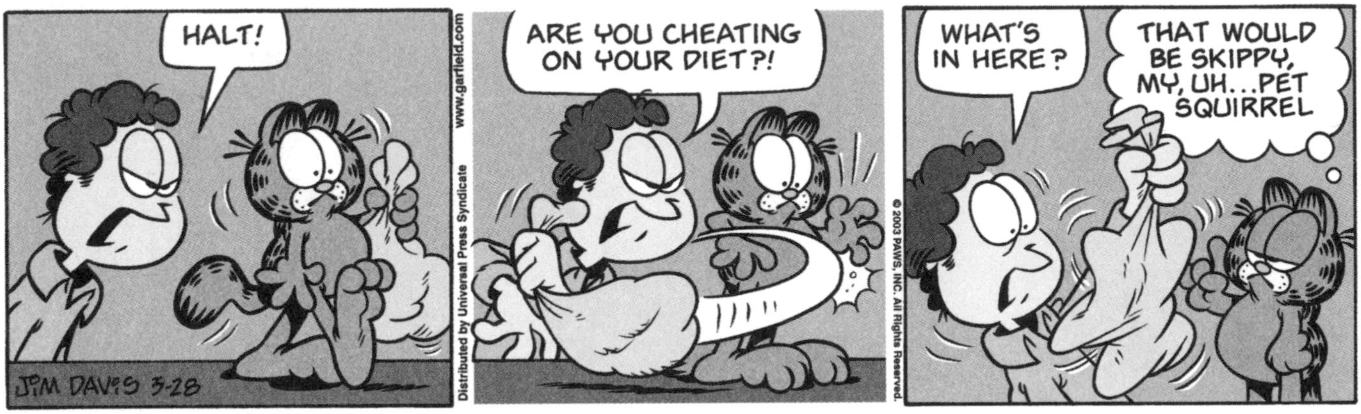
HALT!
ARE YOU CHEATING ON YOUR DIET?!
WHAT'S IN HERE?
THAT WOULD BE SKIPPY, MY, UH...PET SQUIRREL
JIM DAVIS 3-28
Distributed by Universal Press Syndicate www.garfield.com
© 2003 PAWS, INC. All Rights Reserved.

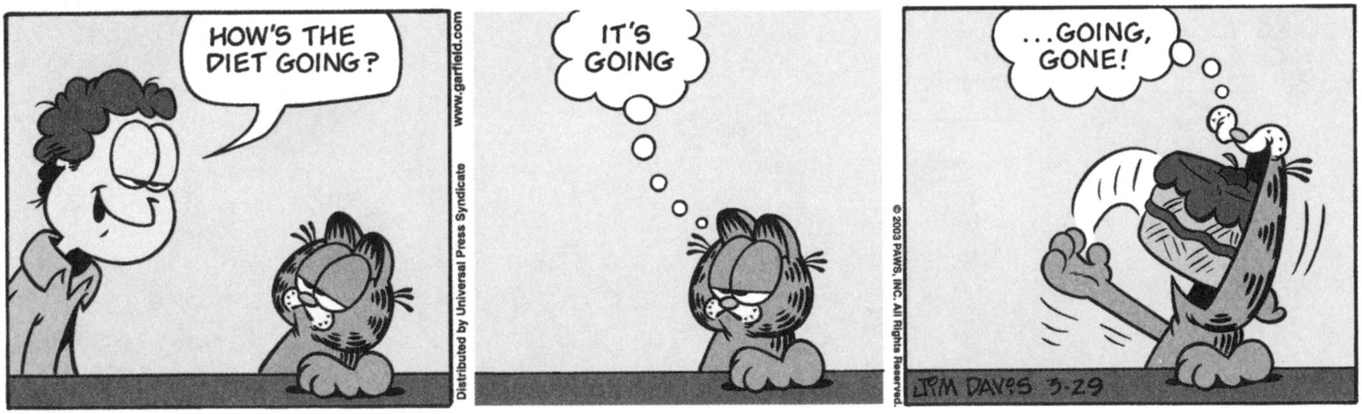
HOW'S THE DIET GOING?
IT'S GOING
...GOING, GONE!
JIM DAVIS 3-29
Distributed by Universal Press Syndicate www.garfield.com
© 2003 PAWS, INC. All Rights Reserved.

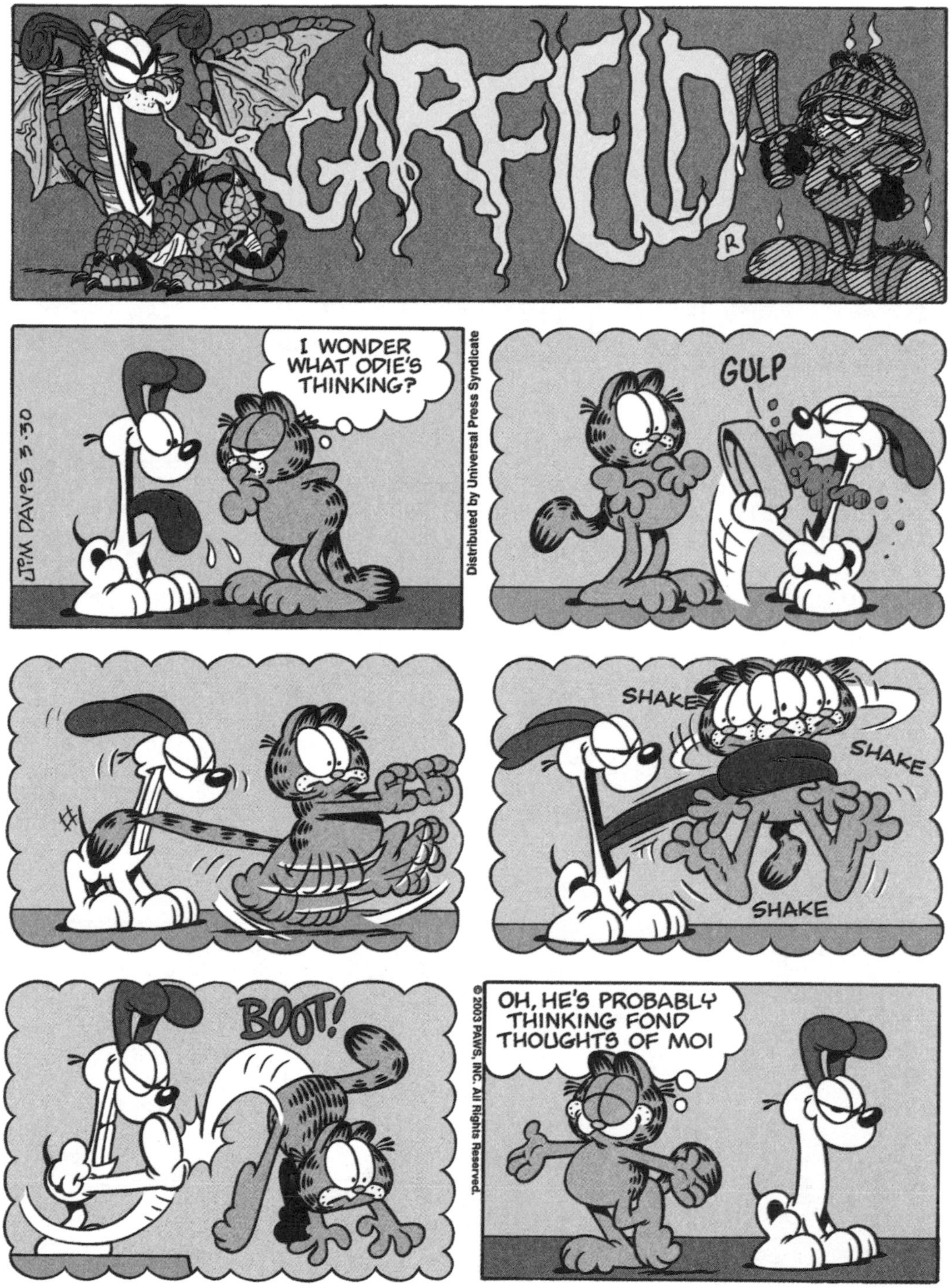
GARFIELD
JIM DAVIS 3·30
Distributed by Universal Press Syndicate
I WONDER WHAT ODIE'S THINKING?
GULP
SHAKE
SHAKE
SHAKE
BOOT!
© 2003 PAWS, INC. All Rights Reserved.
OH, HE'S PROBABLY THINKING FOND THOUGHTS OF MOI

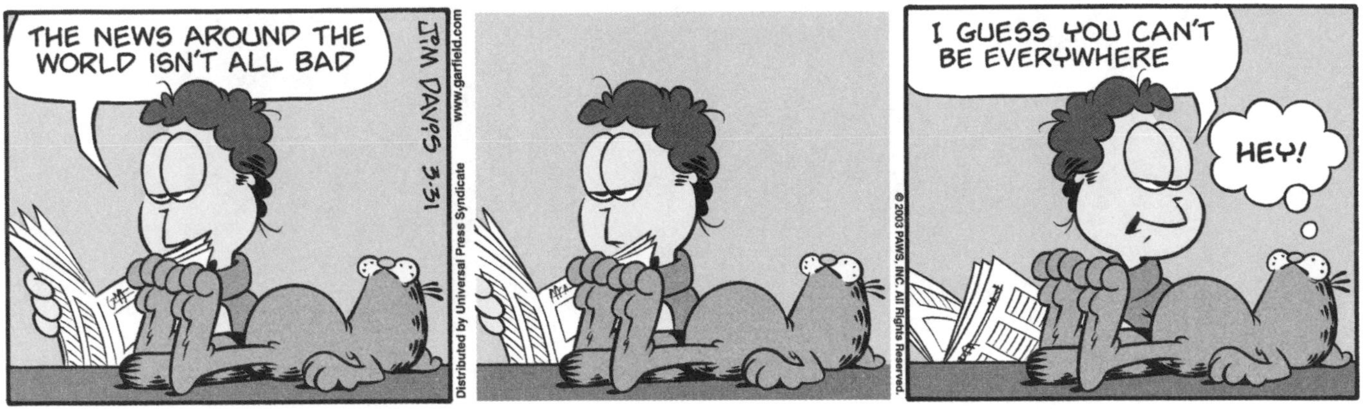
THE NEWS AROUND THE WORLD ISN'T ALL BAD
JIM DAVIS 3-31
www.garfield.com
Distributed by Universal Press Syndicate
© 2003 PAWS, INC. All Rights Reserved.
I GUESS YOU CAN'T BE EVERYWHERE
HEY!

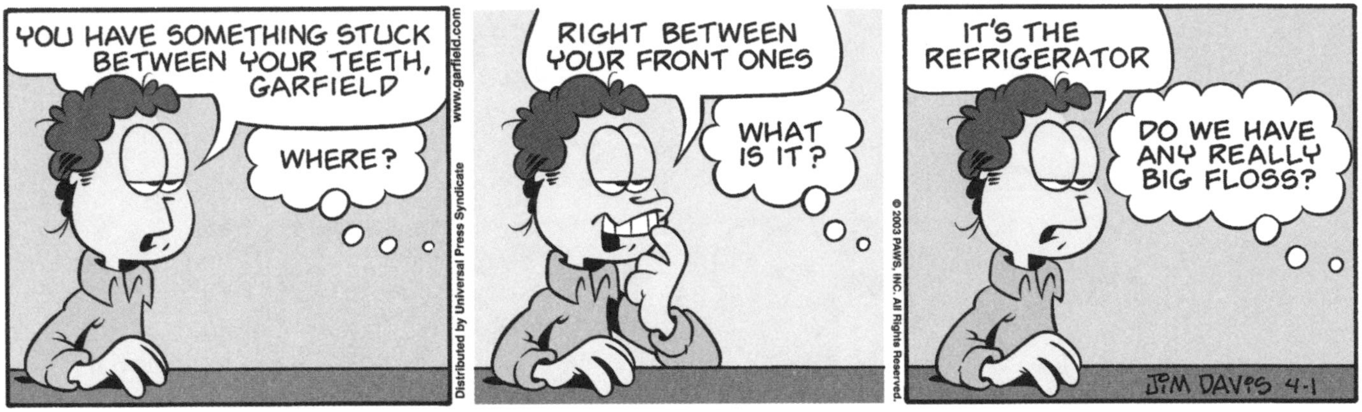
YOU HAVE SOMETHING STUCK BETWEEN YOUR TEETH, GARFIELD
WHERE?
www.garfield.com
Distributed by Universal Press Syndicate
RIGHT BETWEEN YOUR FRONT ONES
WHAT IS IT?
© 2003 PAWS, INC. All Rights Reserved.
IT'S THE REFRIGERATOR
DO WE HAVE ANY REALLY BIG FLOSS?
JIM DAVIS 4-1

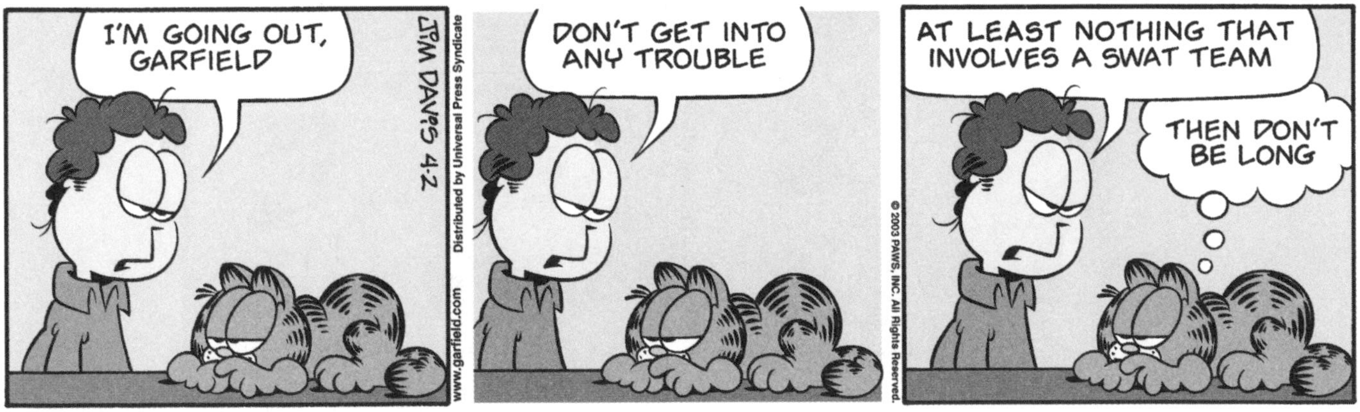
I'M GOING OUT, GARFIELD
JIM DAVIS 4-2
Distributed by Universal Press Syndicate
www.garfield.com
DON'T GET INTO ANY TROUBLE
© 2003 PAWS, INC. All Rights Reserved.
AT LEAST NOTHING THAT INVOLVES A SWAT TEAM
THEN DON'T BE LONG

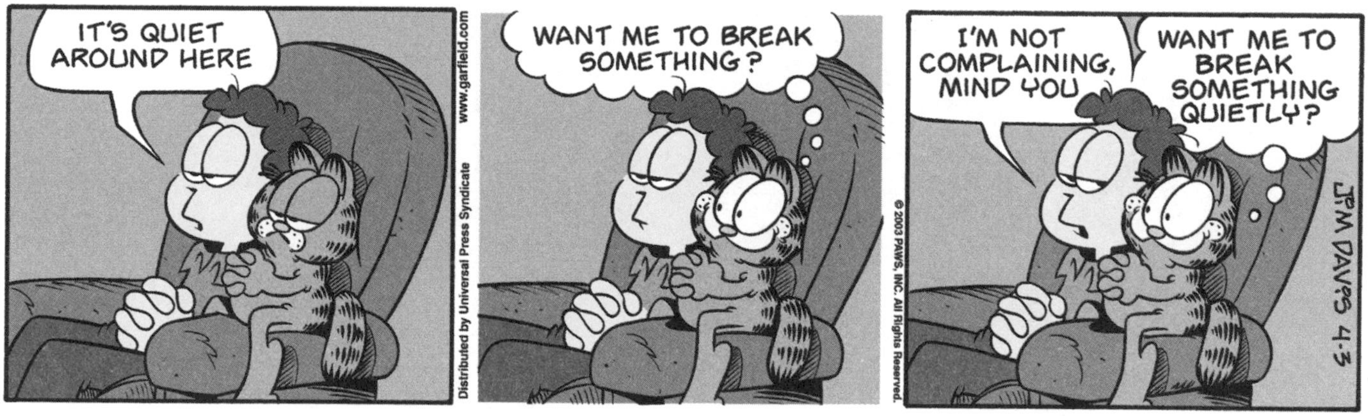
IT'S QUIET AROUND HERE
www.garfield.com
Distributed by Universal Press Syndicate
WANT ME TO BREAK SOMETHING?
© 2003 PAWS, INC. All Rights Reserved.
I'M NOT COMPLAINING, MIND YOU
WANT ME TO BREAK SOMETHING QUIETLY?
JIM DAVIS 4-3

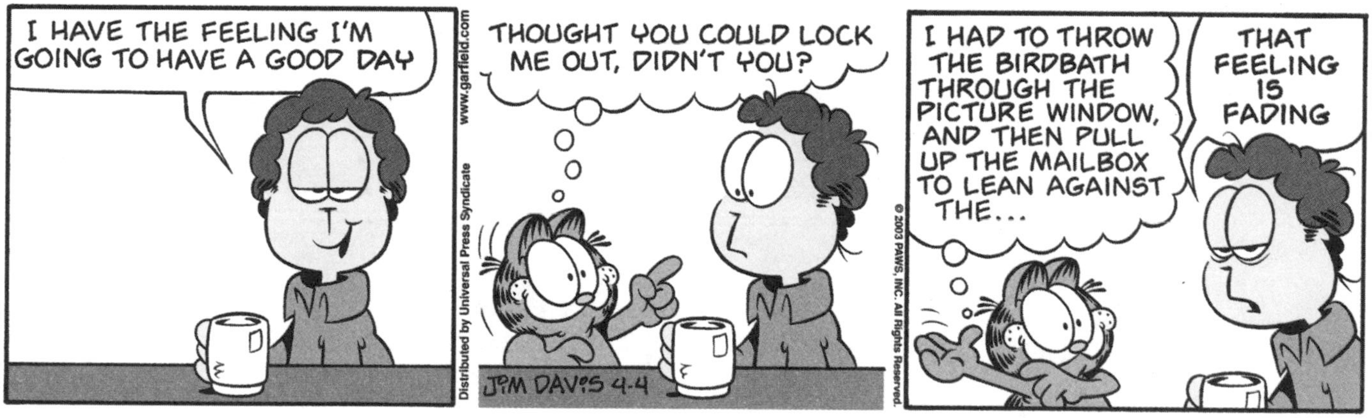
I HAVE THE FEELING I'M GOING TO HAVE A GOOD DAY
www.garfield.com
Distributed by Universal Press Syndicate
THOUGHT YOU COULD LOCK ME OUT, DIDN'T YOU?
JIM DAVIS 4-4
© 2003 PAWS, INC. All Rights Reserved.
I HAD TO THROW THE BIRDBATH THROUGH THE PICTURE WINDOW, AND THEN PULL UP THE MAILBOX TO LEAN AGAINST THE...
THAT FEELING IS FADING

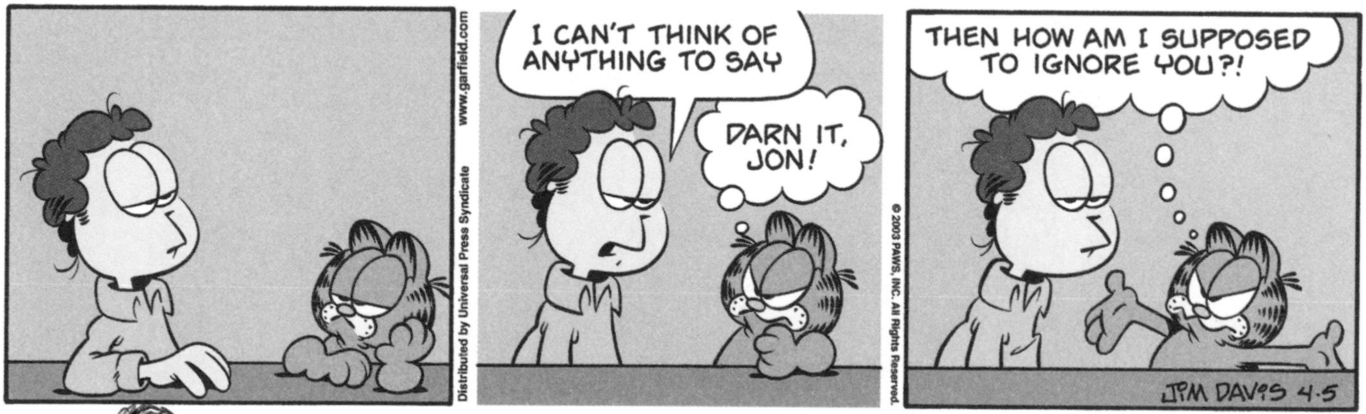
www.garfield.com
Distributed by Universal Press Syndicate
I CAN'T THINK OF ANYTHING TO SAY
DARN IT, JON!
© 2003 PAWS, INC. All Rights Reserved.
THEN HOW AM I SUPPOSED TO IGNORE YOU?!
JIM DAVIS 4-5

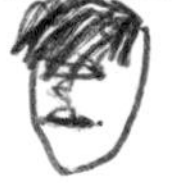

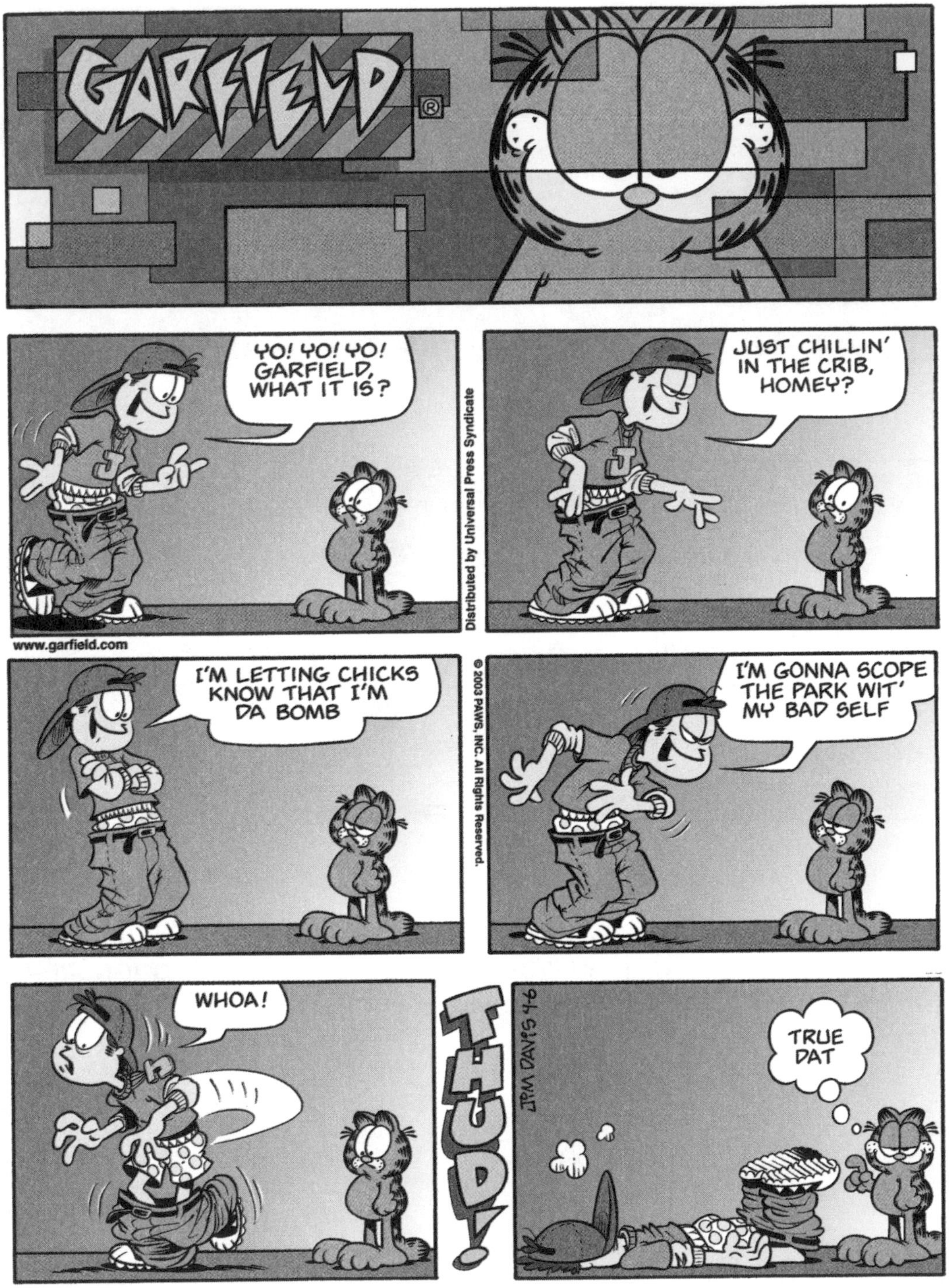
GARFIELD®
YO! YO! YO! GARFIELD, WHAT IT IS?
JUST CHILLIN' IN THE CRIB, HOMEY?
Distributed by Universal Press Syndicate
www.garfield.com
© 2003 PAWS, INC. All Rights Reserved.
I'M LETTING CHICKS KNOW THAT I'M DA BOMB
I'M GONNA SCOPE THE PARK WIT' MY BAD SELF
WHOA!
THUD!
JIM DAVIS 4-6
TRUE DAT

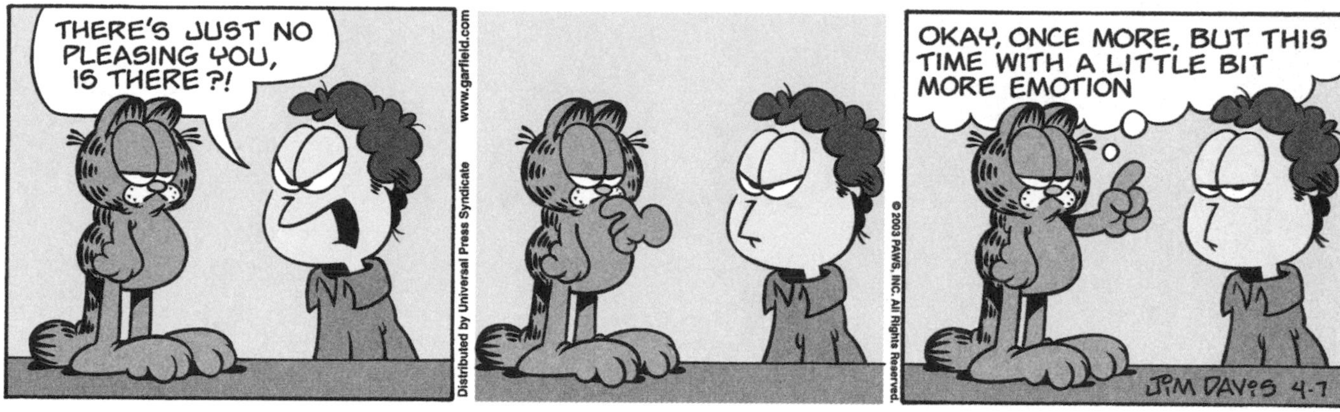
THERE'S JUST NO PLEASING YOU, IS THERE ?!
Distributed by Universal Press Syndicate www.garfield.com
OKAY, ONCE MORE, BUT THIS TIME WITH A LITTLE BIT MORE EMOTION
© 2003 PAWS, INC. All Rights Reserved.
JIM DAVIS 4-7

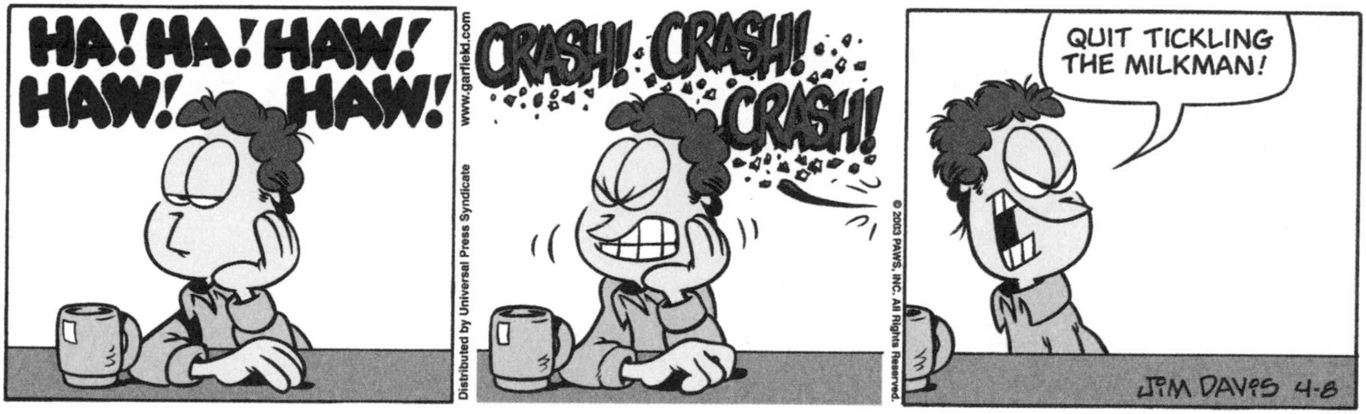
HA! HA! HAW! HAW! HAW!
Distributed by Universal Press Syndicate www.garfield.com
CRASH! CRASH! CRASH!
© 2003 PAWS, INC. All Rights Reserved.
QUIT TICKLING THE MILKMAN!
JIM DAVIS 4-8

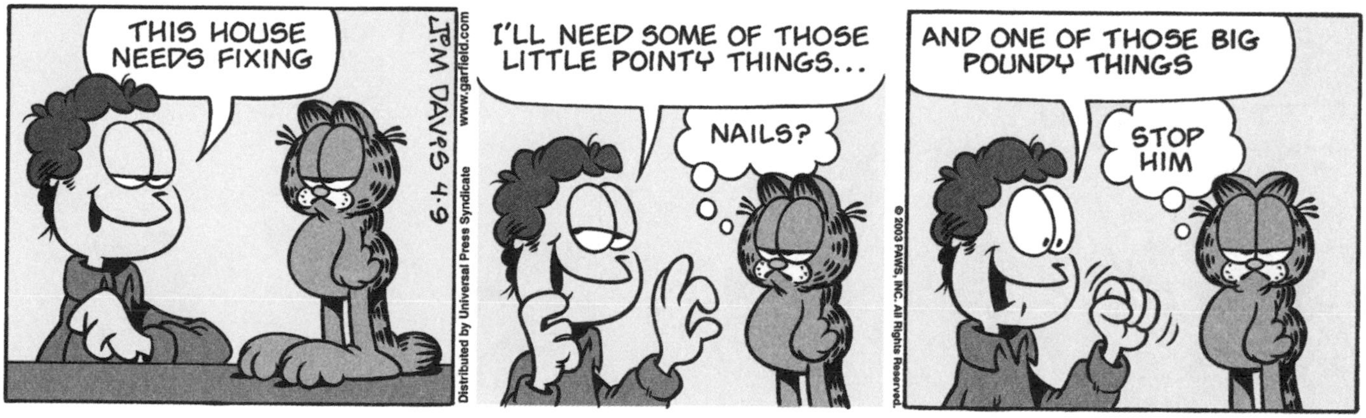
THIS HOUSE NEEDS FIXING
JIM DAVIS 4-9
Distributed by Universal Press Syndicate www.garfield.com
I'LL NEED SOME OF THOSE LITTLE POINTY THINGS...
NAILS?
© 2003 PAWS, INC. All Rights Reserved.
AND ONE OF THOSE BIG POUNDY THINGS
STOP HIM

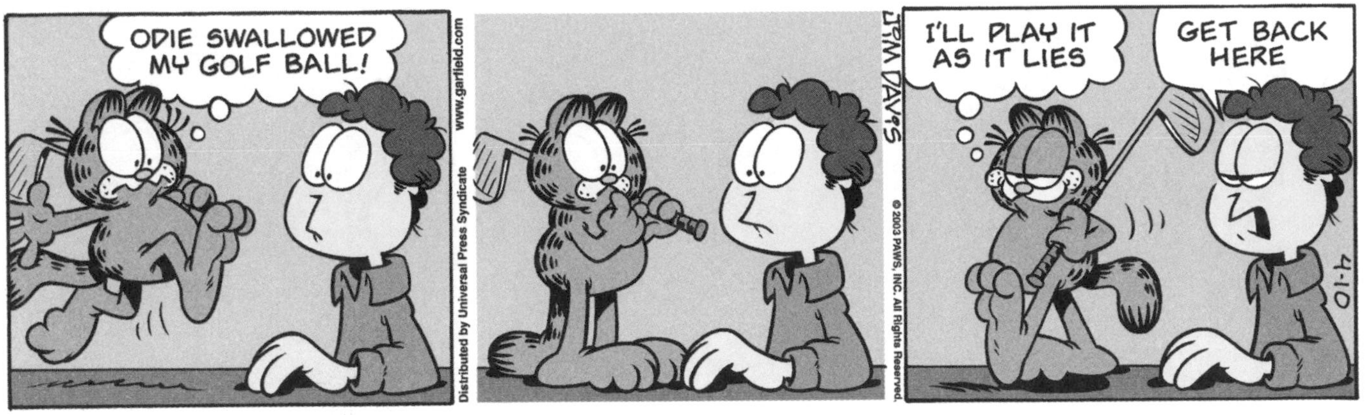
ODIE SWALLOWED MY GOLF BALL!
www.garfield.com
Distributed by Universal Press Syndicate
JIM DAVIS
© 2003 PAWS, INC. All Rights Reserved.
I'LL PLAY IT AS IT LIES
GET BACK HERE
4-10

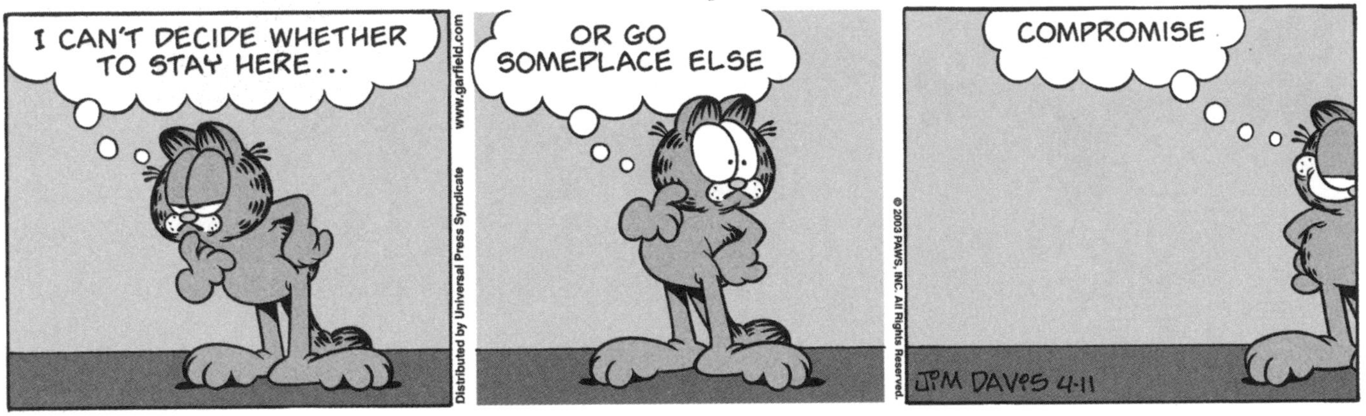
I CAN'T DECIDE WHETHER TO STAY HERE...
www.garfield.com
Distributed by Universal Press Syndicate
OR GO SOMEPLACE ELSE
© 2003 PAWS, INC. All Rights Reserved.
COMPROMISE
JIM DAVIS 4-11

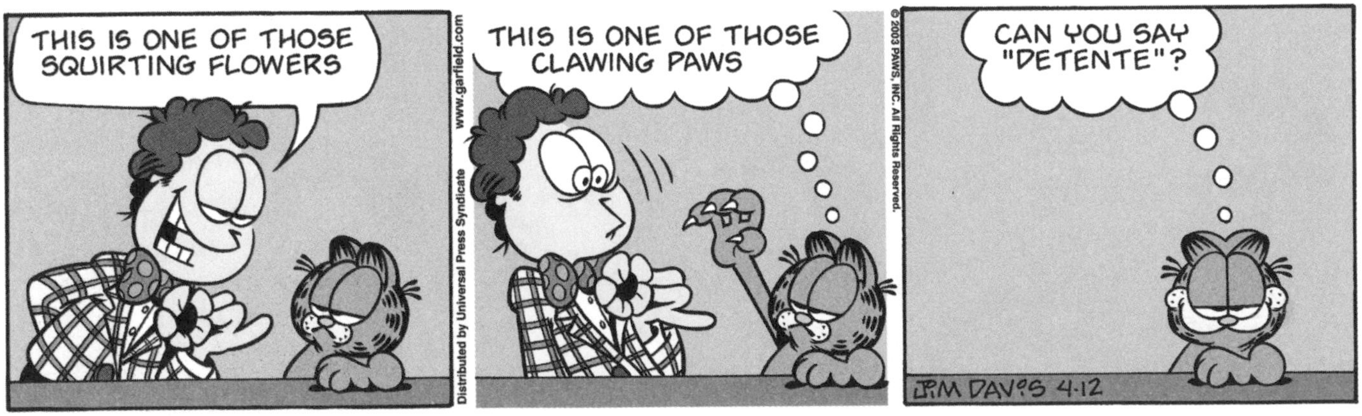
THIS IS ONE OF THOSE SQUIRTING FLOWERS
www.garfield.com
Distributed by Universal Press Syndicate
THIS IS ONE OF THOSE CLAWING PAWS
© 2003 PAWS, INC. All Rights Reserved.
CAN YOU SAY "DETENTE"?
JIM DAVIS 4-12

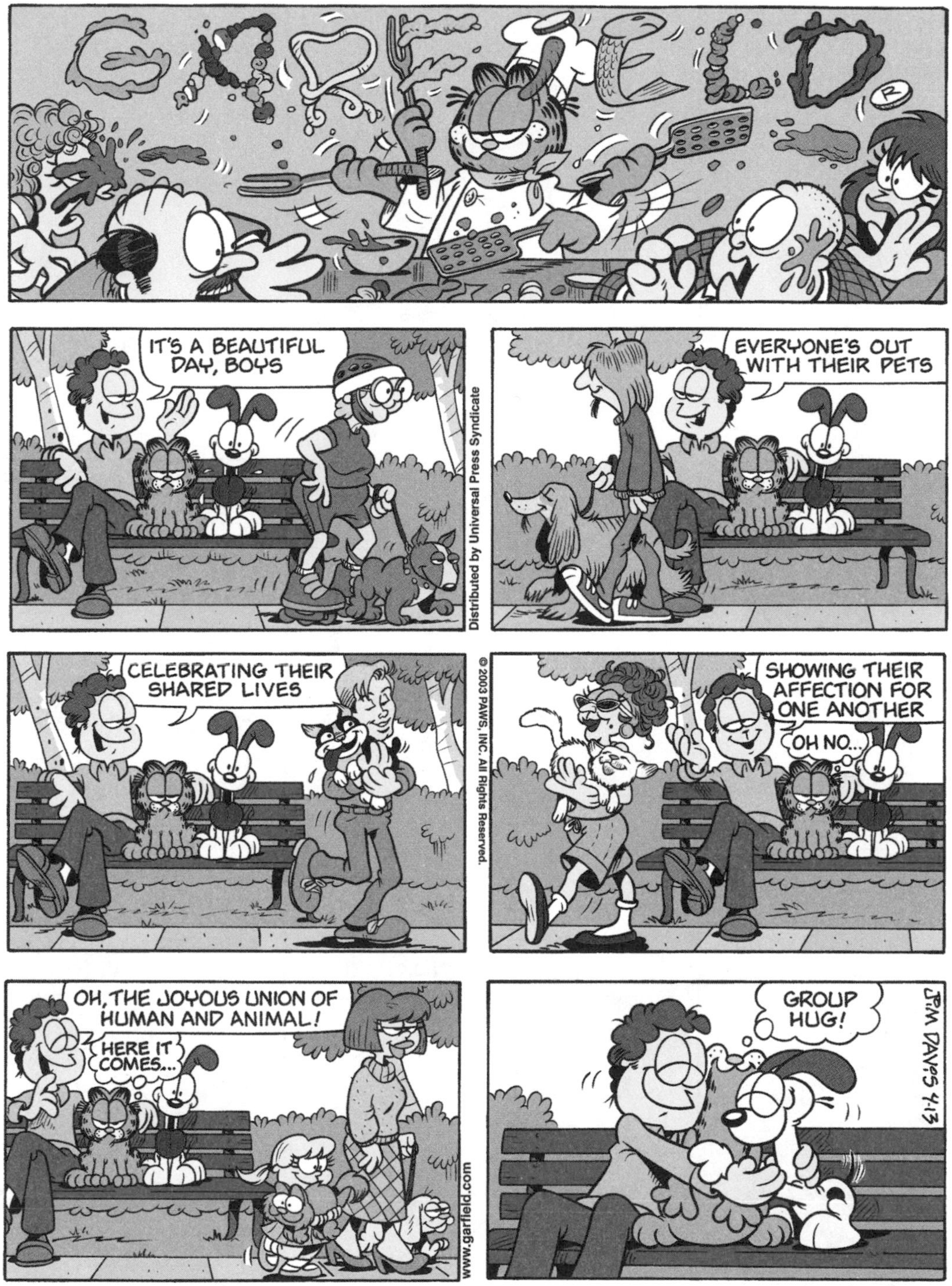
GARFIELD ®
IT'S A BEAUTIFUL DAY, BOYS
Distributed by Universal Press Syndicate
EVERYONE'S OUT WITH THEIR PETS
CELEBRATING THEIR SHARED LIVES
© 2003 PAWS, INC. All Rights Reserved.
SHOWING THEIR AFFECTION FOR ONE ANOTHER
OH NO...
OH, THE JOYOUS UNION OF HUMAN AND ANIMAL!
HERE IT COMES...
www.garfield.com
GROUP HUG!
JIM DAVIS 4-13

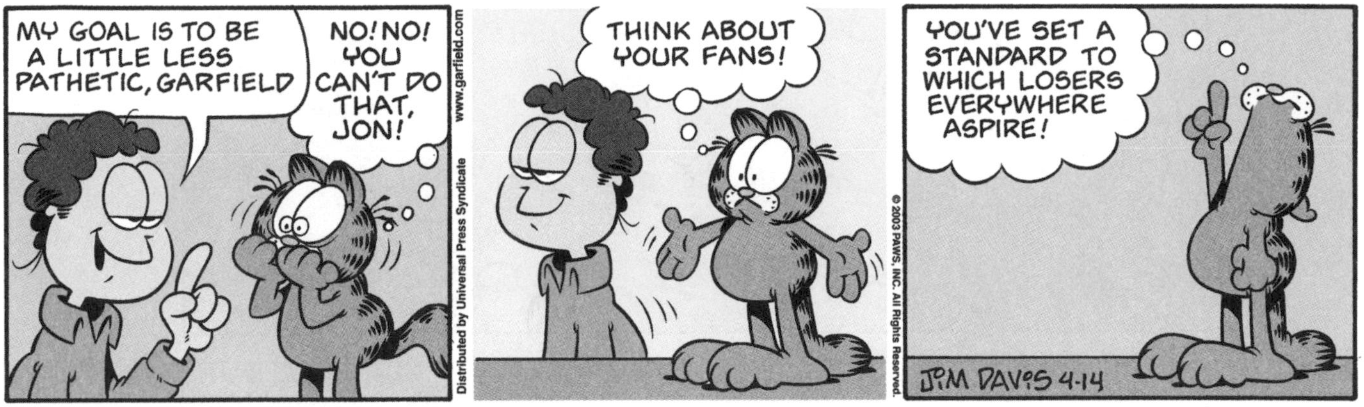
MY GOAL IS TO BE A LITTLE LESS PATHETIC, GARFIELD
NO! NO! YOU CAN'T DO THAT, JON!
www.garfield.com
Distributed by Universal Press Syndicate
THINK ABOUT YOUR FANS!
© 2003 PAWS, INC. All Rights Reserved.
YOU'VE SET A STANDARD TO WHICH LOSERS EVERYWHERE ASPIRE!
JIM DAVIS 4-14

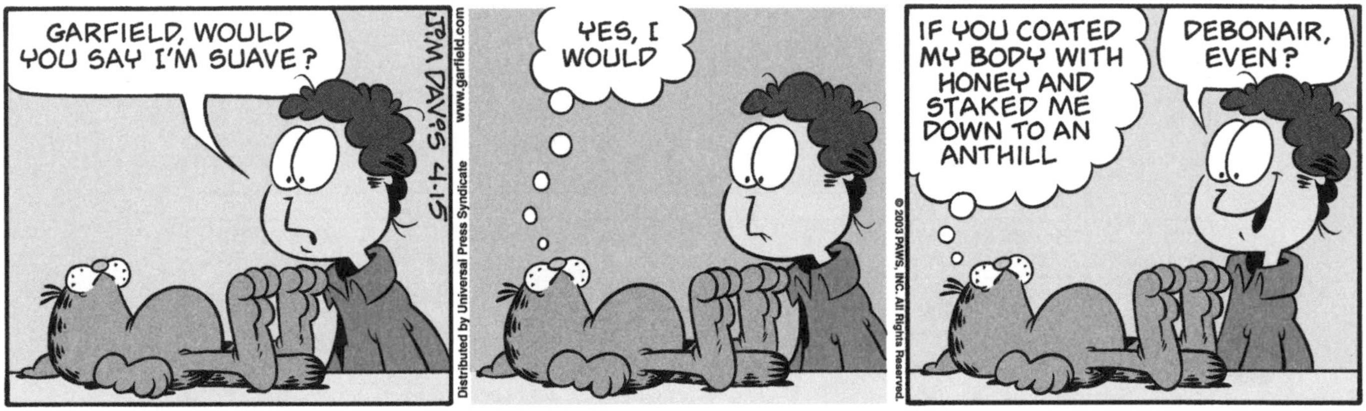
GARFIELD, WOULD YOU SAY I'M SUAVE?
JIM DAVIS 4-15
www.garfield.com
Distributed by Universal Press Syndicate
YES, I WOULD
© 2003 PAWS, INC. All Rights Reserved.
IF YOU COATED MY BODY WITH HONEY AND STAKED ME DOWN TO AN ANTHILL
DEBONAIR, EVEN?

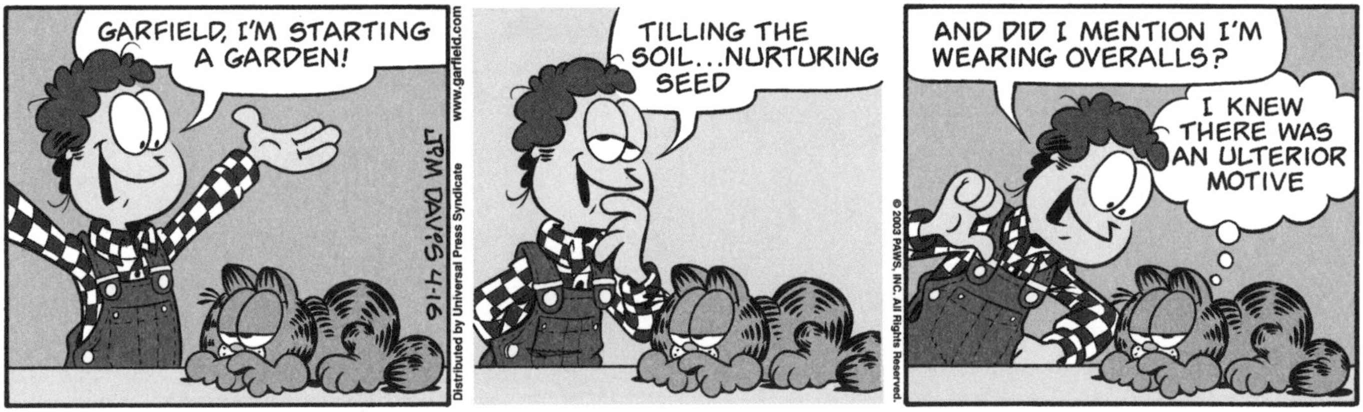
GARFIELD, I'M STARTING A GARDEN!
JIM DAVIS 4-16
www.garfield.com
Distributed by Universal Press Syndicate
TILLING THE SOIL...NURTURING SEED
© 2003 PAWS, INC. All Rights Reserved.
AND DID I MENTION I'M WEARING OVERALLS?
I KNEW THERE WAS AN ULTERIOR MOTIVE

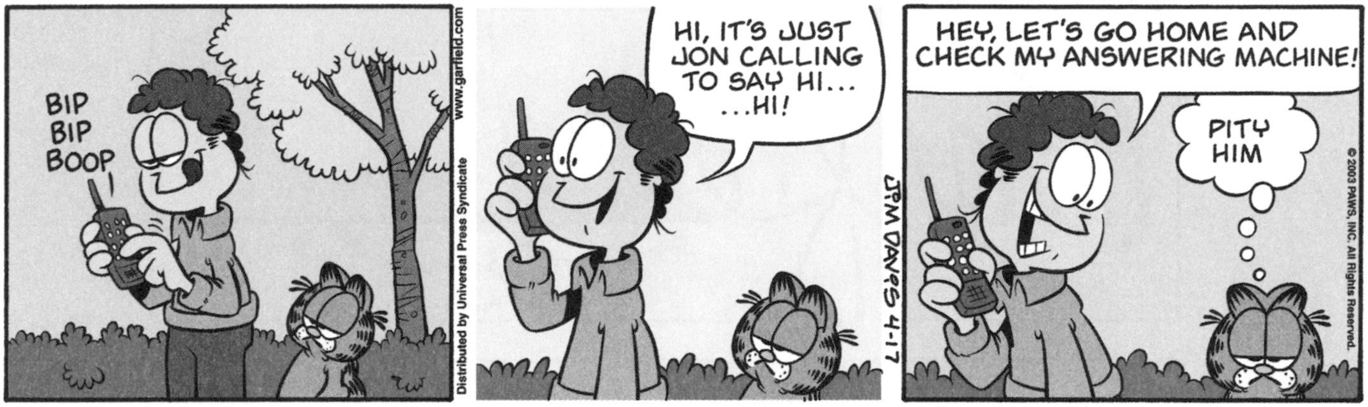
BIP
BIP
BOOP
Distributed by Universal Press Syndicate www.garfield.com
HI, IT'S JUST JON CALLING TO SAY HI... ...HI!
JIM DAVIS 4-17
HEY, LET'S GO HOME AND CHECK MY ANSWERING MACHINE!
PITY HIM
© 2003 PAWS, INC. All Rights Reserved.

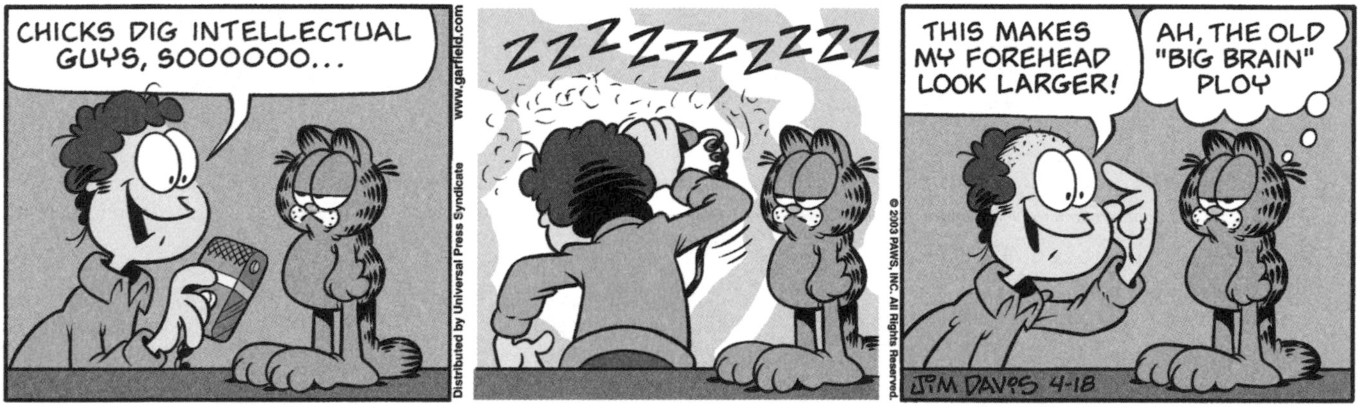
CHICKS DIG INTELLECTUAL GUYS, SOOOOOO...
Distributed by Universal Press Syndicate www.garfield.com
ZZZZZZZZZZZ
© 2003 PAWS, INC. All Rights Reserved.
THIS MAKES MY FOREHEAD LOOK LARGER!
AH, THE OLD "BIG BRAIN" PLOY
JIM DAVIS 4-18

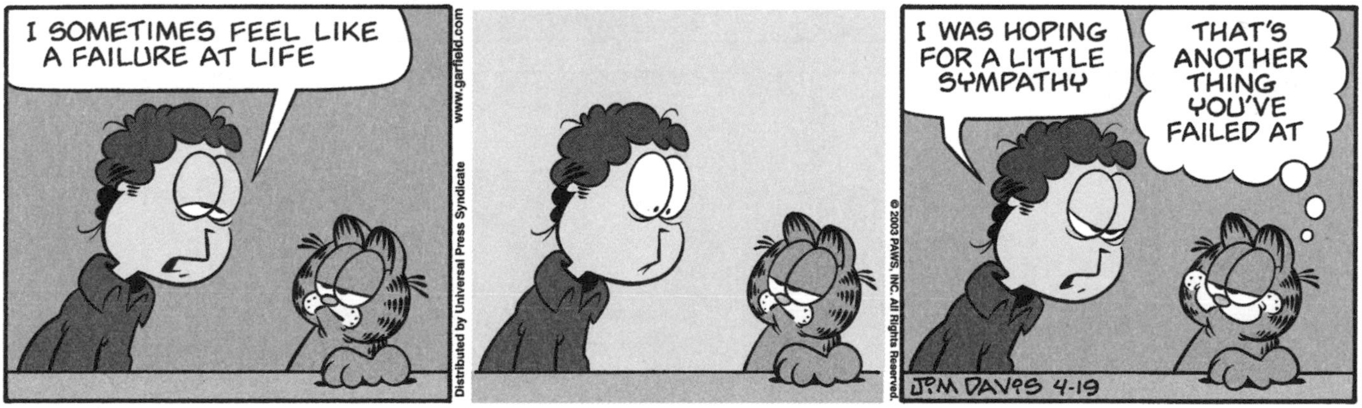
I SOMETIMES FEEL LIKE A FAILURE AT LIFE
Distributed by Universal Press Syndicate www.garfield.com
© 2003 PAWS, INC. All Rights Reserved.
I WAS HOPING FOR A LITTLE SYMPATHY
THAT'S ANOTHER THING YOU'VE FAILED AT
JIM DAVIS 4-19

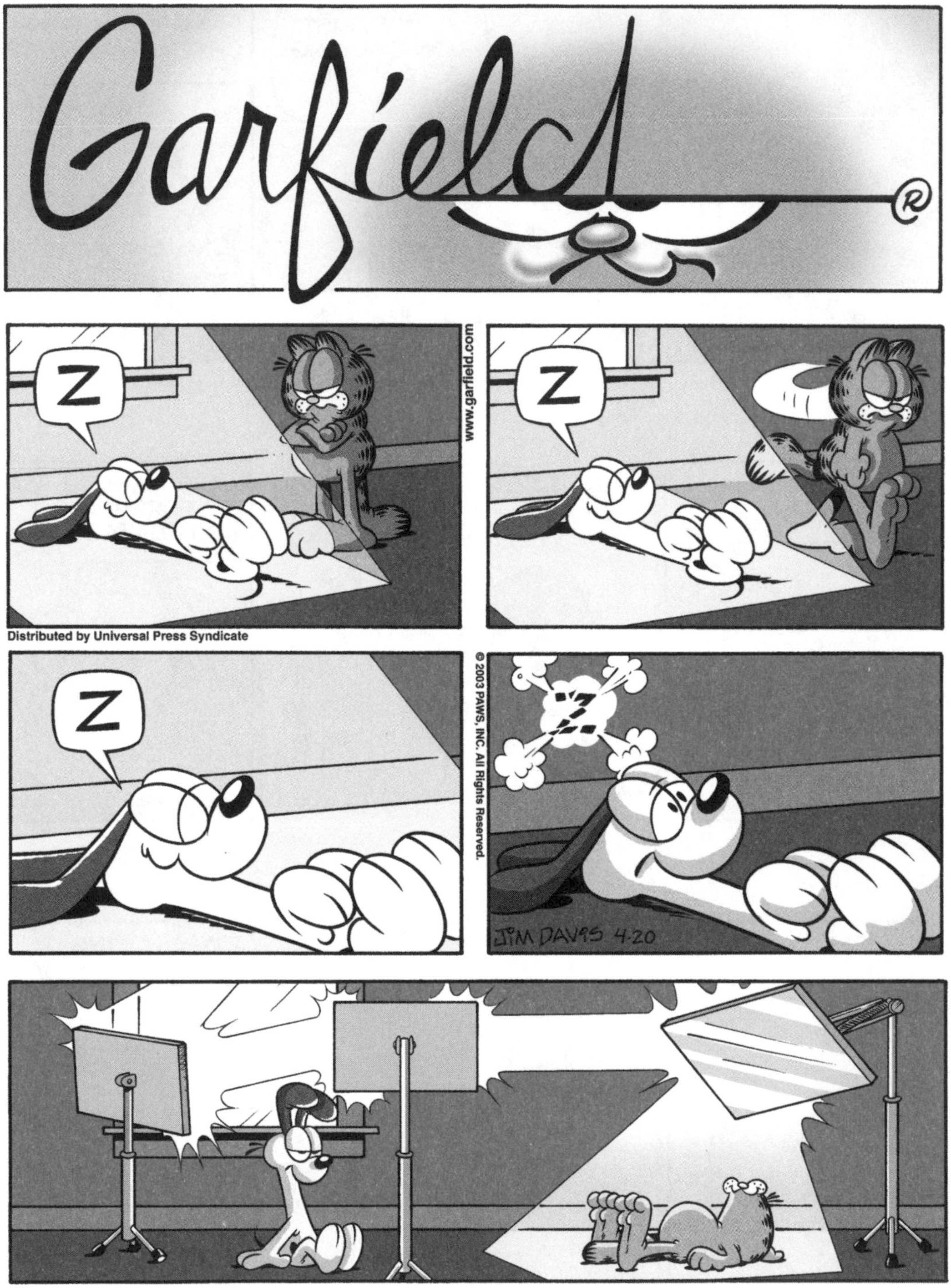
Garfield
Z
Z
Z
www.garfield.com
Distributed by Universal Press Syndicate
© 2003 PAWS, INC. All Rights Reserved.
JIM DAVIS 4-20

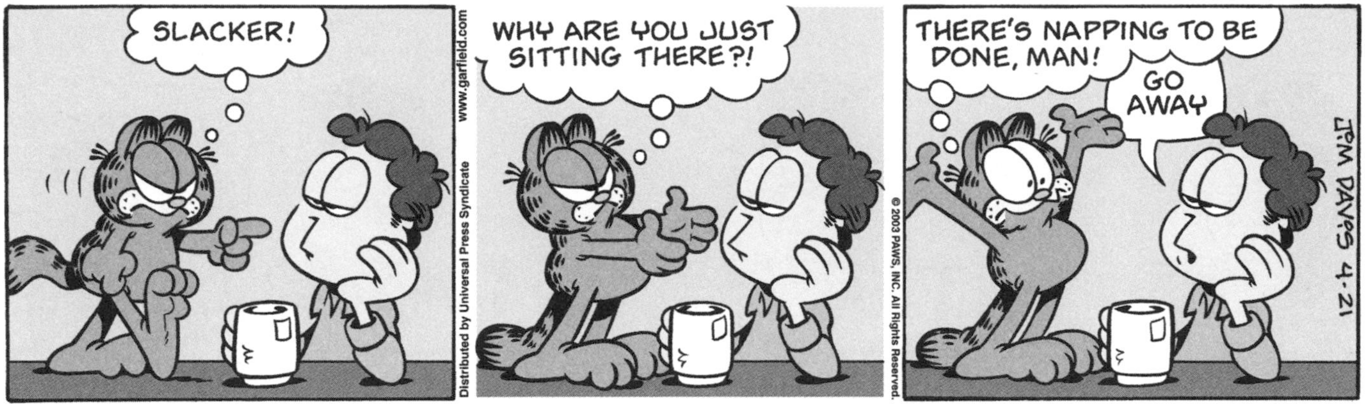
SLACKER!
WHY ARE YOU JUST SITTING THERE?!
THERE'S NAPPING TO BE DONE, MAN!
GO AWAY
JIM DAVIS 4-21
www.garfield.com
Distributed by Universal Press Syndicate
© 2003 PAWS, INC. All Rights Reserved.

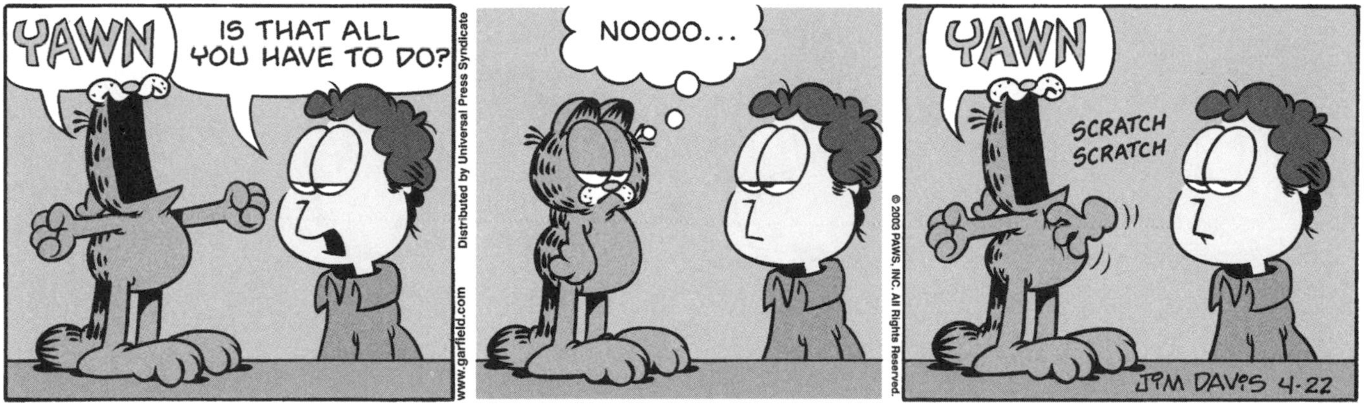
YAWN
IS THAT ALL YOU HAVE TO DO?
NOOOO...
YAWN
SCRATCH SCRATCH
JIM DAVIS 4-22
www.garfield.com
Distributed by Universal Press Syndicate
© 2003 PAWS, INC. All Rights Reserved.

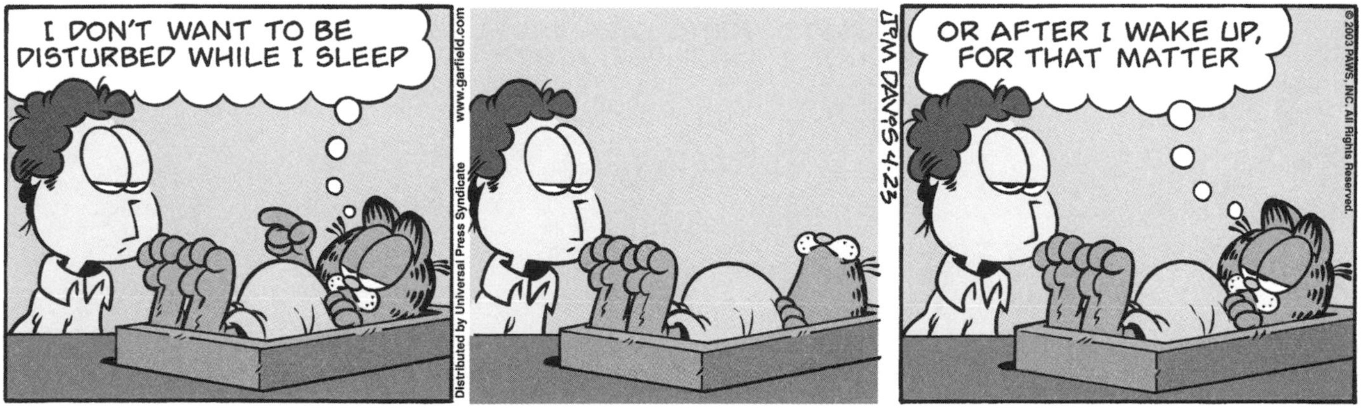
I DON'T WANT TO BE DISTURBED WHILE I SLEEP
OR AFTER I WAKE UP, FOR THAT MATTER
JIM DAVIS 4-23
www.garfield.com
Distributed by Universal Press Syndicate
© 2003 PAWS, INC. All Rights Reserved.

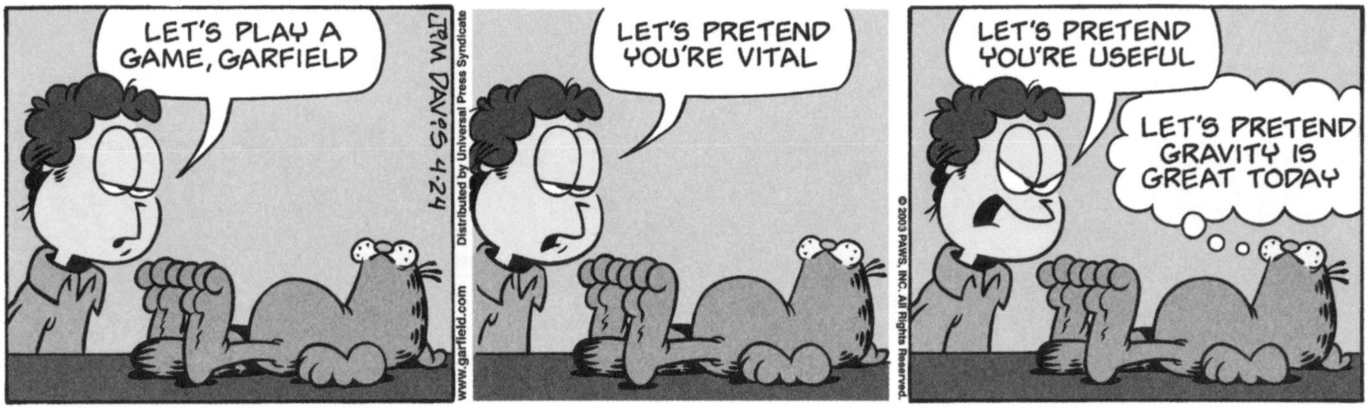
LET'S PLAY A GAME, GARFIELD
JIM DAVIS 4-24
Distributed by Universal Press Syndicate
www.garfield.com
LET'S PRETEND YOU'RE VITAL
LET'S PRETEND YOU'RE USEFUL
LET'S PRETEND GRAVITY IS GREAT TODAY
© 2003 PAWS, INC. All Rights Reserved.

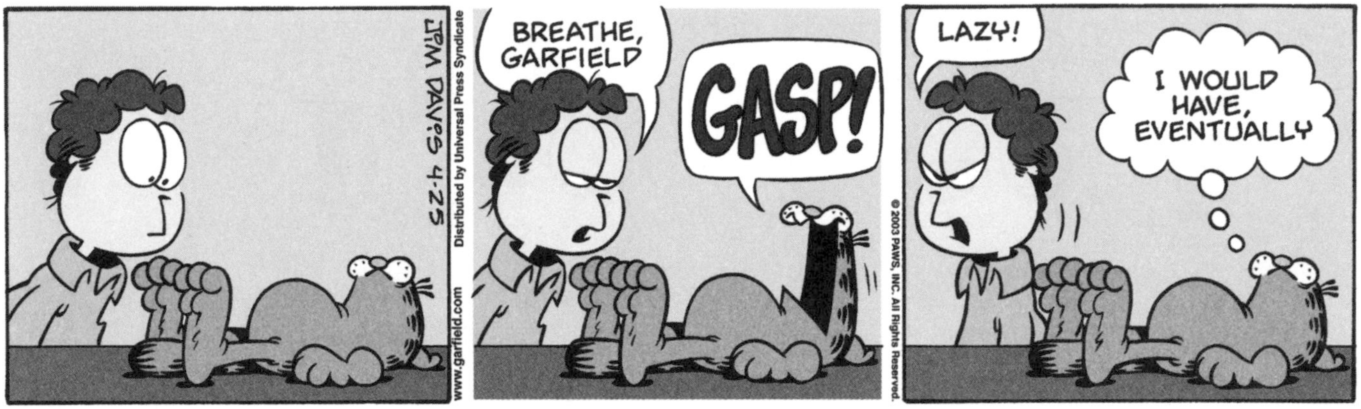
JIM DAVIS 4-25
Distributed by Universal Press Syndicate
www.garfield.com
BREATHE, GARFIELD
GASP!
© 2003 PAWS, INC. All Rights Reserved.
LAZY!
I WOULD HAVE, EVENTUALLY

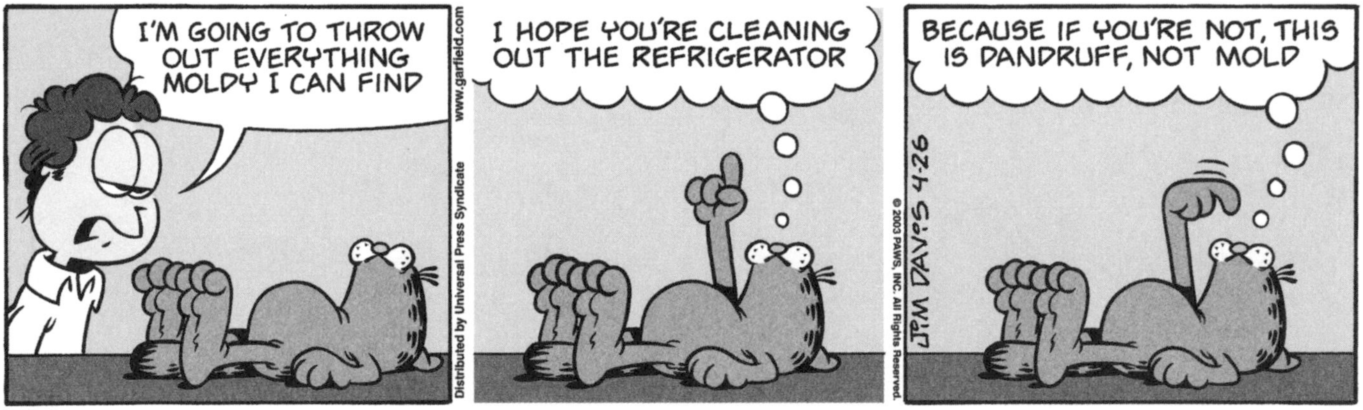
I'M GOING TO THROW OUT EVERYTHING MOLDY I CAN FIND
www.garfield.com
Distributed by Universal Press Syndicate
I HOPE YOU'RE CLEANING OUT THE REFRIGERATOR
© 2003 PAWS, INC. All Rights Reserved.
JIM DAVIS 4-26
BECAUSE IF YOU'RE NOT, THIS IS DANDRUFF, NOT MOLD

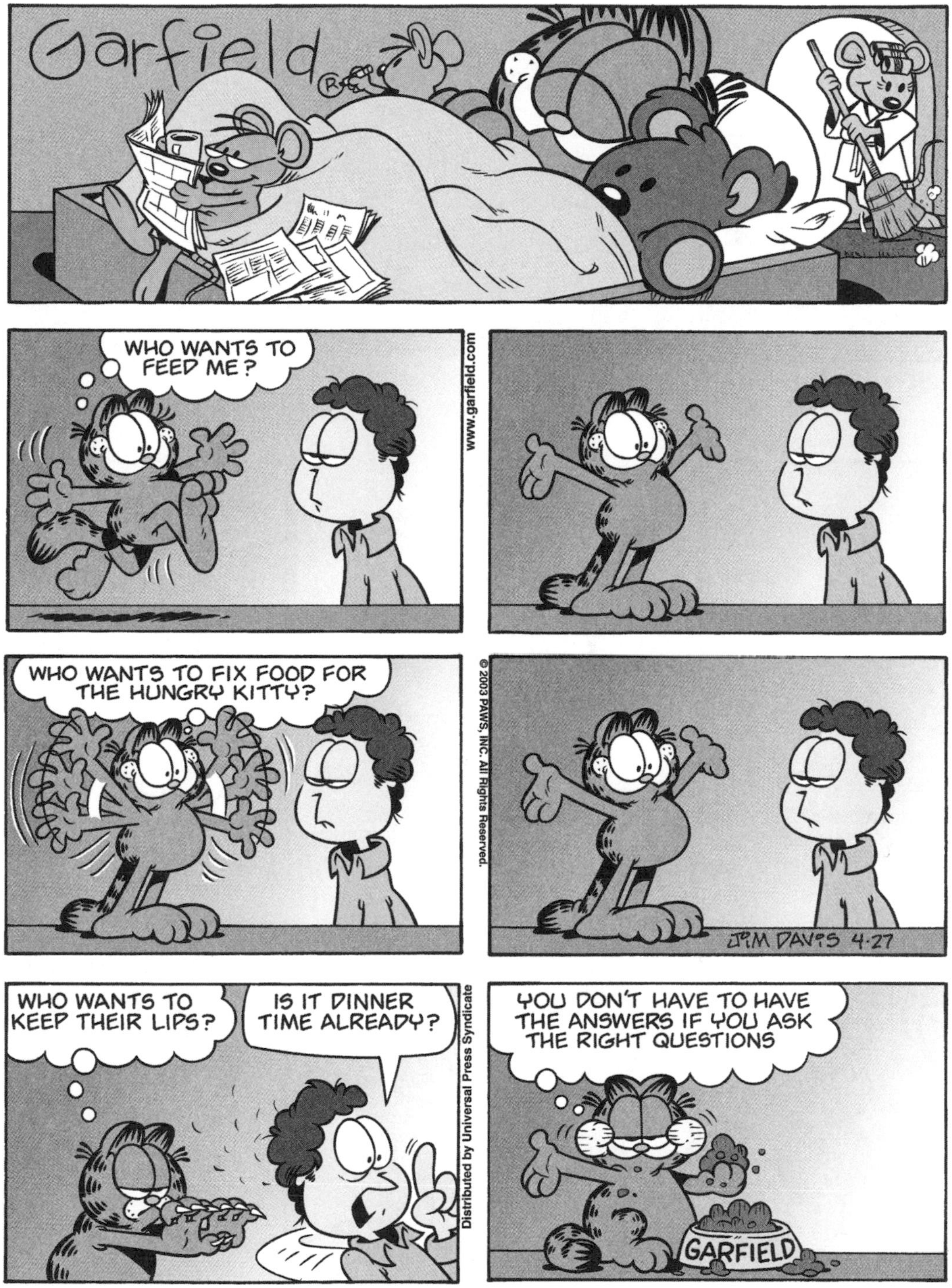
Garfield
WHO WANTS TO FEED ME?
www.garfield.com
WHO WANTS TO FIX FOOD FOR THE HUNGRY KITTY?
© 2003 PAWS, INC. All Rights Reserved.
JIM DAVIS 4-27
WHO WANTS TO KEEP THEIR LIPS?
IS IT DINNER TIME ALREADY?
Distributed by Universal Press Syndicate
YOU DON'T HAVE TO HAVE THE ANSWERS IF YOU ASK THE RIGHT QUESTIONS
GARFIELD

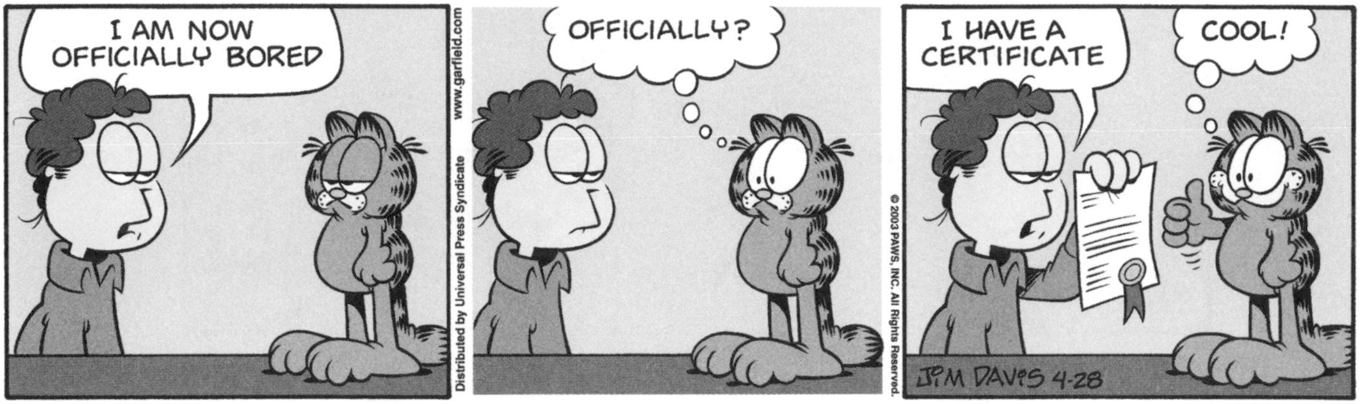
I AM NOW OFFICIALLY BORED
Distributed by Universal Press Syndicate www.garfield.com
OFFICIALLY?
© 2003 PAWS, INC. All Rights Reserved.
I HAVE A CERTIFICATE
COOL!
JIM DAVIS 4-28

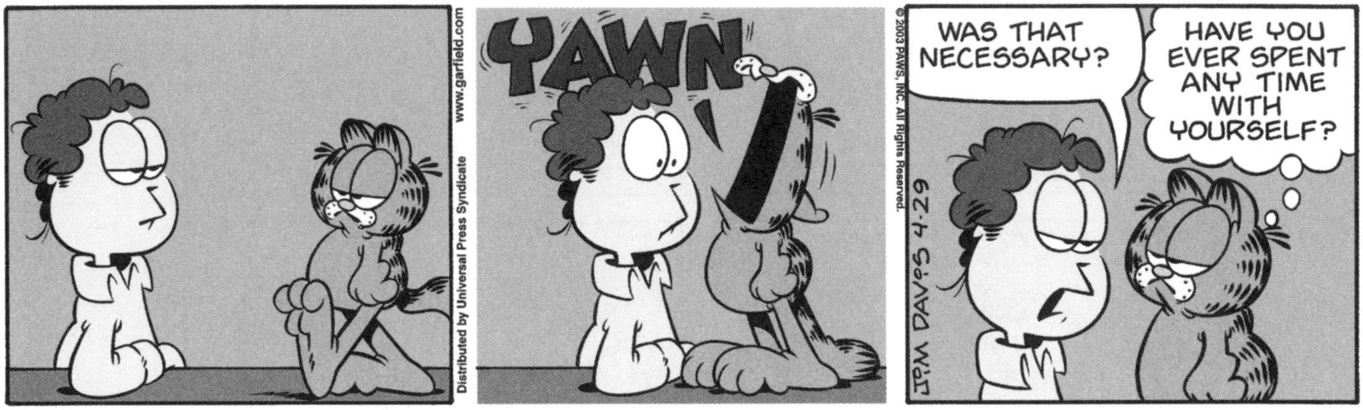
Distributed by Universal Press Syndicate www.garfield.com
YAWN
© 2003 PAWS, INC. All Rights Reserved.
JIM DAVIS 4-29
WAS THAT NECESSARY?
HAVE YOU EVER SPENT ANY TIME WITH YOURSELF?

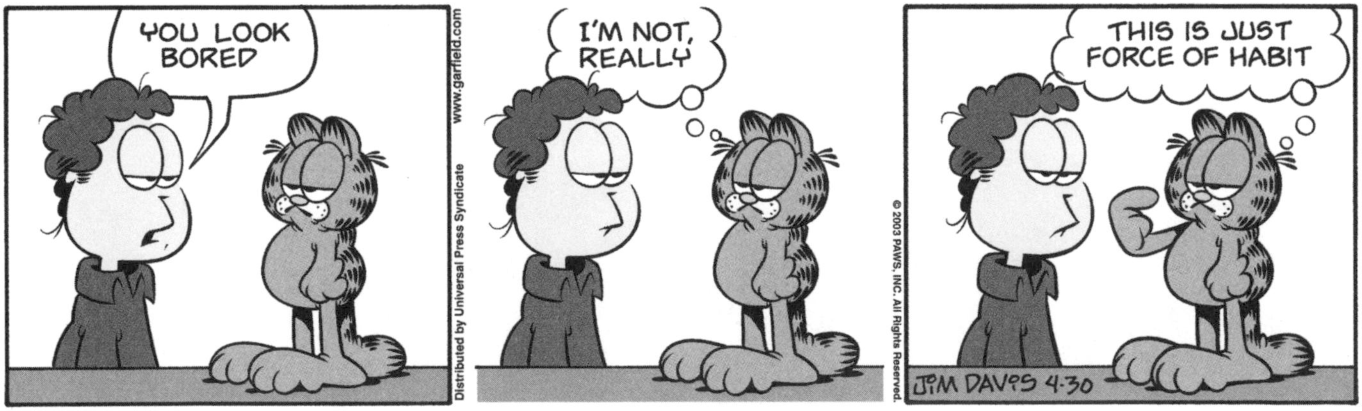
YOU LOOK BORED
Distributed by Universal Press Syndicate www.garfield.com
I'M NOT, REALLY
© 2003 PAWS, INC. All Rights Reserved.
THIS IS JUST FORCE OF HABIT
JIM DAVIS 4-30

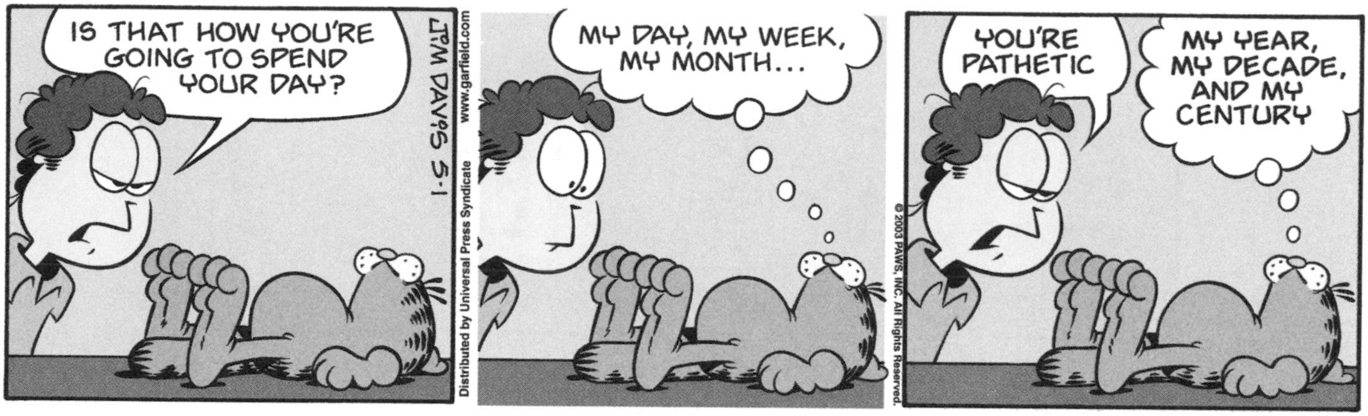
IS THAT HOW YOU'RE GOING TO SPEND YOUR DAY?
JIM DAVIS 5-1
www.garfield.com
Distributed by Universal Press Syndicate
MY DAY, MY WEEK, MY MONTH...
© 2003 PAWS, INC. All Rights Reserved.
YOU'RE PATHETIC
MY YEAR, MY DECADE, AND MY CENTURY

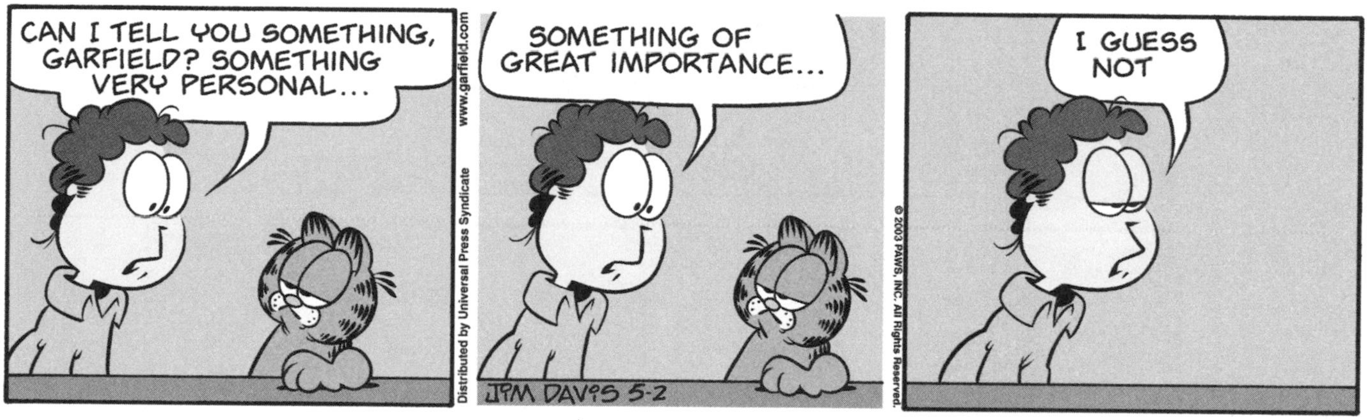
CAN I TELL YOU SOMETHING, GARFIELD? SOMETHING VERY PERSONAL...
www.garfield.com
Distributed by Universal Press Syndicate
SOMETHING OF GREAT IMPORTANCE...
JIM DAVIS 5-2
© 2003 PAWS, INC. All Rights Reserved.
I GUESS NOT

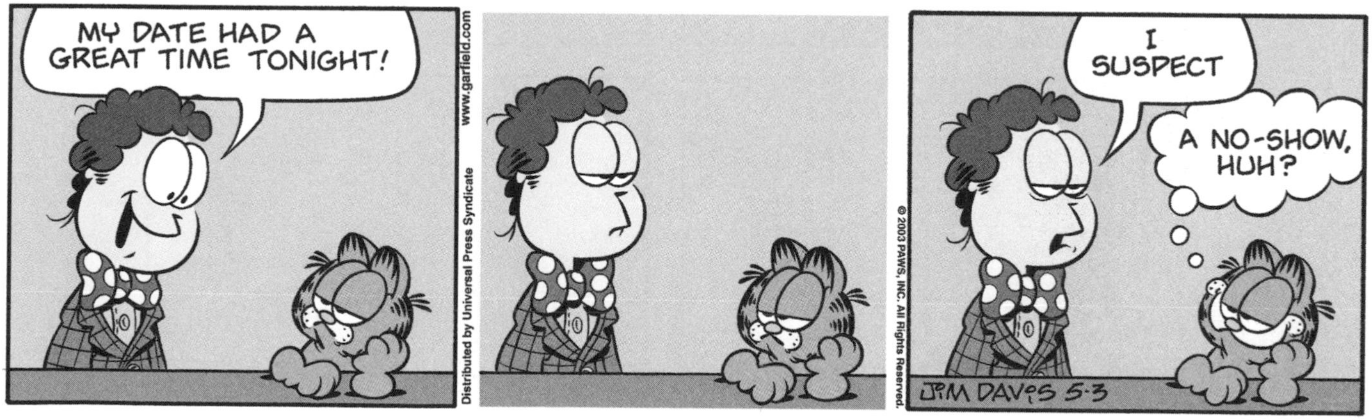
MY DATE HAD A GREAT TIME TONIGHT!
www.garfield.com
Distributed by Universal Press Syndicate
© 2003 PAWS, INC. All Rights Reserved.
I SUSPECT
A NO-SHOW, HUH?
JIM DAVIS 5-3

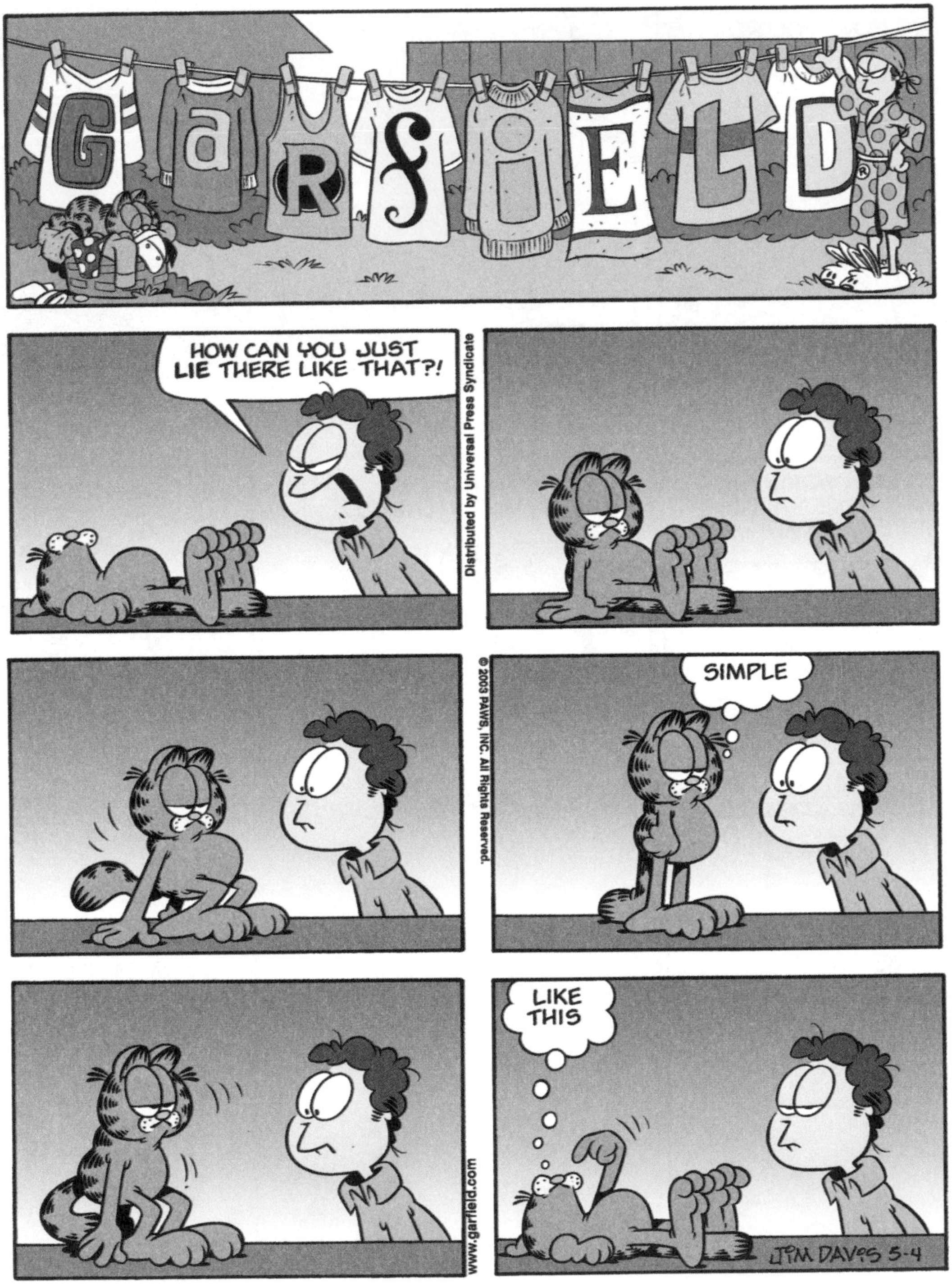
GARFIELD
HOW CAN YOU JUST LIE THERE LIKE THAT?!
Distributed by Universal Press Syndicate
© 2003 PAWS, INC. All Rights Reserved.
SIMPLE
LIKE THIS
www.garfield.com
JIM DAVIS 5-4

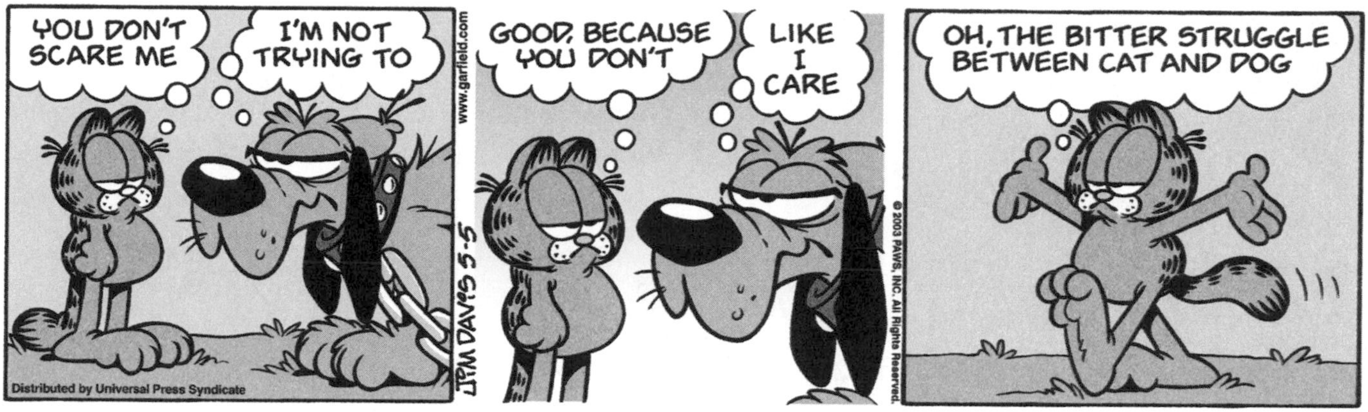
YOU DON'T SCARE ME
I'M NOT TRYING TO
GOOD, BECAUSE YOU DON'T
LIKE I CARE
OH, THE BITTER STRUGGLE BETWEEN CAT AND DOG
Distributed by Universal Press Syndicate
www.garfield.com
JPM DAVIS 5-5
© 2003 PAWS, INC. All Rights Reserved.

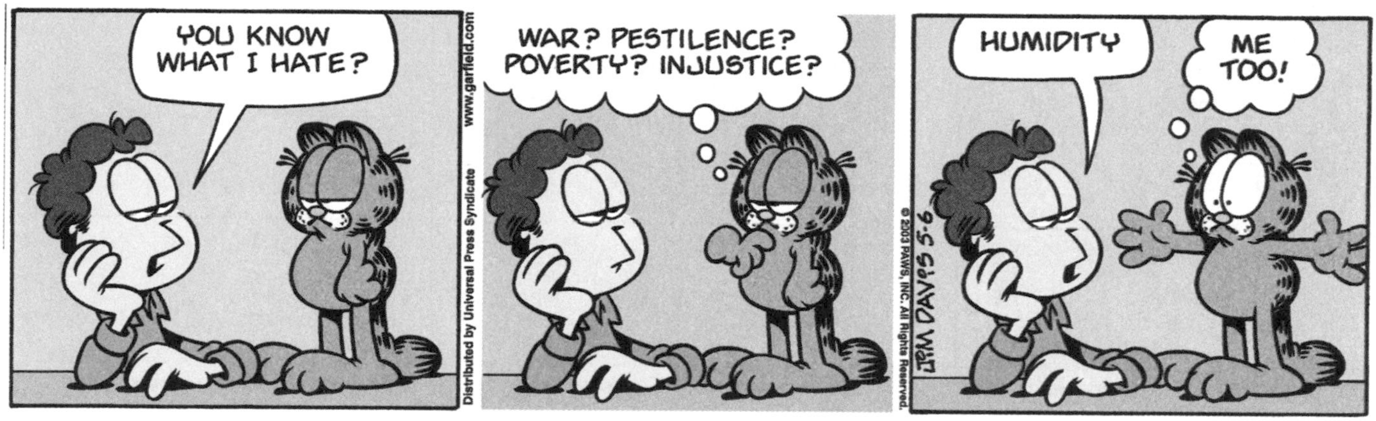
YOU KNOW WHAT I HATE?
WAR? PESTILENCE? POVERTY? INJUSTICE?
HUMIDITY
ME TOO!
www.garfield.com
Distributed by Universal Press Syndicate
© 2003 PAWS, INC. All Rights Reserved.
JPM DAVIS 5-6

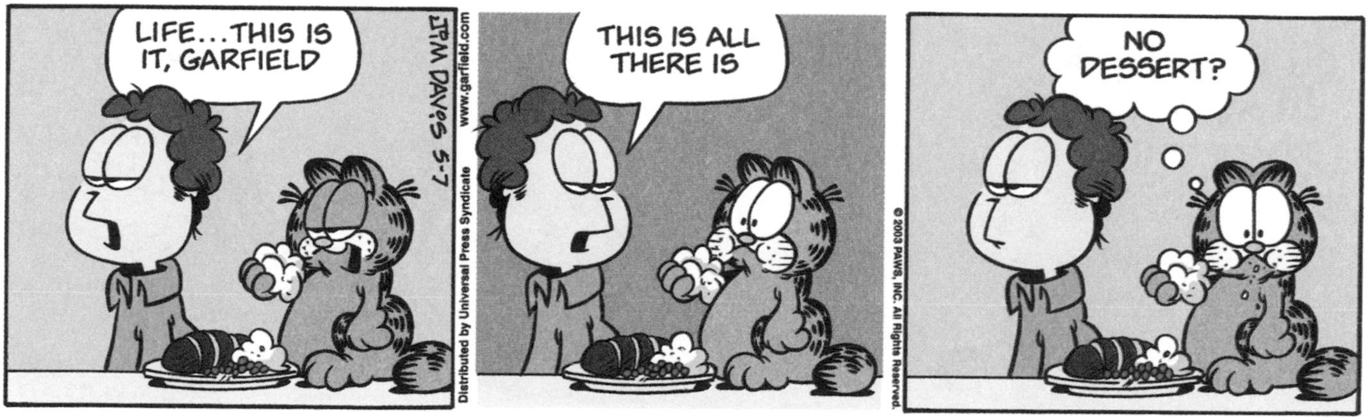
LIFE... THIS IS IT, GARFIELD
THIS IS ALL THERE IS
NO DESSERT?
JPM DAVIS 5-7
www.garfield.com
Distributed by Universal Press Syndicate
© 2003 PAWS, INC. All Rights Reserved.

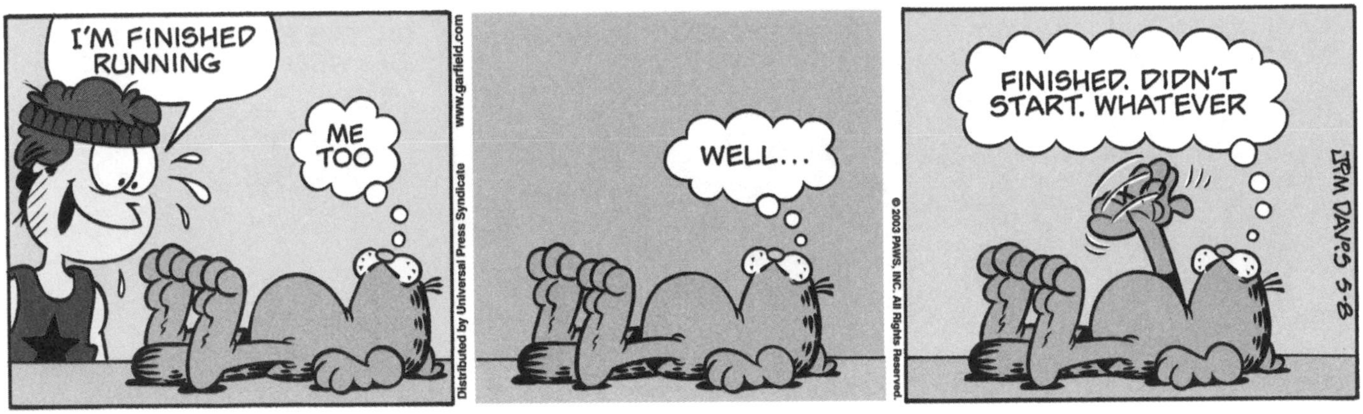
I'M FINISHED RUNNING
ME TOO
www.garfield.com
Distributed by Universal Press Syndicate
WELL...
© 2003 PAWS, INC. All Rights Reserved.
FINISHED. DIDN'T START. WHATEVER
JIM DAVIS 5-8

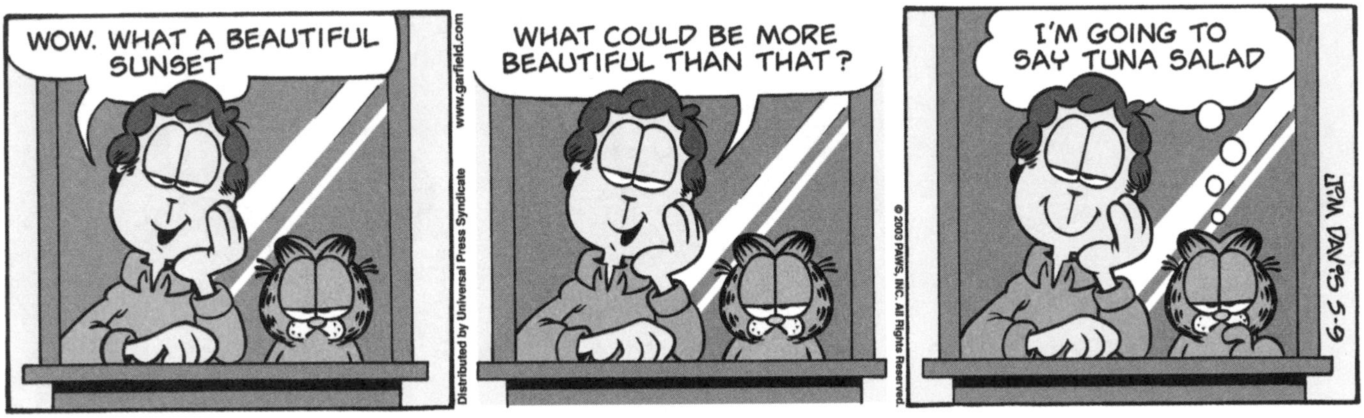
WOW. WHAT A BEAUTIFUL SUNSET
www.garfield.com
Distributed by Universal Press Syndicate
WHAT COULD BE MORE BEAUTIFUL THAN THAT?
© 2003 PAWS, INC. All Rights Reserved.
I'M GOING TO SAY TUNA SALAD
JIM DAVIS 5-9

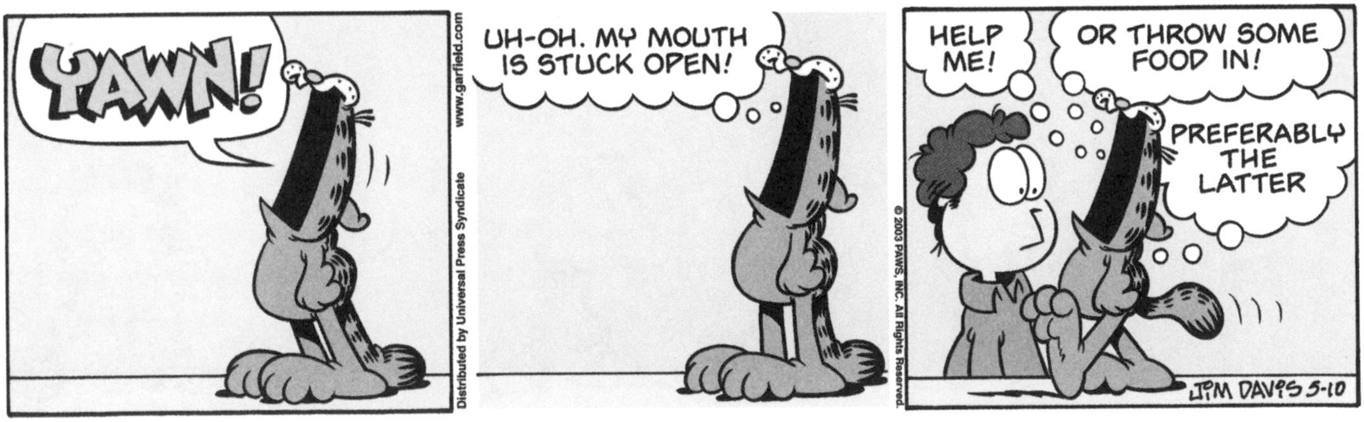
YAWN!
www.garfield.com
Distributed by Universal Press Syndicate
UH-OH. MY MOUTH IS STUCK OPEN!
© 2003 PAWS, INC. All Rights Reserved.
HELP ME!
OR THROW SOME FOOD IN!
PREFERABLY THE LATTER
JIM DAVIS 5-10

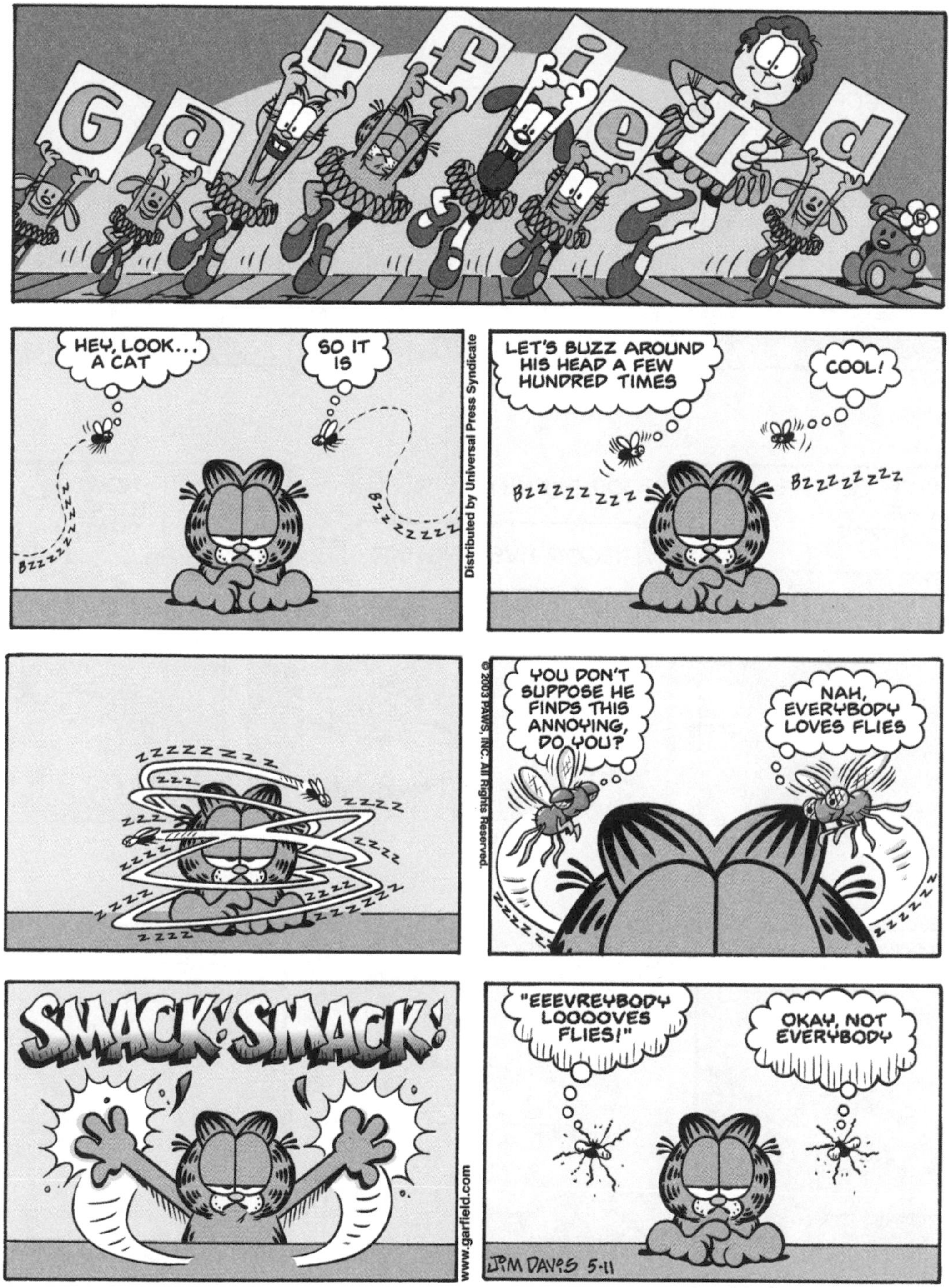
Garfield
HEY, LOOK... A CAT
SO IT IS
BZZZZZZZ
BZZZZZZZ
LET'S BUZZ AROUND HIS HEAD A FEW HUNDRED TIMES
COOL!
BZZZZZZZ
BZZZZZZZZ
ZZZZZZZZZ
YOU DON'T SUPPOSE HE FINDS THIS ANNOYING, DO YOU?
NAH, EVERYBODY LOVES FLIES
SMACK! SMACK!
"EEEVREYBODY LOOOOVES FLIES!"
OKAY, NOT EVERYBODY
JIM DAVIS 5-11
Distributed by Universal Press Syndicate
© 2003 PAWS, INC. All Rights Reserved.
www.garfield.com

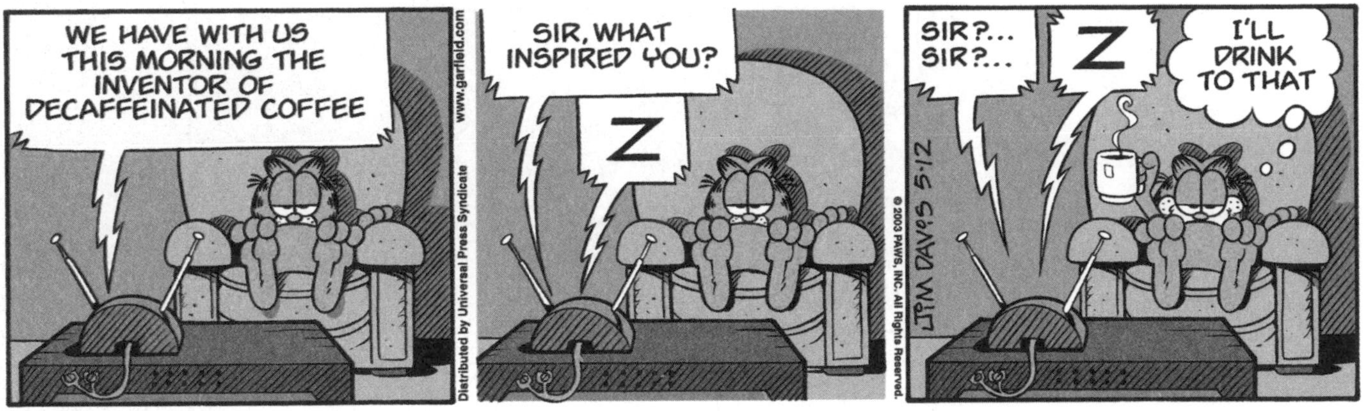
WE HAVE WITH US THIS MORNING THE INVENTOR OF DECAFFEINATED COFFEE
www.garfield.com
Distributed by Universal Press Syndicate
SIR, WHAT INSPIRED YOU?
Z
© 2003 PAWS, INC. All Rights Reserved.
JPM DAVIS 5-12
SIR?... SIR?...
Z
I'LL DRINK TO THAT

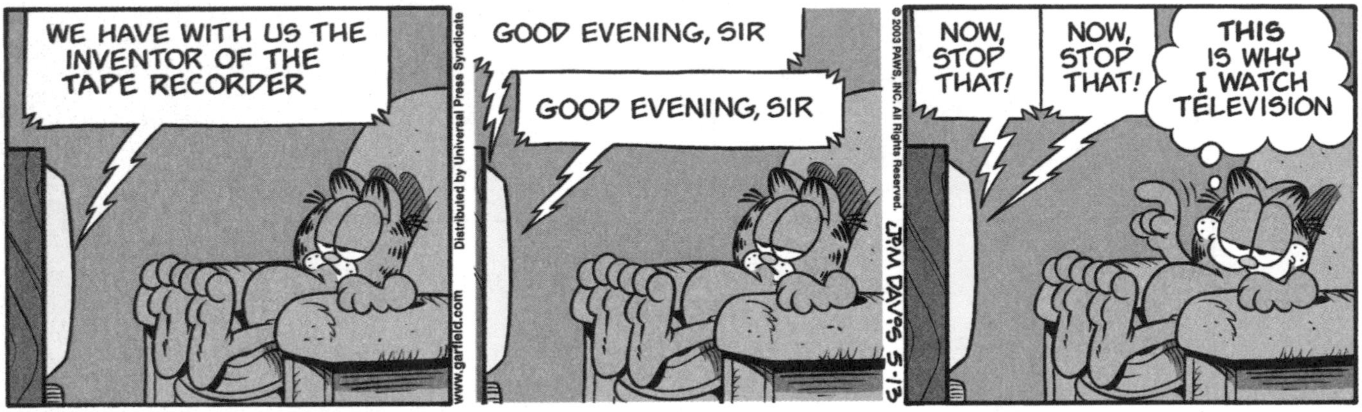
WE HAVE WITH US THE INVENTOR OF THE TAPE RECORDER
www.garfield.com
Distributed by Universal Press Syndicate
GOOD EVENING, SIR
GOOD EVENING, SIR
© 2003 PAWS, INC. All Rights Reserved.
JPM DAVIS 5-13
NOW, STOP THAT!
NOW, STOP THAT!
THIS IS WHY I WATCH TELEVISION

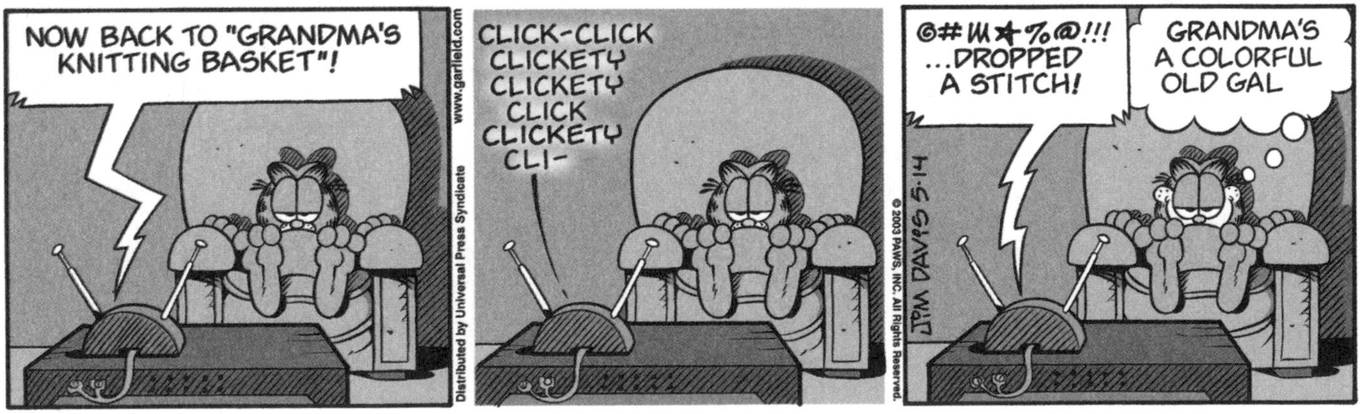
NOW BACK TO "GRANDMA'S KNITTING BASKET"!
www.garfield.com
Distributed by Universal Press Syndicate
CLICK-CLICK CLICKETY CLICKETY CLICK CLICKETY CLI-
© 2003 PAWS, INC. All Rights Reserved.
JPM DAVIS 5-14
@#Ш✱%@!!! ...DROPPED A STITCH!
GRANDMA'S A COLORFUL OLD GAL

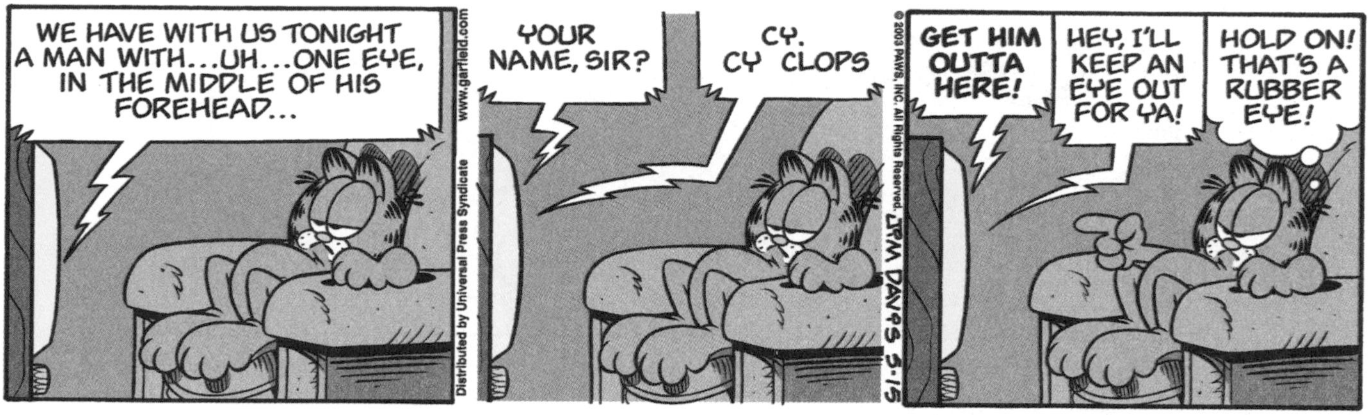
WE HAVE WITH US TONIGHT A MAN WITH...UH...ONE EYE, IN THE MIDDLE OF HIS FOREHEAD...
www.garfield.com
Distributed by Universal Press Syndicate
YOUR NAME, SIR?
CY. CY CLOPS
JPM DAVPS 5-15
© 2003 PAWS, INC. All Rights Reserved.
GET HIM OUTTA HERE!
HEY, I'LL KEEP AN EYE OUT FOR YA!
HOLD ON! THAT'S A RUBBER EYE!

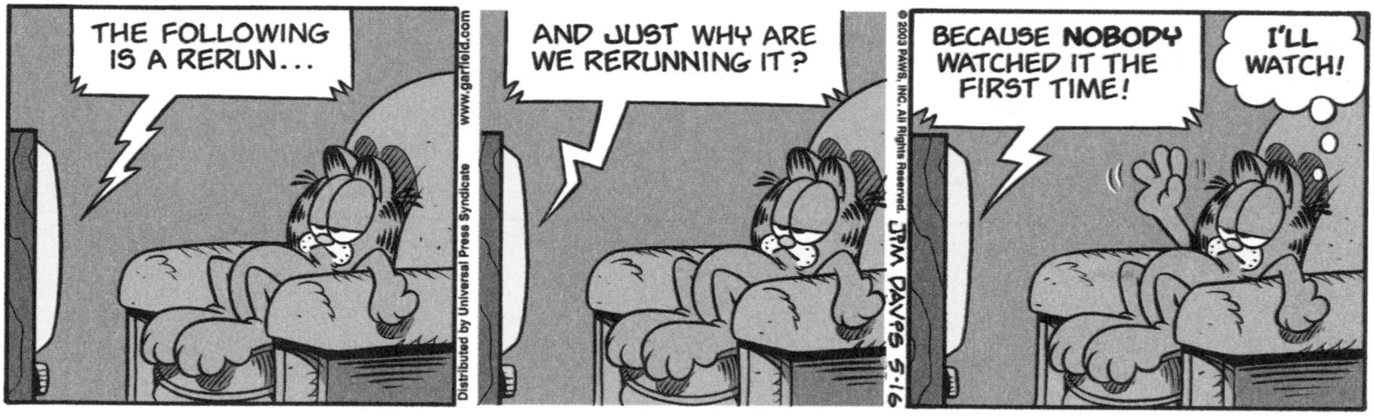
THE FOLLOWING IS A RERUN...
www.garfield.com
Distributed by Universal Press Syndicate
AND JUST WHY ARE WE RERUNNING IT?
JPM DAVPS 5-16
© 2003 PAWS, INC. All Rights Reserved.
BECAUSE **NOBODY** WATCHED IT THE FIRST TIME!
I'LL WATCH!

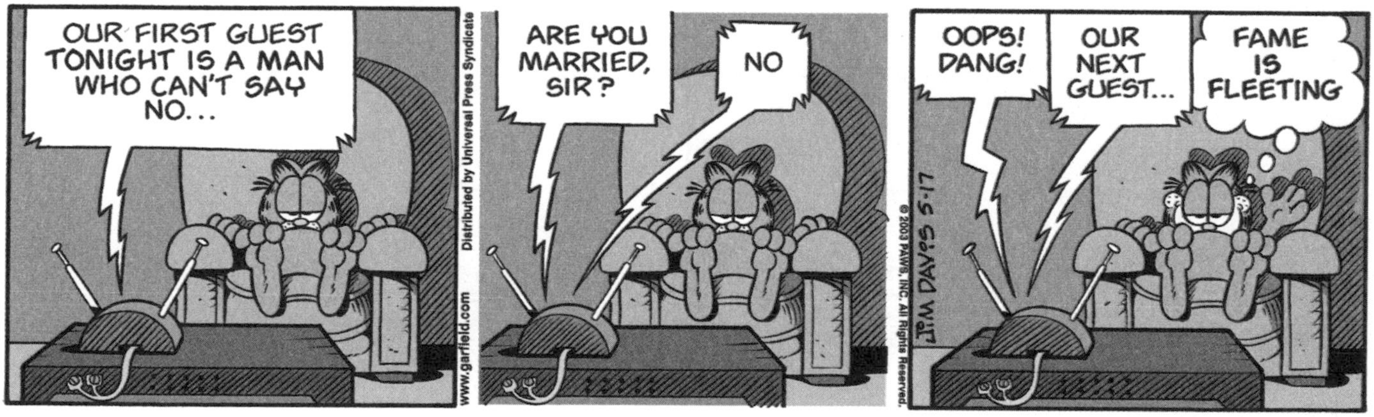
OUR FIRST GUEST TONIGHT IS A MAN WHO CAN'T SAY NO...
Distributed by Universal Press Syndicate
www.garfield.com
ARE YOU MARRIED, SIR?
NO
JPM DAVPS 5-17
© 2003 PAWS, INC. All Rights Reserved.
OOPS! DANG!
OUR NEXT GUEST...
FAME IS FLEETING

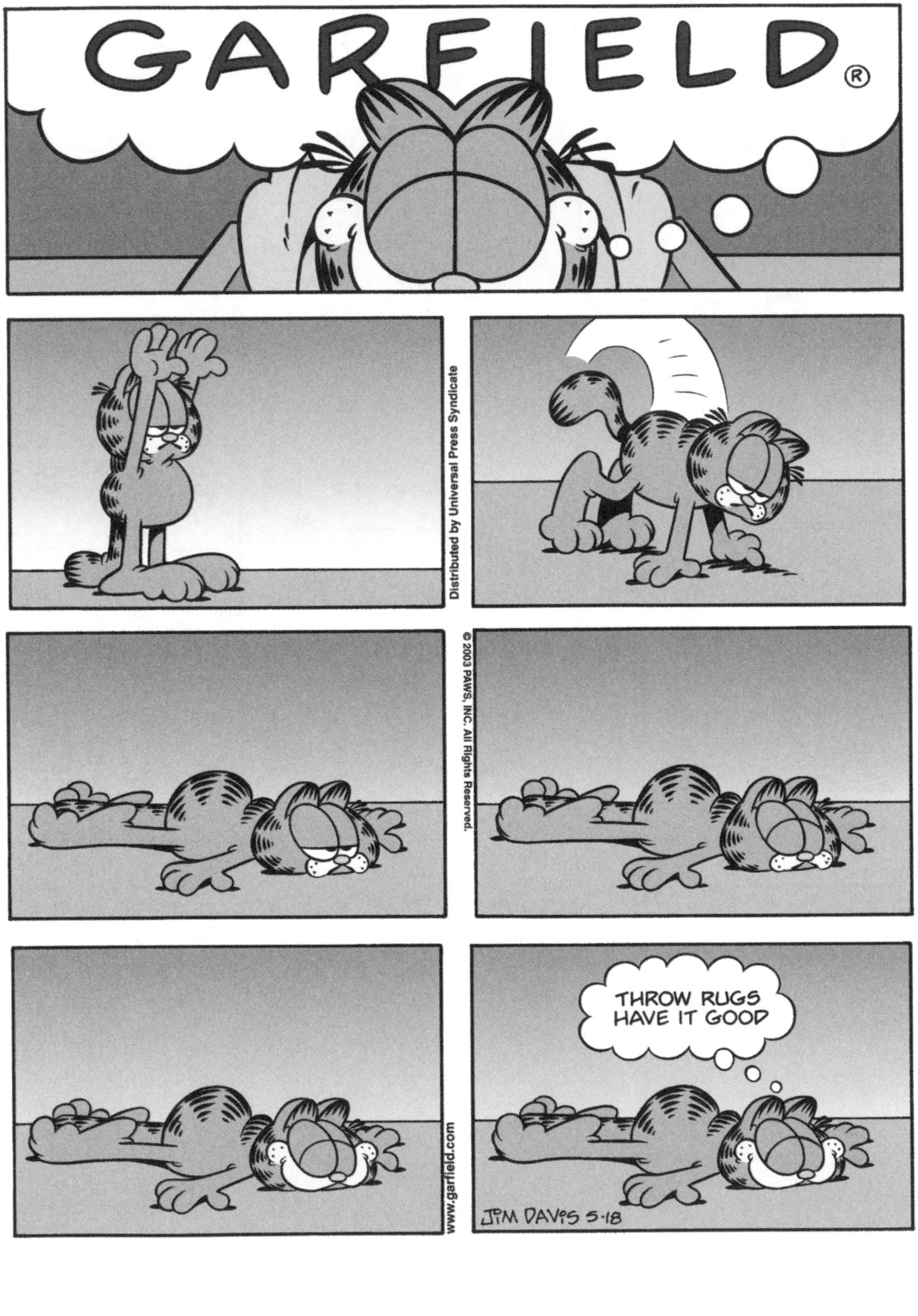
GARFIELD®
Distributed by Universal Press Syndicate
© 2003 PAWS, INC. All Rights Reserved.
www.garfield.com
THROW RUGS HAVE IT GOOD
JIM DAVIS 5-18

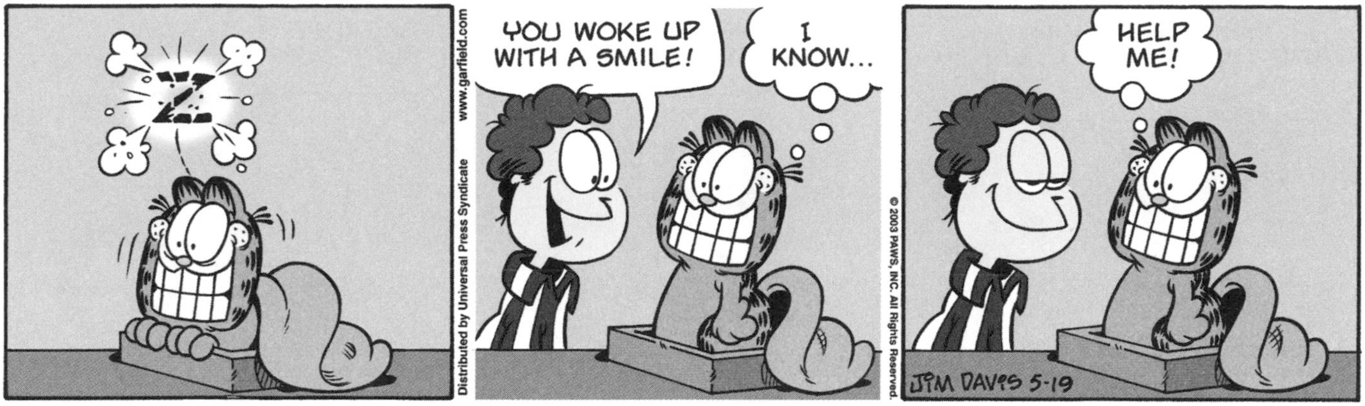
www.garfield.com
Distributed by Universal Press Syndicate
YOU WOKE UP WITH A SMILE!
I KNOW...
© 2003 PAWS, INC. All Rights Reserved.
HELP ME!
JIM DAVIS 5-19

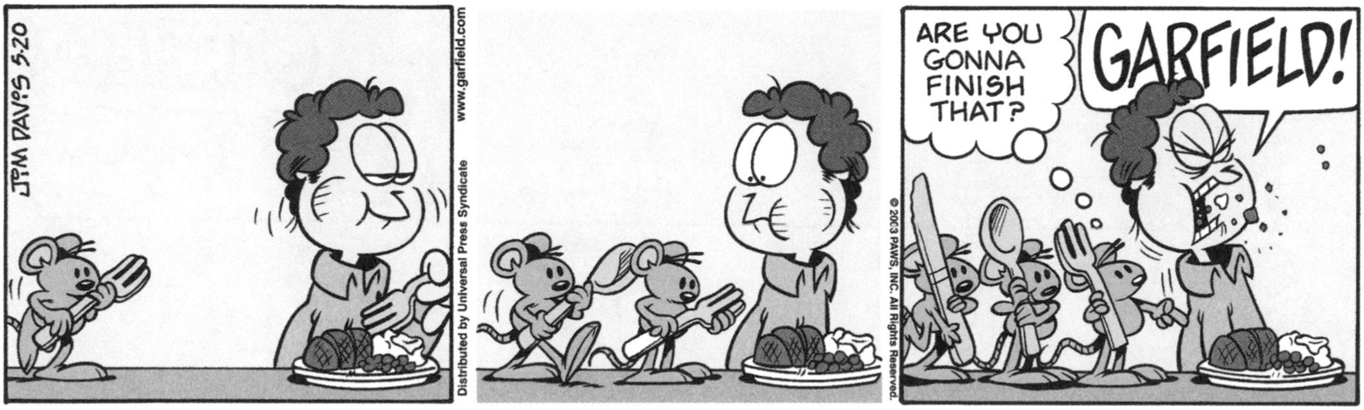
JIM DAVIS 5-20
www.garfield.com
Distributed by Universal Press Syndicate
© 2003 PAWS, INC. All Rights Reserved.
ARE YOU GONNA FINISH THAT?
GARFIELD!

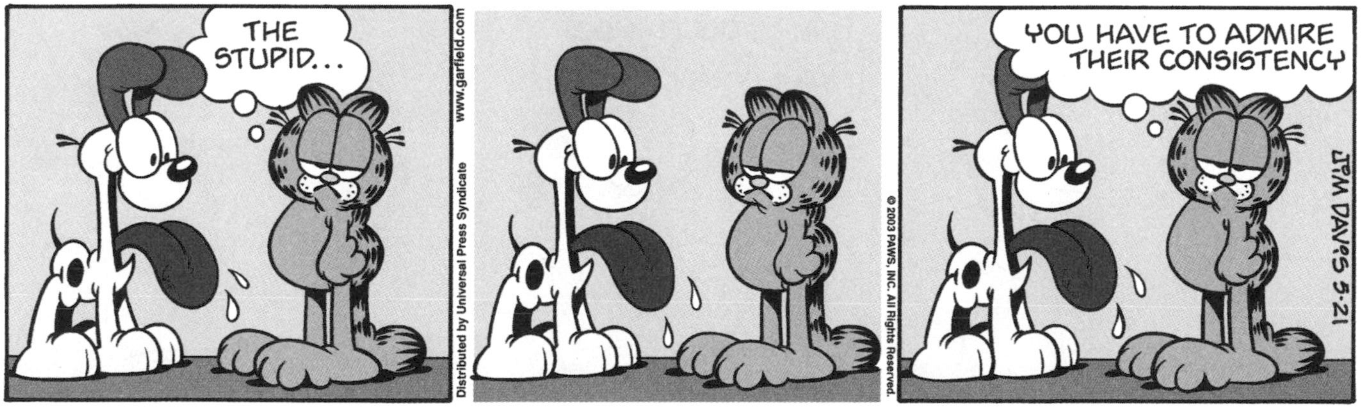
THE STUPID...
www.garfield.com
Distributed by Universal Press Syndicate
© 2003 PAWS, INC. All Rights Reserved.
YOU HAVE TO ADMIRE THEIR CONSISTENCY
JIM DAVIS 5-21

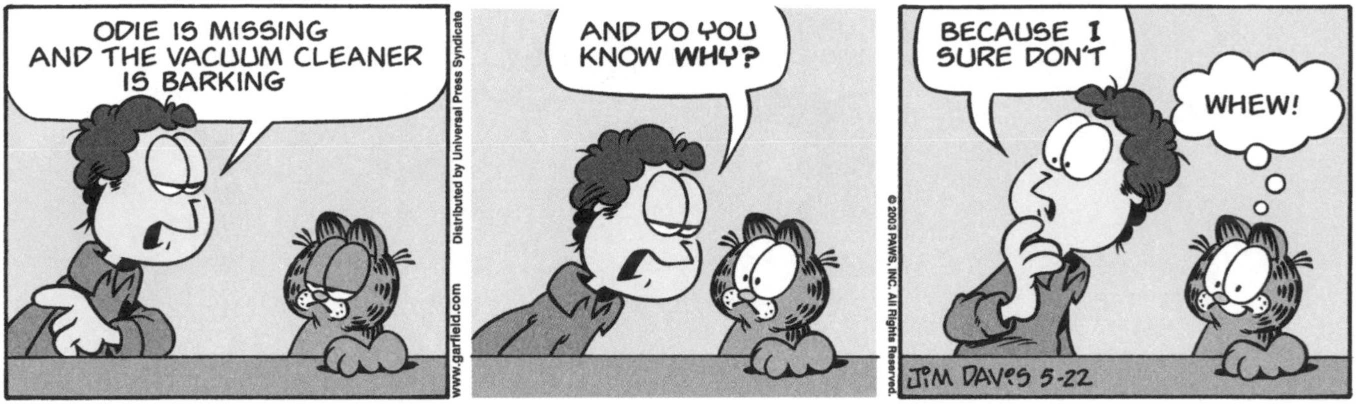
ODIE IS MISSING AND THE VACUUM CLEANER IS BARKING
www.garfield.com Distributed by Universal Press Syndicate
AND DO YOU KNOW WHY?
© 2003 PAWS, INC. All Rights Reserved.
BECAUSE I SURE DON'T
WHEW!
JIM DAVIS 5-22

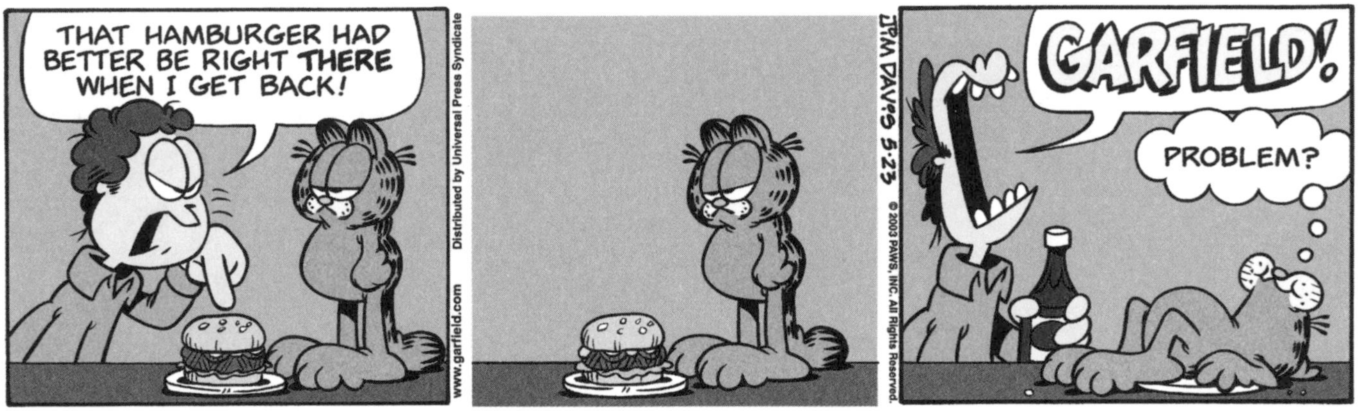
THAT HAMBURGER HAD BETTER BE RIGHT THERE WHEN I GET BACK!
www.garfield.com Distributed by Universal Press Syndicate
JIM DAVIS 5-23
© 2003 PAWS, INC. All Rights Reserved.
GARFIELD!
PROBLEM?

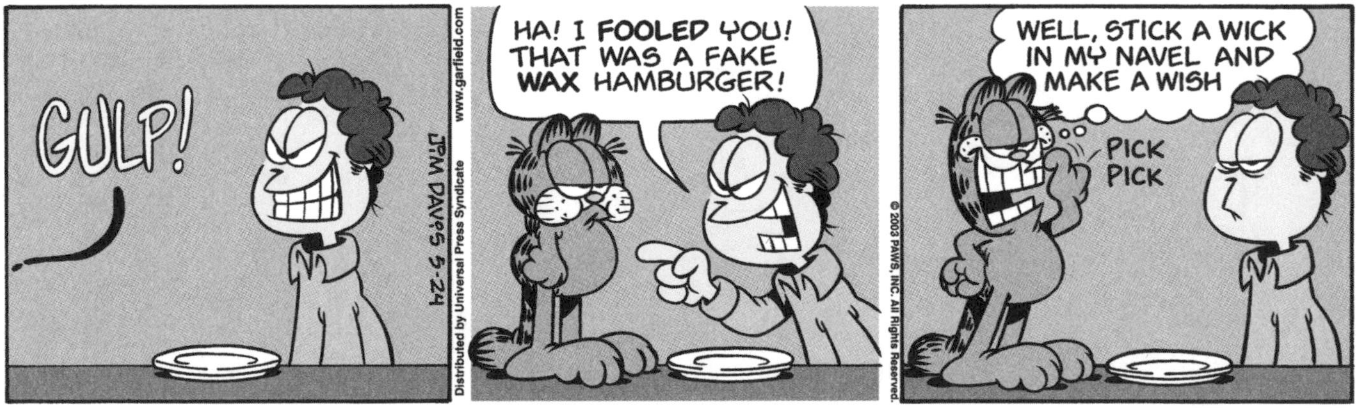
GULP!
JIM DAVIS 5-24
www.garfield.com Distributed by Universal Press Syndicate
HA! I FOOLED YOU! THAT WAS A FAKE WAX HAMBURGER!
© 2003 PAWS, INC. All Rights Reserved.
WELL, STICK A WICK IN MY NAVEL AND MAKE A WISH
PICK PICK

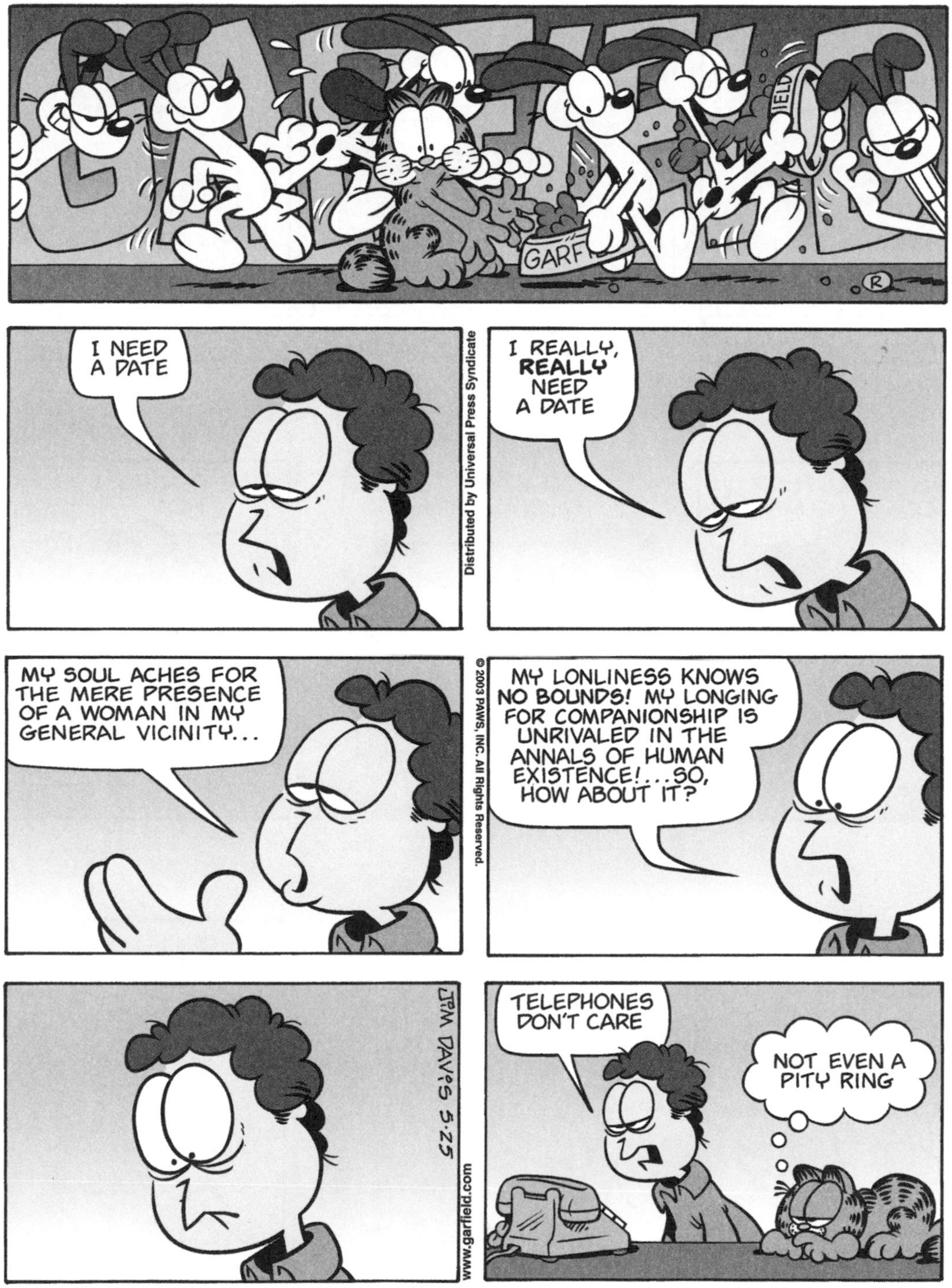
GARF
I NEED A DATE
I REALLY, **REALLY** NEED A DATE
Distributed by Universal Press Syndicate
MY SOUL ACHES FOR THE MERE PRESENCE OF A WOMAN IN MY GENERAL VICINITY...
© 2003 PAWS, INC. All Rights Reserved.
MY LONLINESS KNOWS NO BOUNDS! MY LONGING FOR COMPANIONSHIP IS UNRIVALED IN THE ANNALS OF HUMAN EXISTENCE!...SO, HOW ABOUT IT?
JIM DAVIS 5-25
www.garfield.com
TELEPHONES DON'T CARE
NOT EVEN A PITY RING

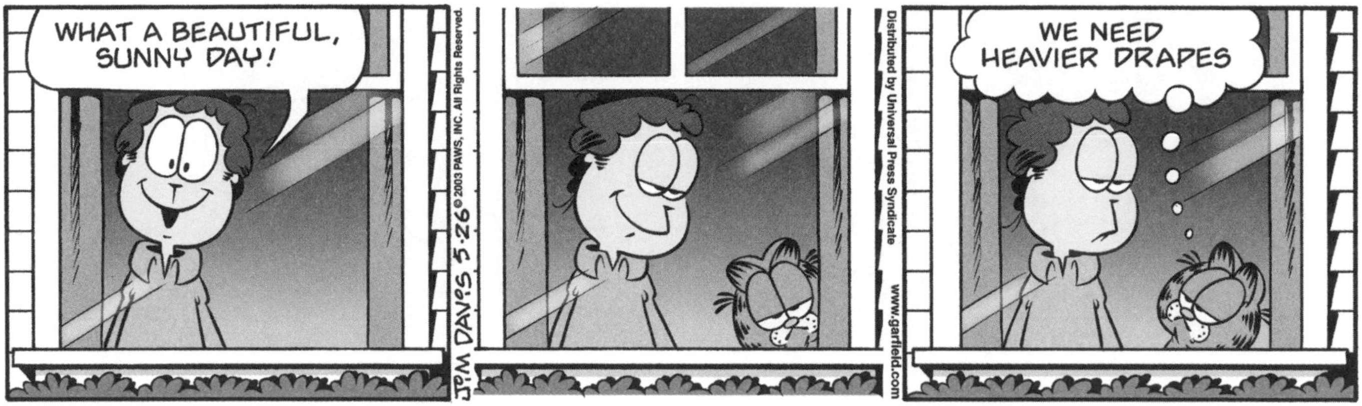
WHAT A BEAUTIFUL, SUNNY DAY!
JIM DAVIS 5·26 © 2003 PAWS, INC. All Rights Reserved.
Distributed by Universal Press Syndicate www.garfield.com
WE NEED HEAVIER DRAPES

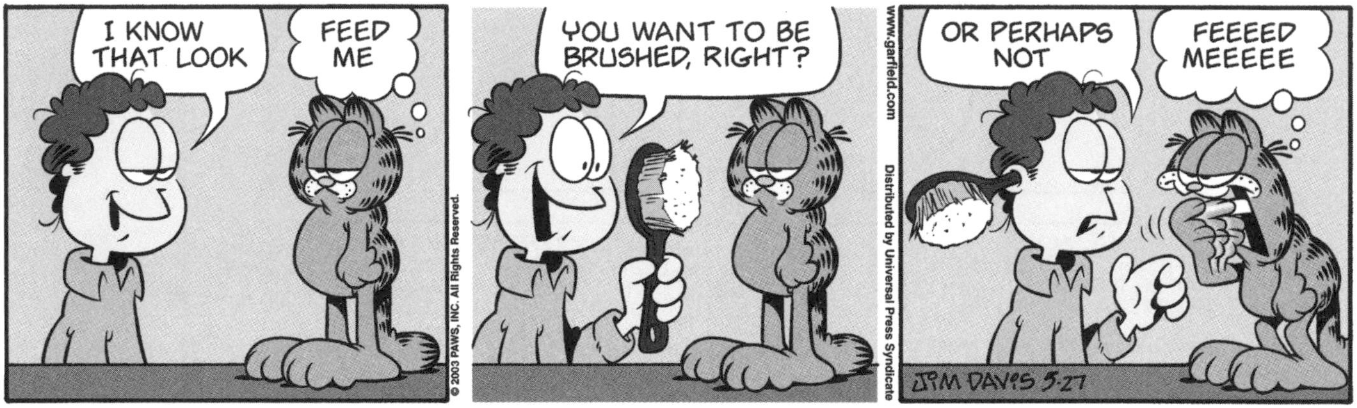
I KNOW THAT LOOK
FEED ME
© 2003 PAWS, INC. All Rights Reserved.
YOU WANT TO BE BRUSHED, RIGHT?
www.garfield.com Distributed by Universal Press Syndicate
OR PERHAPS NOT
FEEEED MEEEEE
JIM DAVIS 5·27

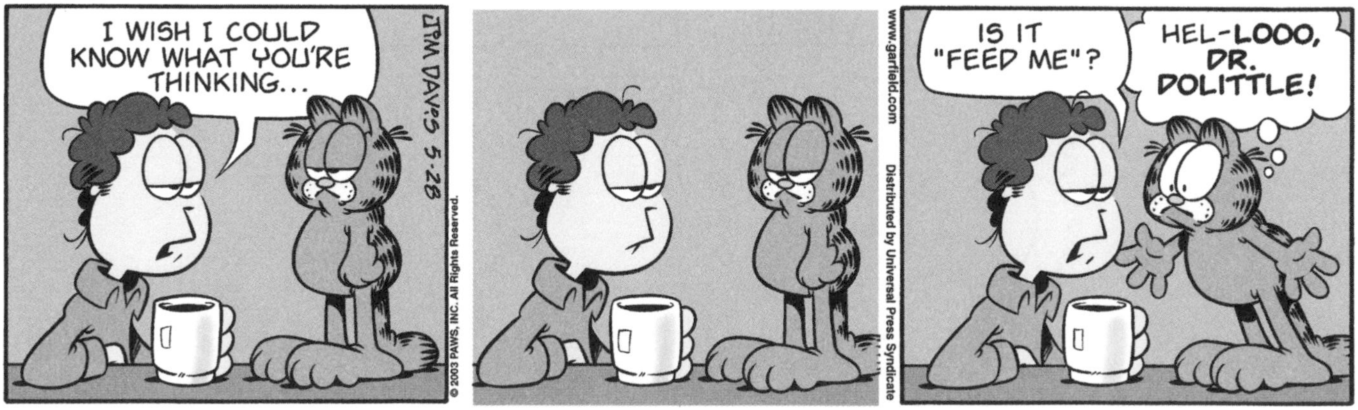
I WISH I COULD KNOW WHAT YOU'RE THINKING...
JIM DAVIS 5·28
© 2003 PAWS, INC. All Rights Reserved.
www.garfield.com Distributed by Universal Press Syndicate
IS IT "FEED ME"?
HEL-**LOOO, DR. DOLITTLE!**

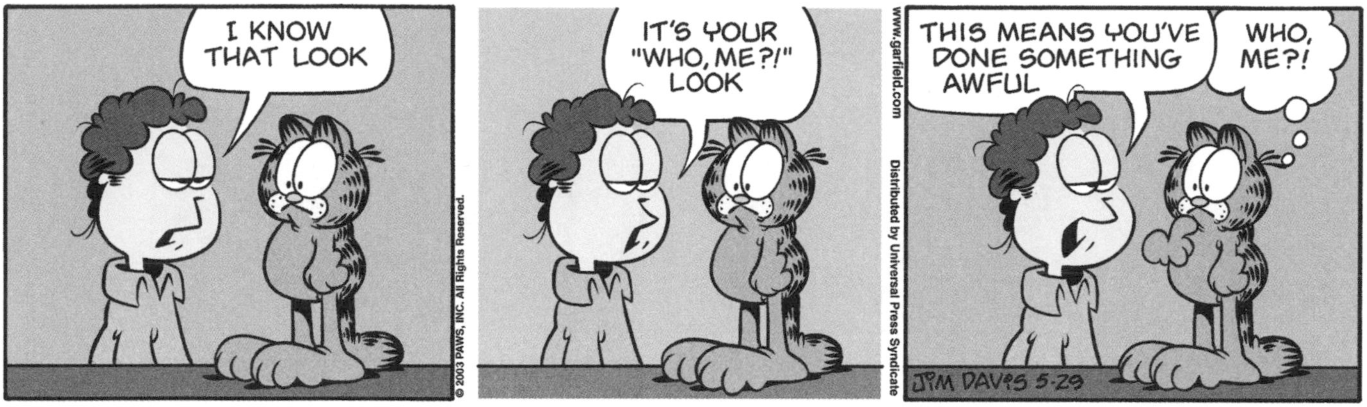
I KNOW THAT LOOK
IT'S YOUR "WHO, ME?!" LOOK
THIS MEANS YOU'VE DONE SOMETHING AWFUL
WHO, ME?!
© 2003 PAWS, INC. All Rights Reserved.
www.garfield.com Distributed by Universal Press Syndicate
JIM DAVIS 5-29

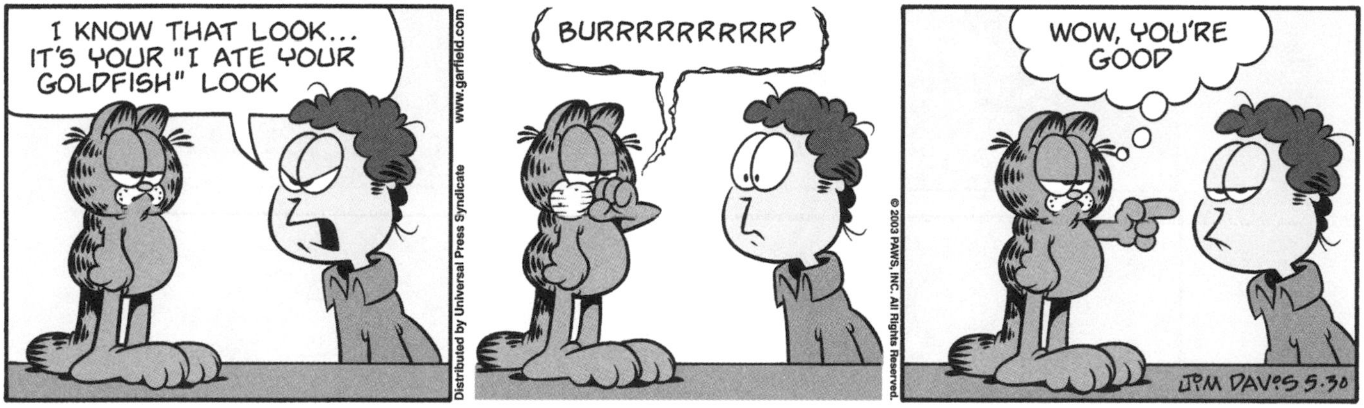
I KNOW THAT LOOK... IT'S YOUR "I ATE YOUR GOLDFISH" LOOK
BURRRRRRRRRP
WOW, YOU'RE GOOD
Distributed by Universal Press Syndicate www.garfield.com
© 2003 PAWS, INC. All Rights Reserved.
JIM DAVIS 5-30

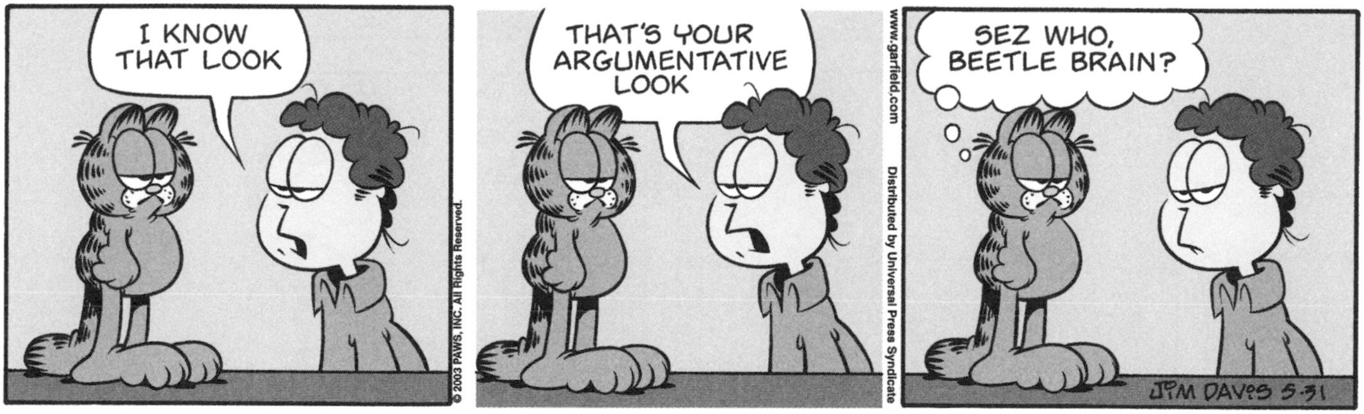
I KNOW THAT LOOK
THAT'S YOUR ARGUMENTATIVE LOOK
SEZ WHO, BEETLE BRAIN?
© 2003 PAWS, INC. All Rights Reserved.
www.garfield.com Distributed by Universal Press Syndicate
JIM DAVIS 5-31

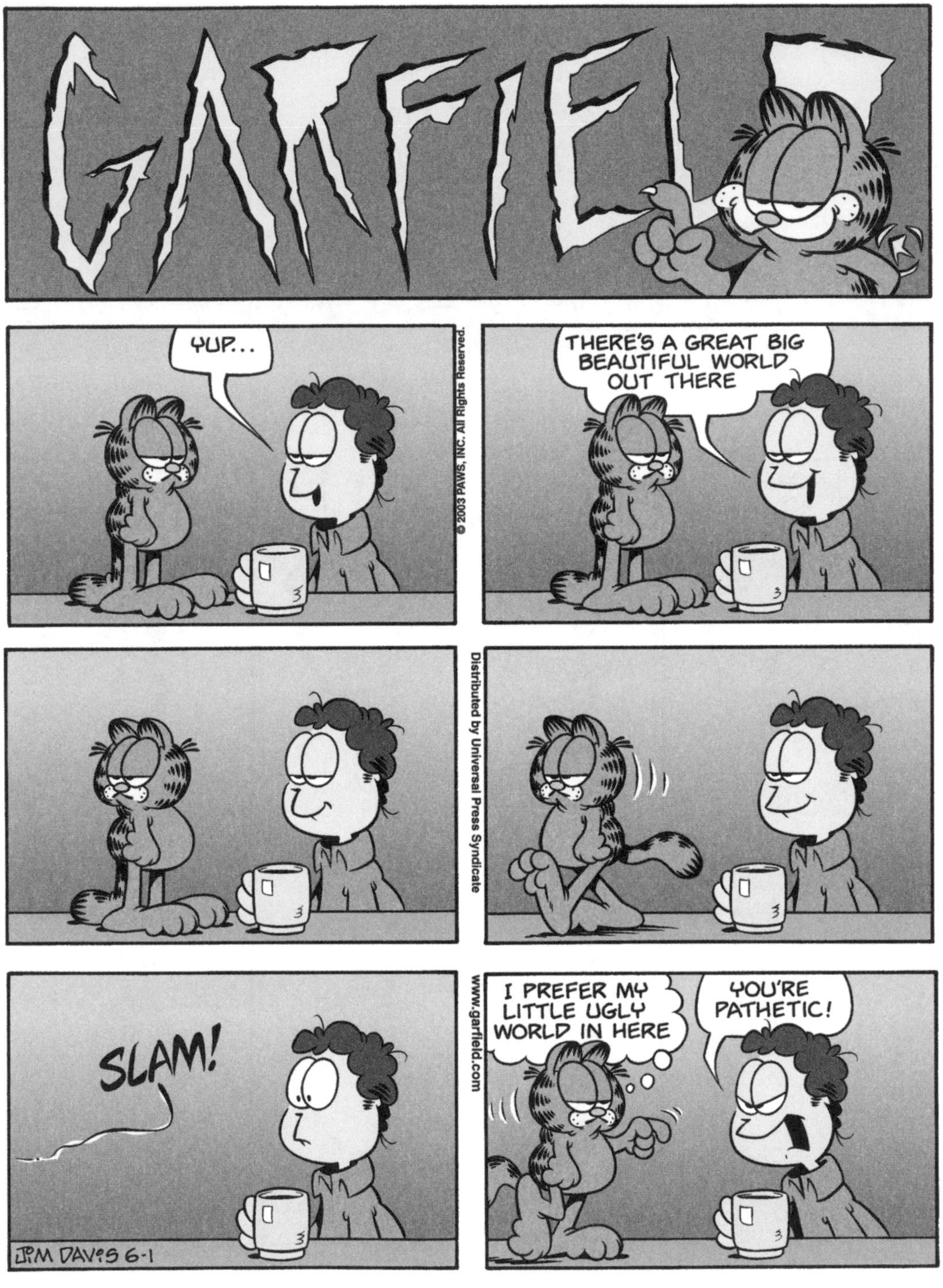
GARFIELD
YUP...
THERE'S A GREAT BIG BEAUTIFUL WORLD OUT THERE
SLAM!
I PREFER MY LITTLE UGLY WORLD IN HERE
YOU'RE PATHETIC!
JIM DAVIS 6-1

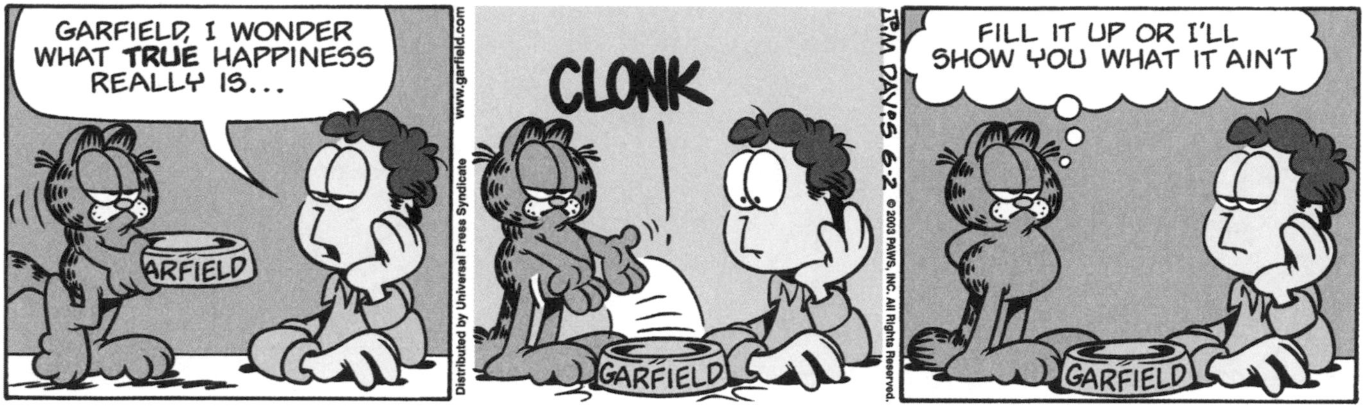
GARFIELD, I WONDER WHAT **TRUE** HAPPINESS REALLY IS...
CLONK
FILL IT UP OR I'LL SHOW YOU WHAT IT AIN'T
GARFIELD
JPM DAVIS 6-2

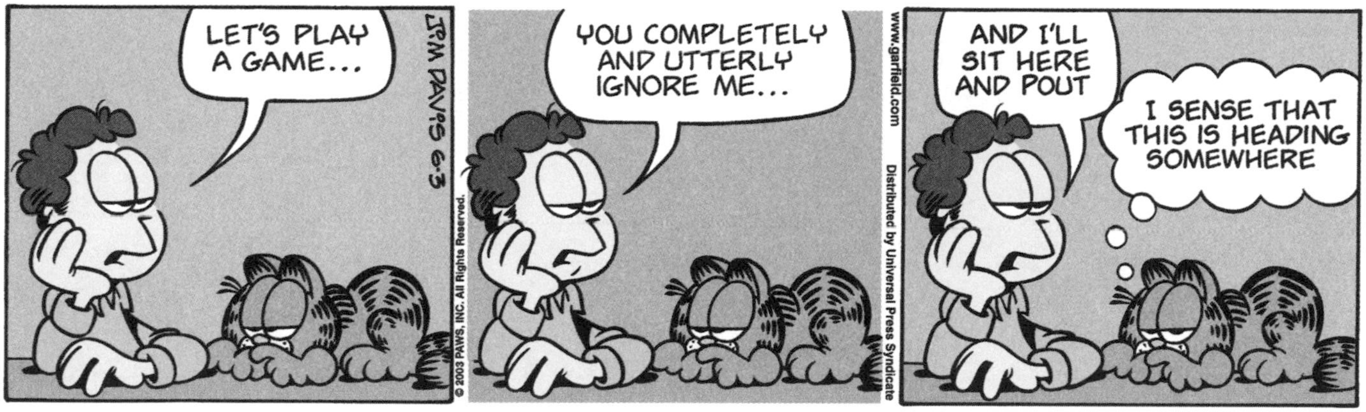
LET'S PLAY A GAME...
YOU COMPLETELY AND UTTERLY IGNORE ME...
AND I'LL SIT HERE AND POUT
I SENSE THAT THIS IS HEADING SOMEWHERE
JPM DAVIS 6-3

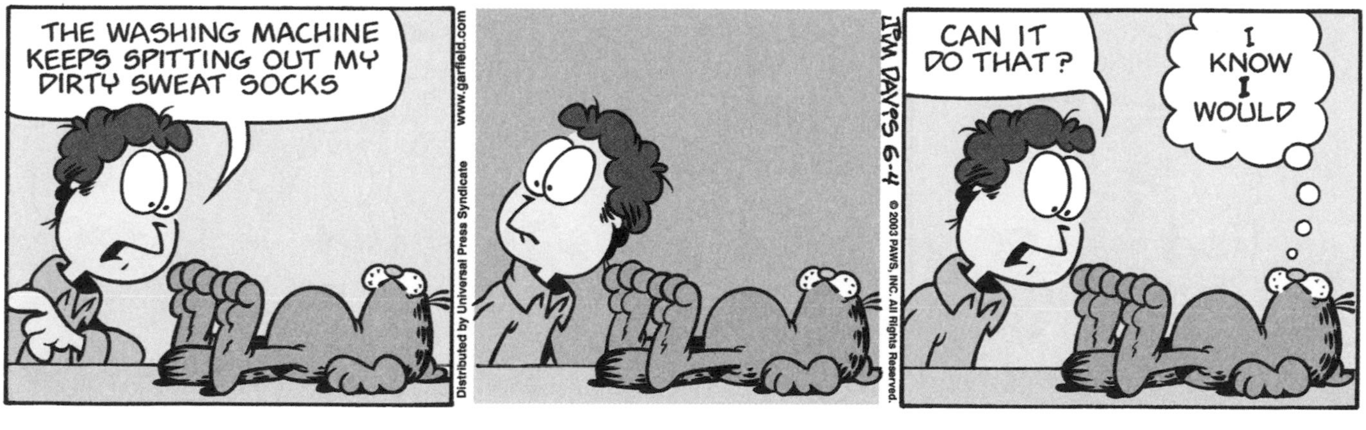
THE WASHING MACHINE KEEPS SPITTING OUT MY DIRTY SWEAT SOCKS
CAN IT DO THAT?
I KNOW **I** WOULD
JPM DAVIS 6-4

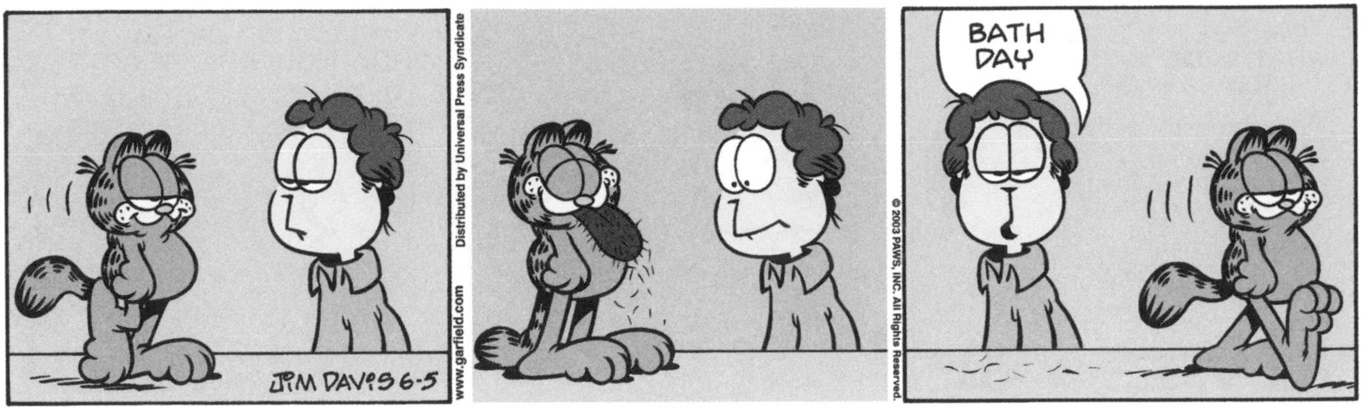
JIM DAVIS 6-5
www.garfield.com
Distributed by Universal Press Syndicate
BATH DAY
© 2003 PAWS, INC. All Rights Reserved.

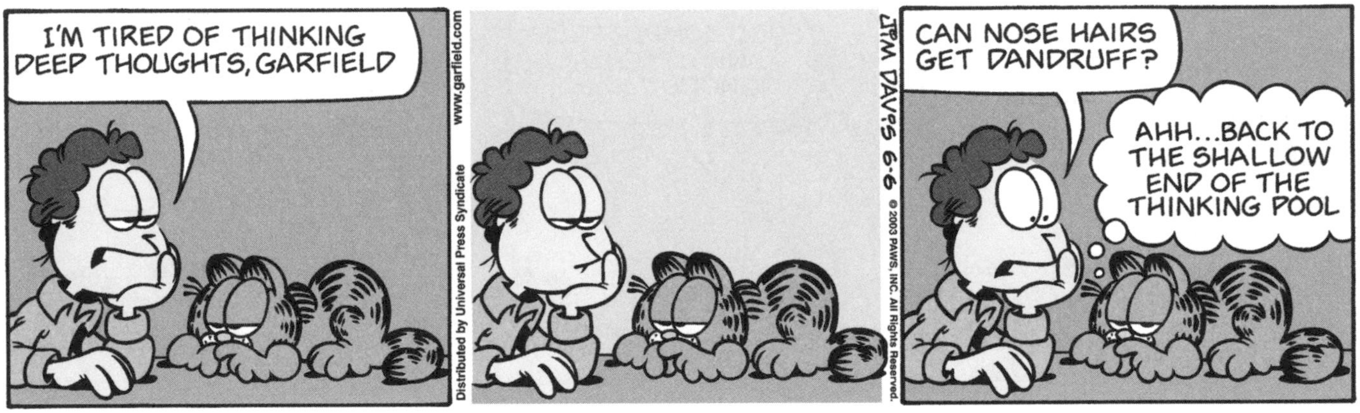
I'M TIRED OF THINKING DEEP THOUGHTS, GARFIELD
www.garfield.com
Distributed by Universal Press Syndicate
JIM DAVIS 6-6
© 2003 PAWS, INC. All Rights Reserved.
CAN NOSE HAIRS GET DANDRUFF?
AHH...BACK TO THE SHALLOW END OF THE THINKING POOL

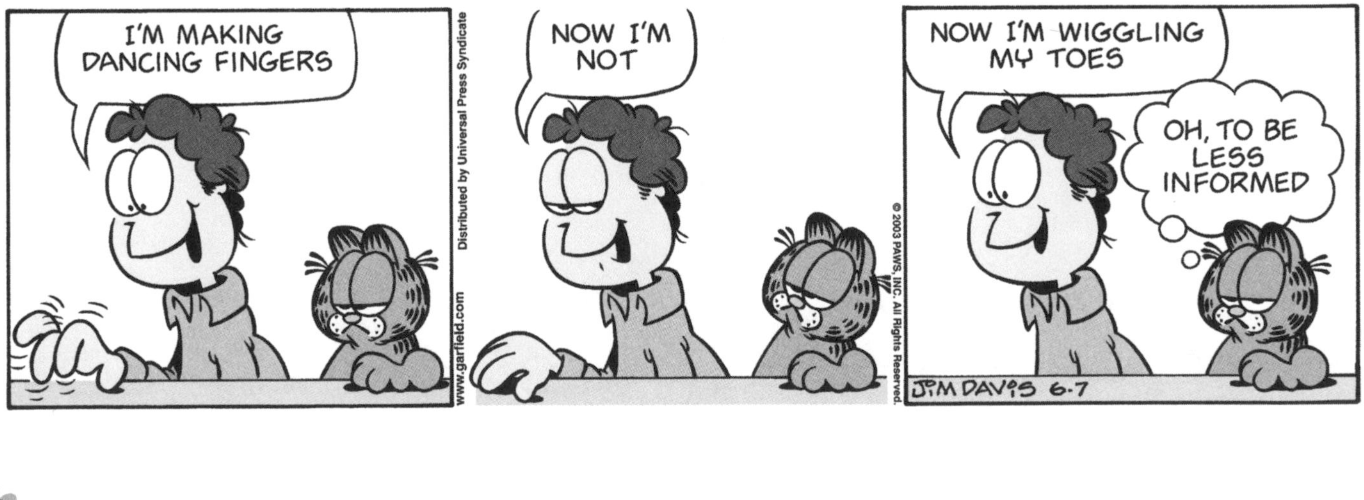
I'M MAKING DANCING FINGERS
Distributed by Universal Press Syndicate
www.garfield.com
NOW I'M NOT
© 2003 PAWS, INC. All Rights Reserved.
NOW I'M WIGGLING MY TOES
OH, TO BE LESS INFORMED
JIM DAVIS 6-7

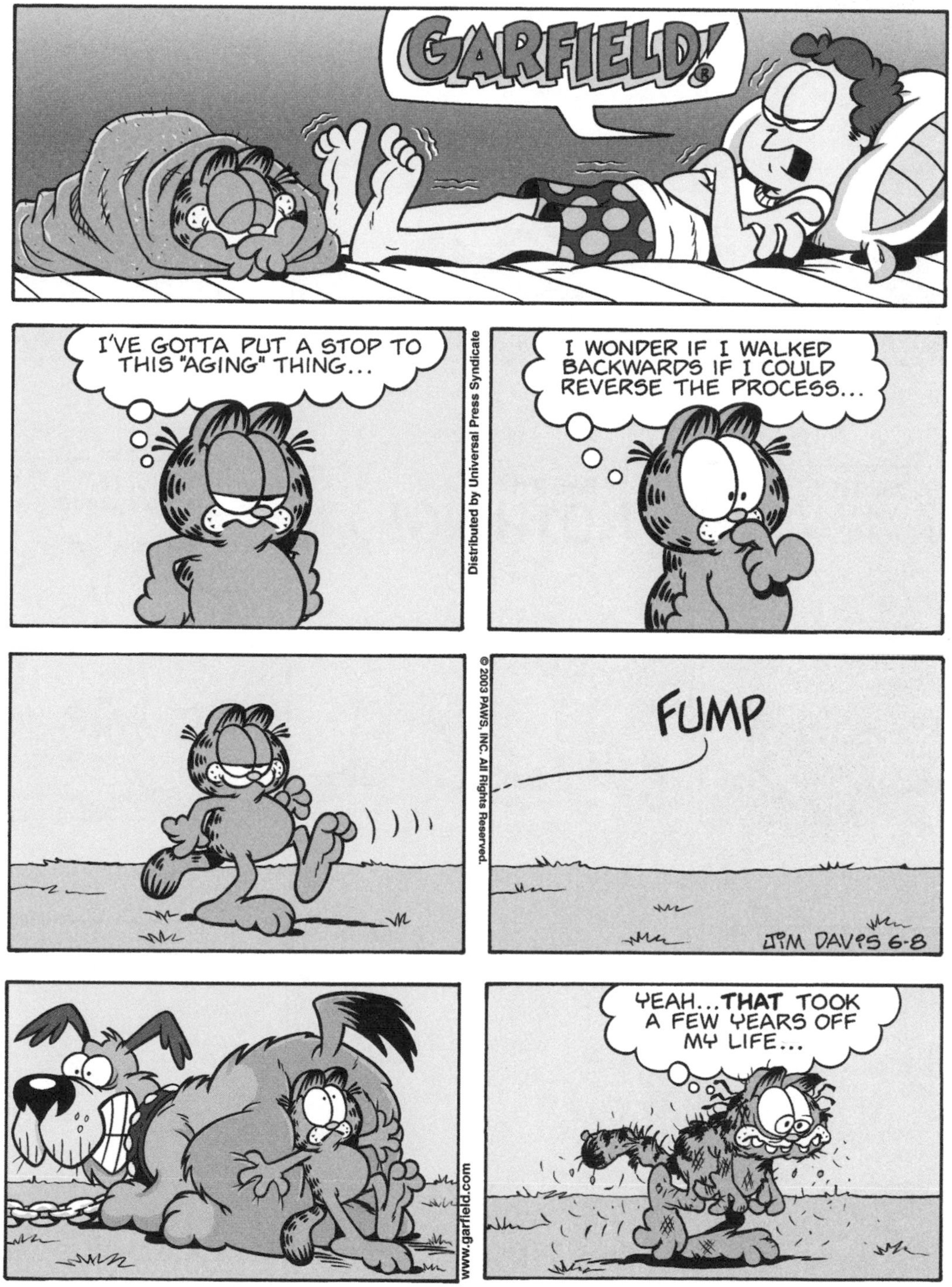

GARFIELD®
I'VE GOTTA PUT A STOP TO THIS "AGING" THING...
I WONDER IF I WALKED BACKWARDS IF I COULD REVERSE THE PROCESS...
FUMP
JIM DAVIS 6-8
YEAH...THAT TOOK A FEW YEARS OFF MY LIFE...

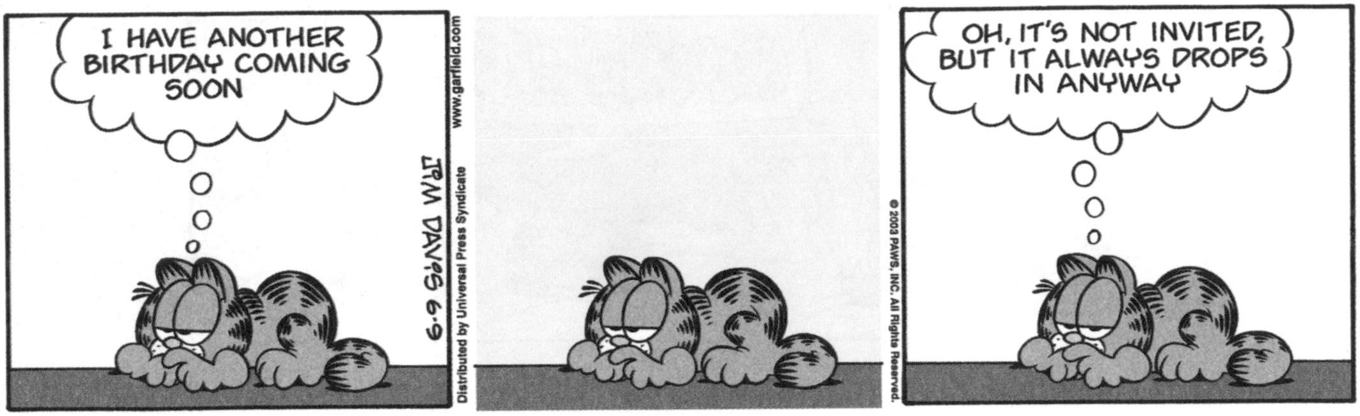
I HAVE ANOTHER BIRTHDAY COMING SOON
JIM DAVIS 6-9
www.garfield.com
Distributed by Universal Press Syndicate
© 2003 PAWS, INC. All Rights Reserved.
OH, IT'S NOT INVITED, BUT IT ALWAYS DROPS IN ANYWAY

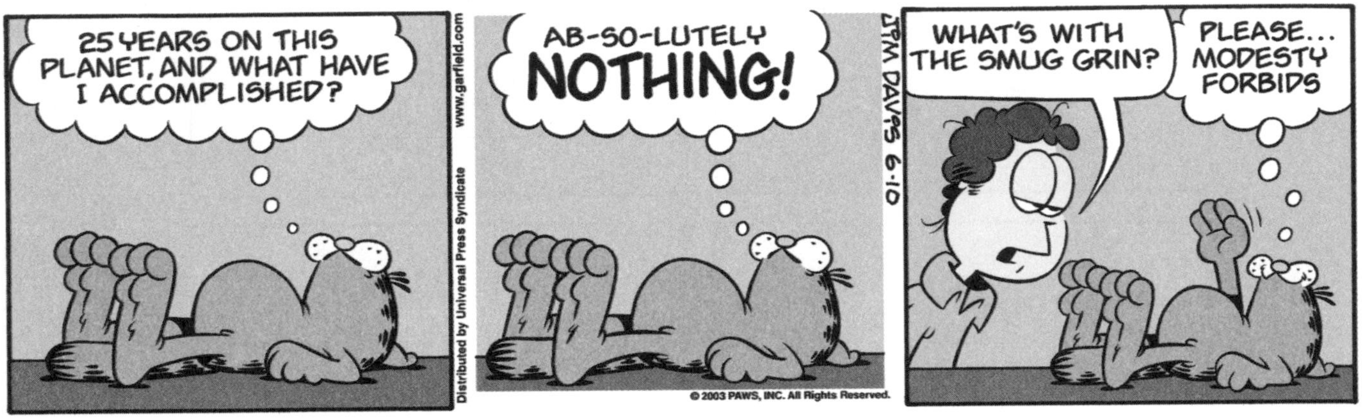
25 YEARS ON THIS PLANET, AND WHAT HAVE I ACCOMPLISHED?
www.garfield.com
Distributed by Universal Press Syndicate
AB-SO-LUTELY NOTHING!
© 2003 PAWS, INC. All Rights Reserved.
JIM DAVIS 6-10
WHAT'S WITH THE SMUG GRIN?
PLEASE... MODESTY FORBIDS

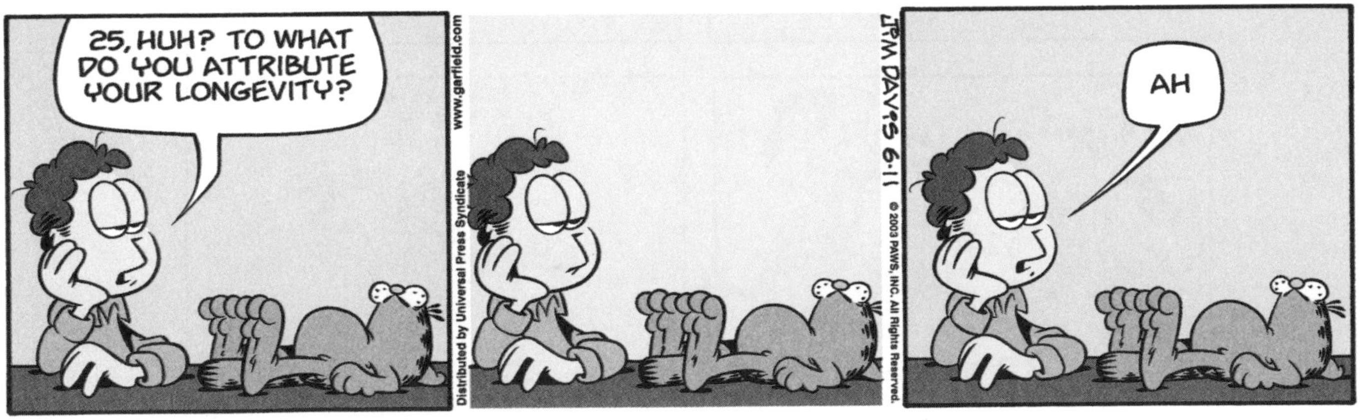
25, HUH? TO WHAT DO YOU ATTRIBUTE YOUR LONGEVITY?
www.garfield.com
Distributed by Universal Press Syndicate
JIM DAVIS 6-11
© 2003 PAWS, INC. All Rights Reserved.
AH

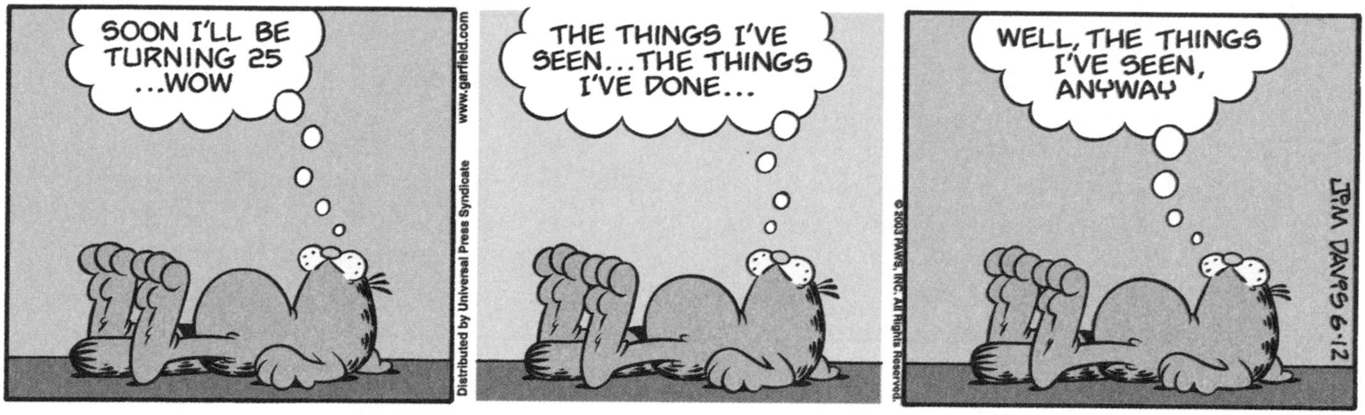
SOON I'LL BE TURNING 25 ...WOW
www.garfield.com Distributed by Universal Press Syndicate
THE THINGS I'VE SEEN...THE THINGS I'VE DONE...
© 2003 PAWS, INC. All Rights Reserved.
WELL, THE THINGS I'VE SEEN, ANYWAY
JIM DAVIS 6-12

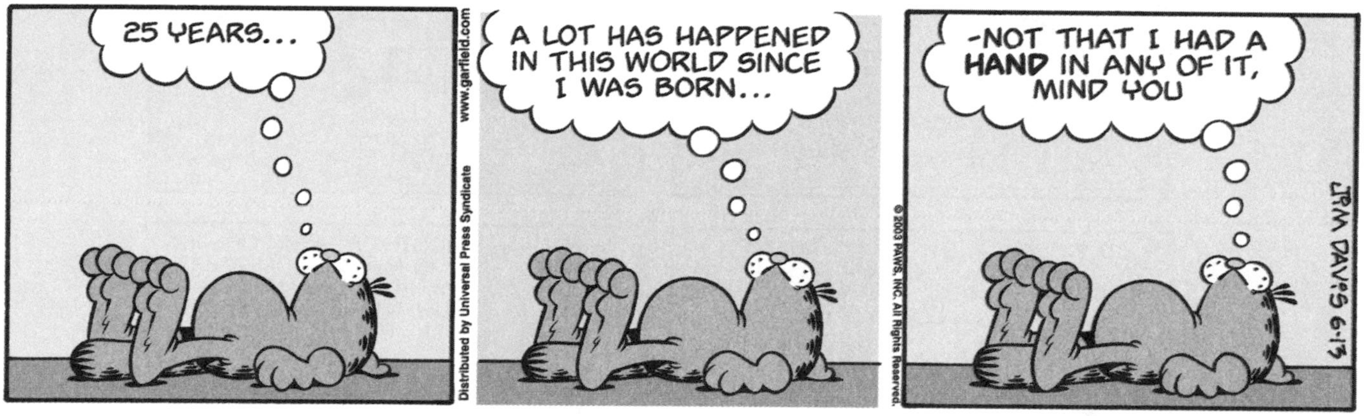
25 YEARS...
www.garfield.com Distributed by Universal Press Syndicate
A LOT HAS HAPPENED IN THIS WORLD SINCE I WAS BORN...
© 2003 PAWS, INC. All Rights Reserved.
-NOT THAT I HAD A **HAND** IN ANY OF IT, MIND YOU
JIM DAVIS 6-13

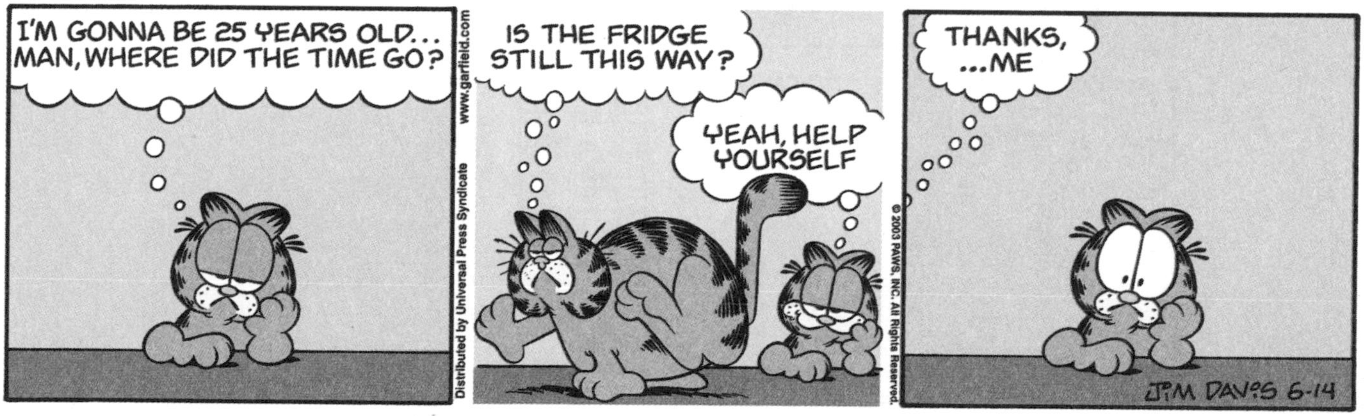
I'M GONNA BE 25 YEARS OLD... MAN, WHERE DID THE TIME GO?
www.garfield.com Distributed by Universal Press Syndicate
IS THE FRIDGE STILL THIS WAY?
YEAH, HELP YOURSELF
© 2003 PAWS, INC. All Rights Reserved.
THANKS, ...ME
JIM DAVIS 6-14

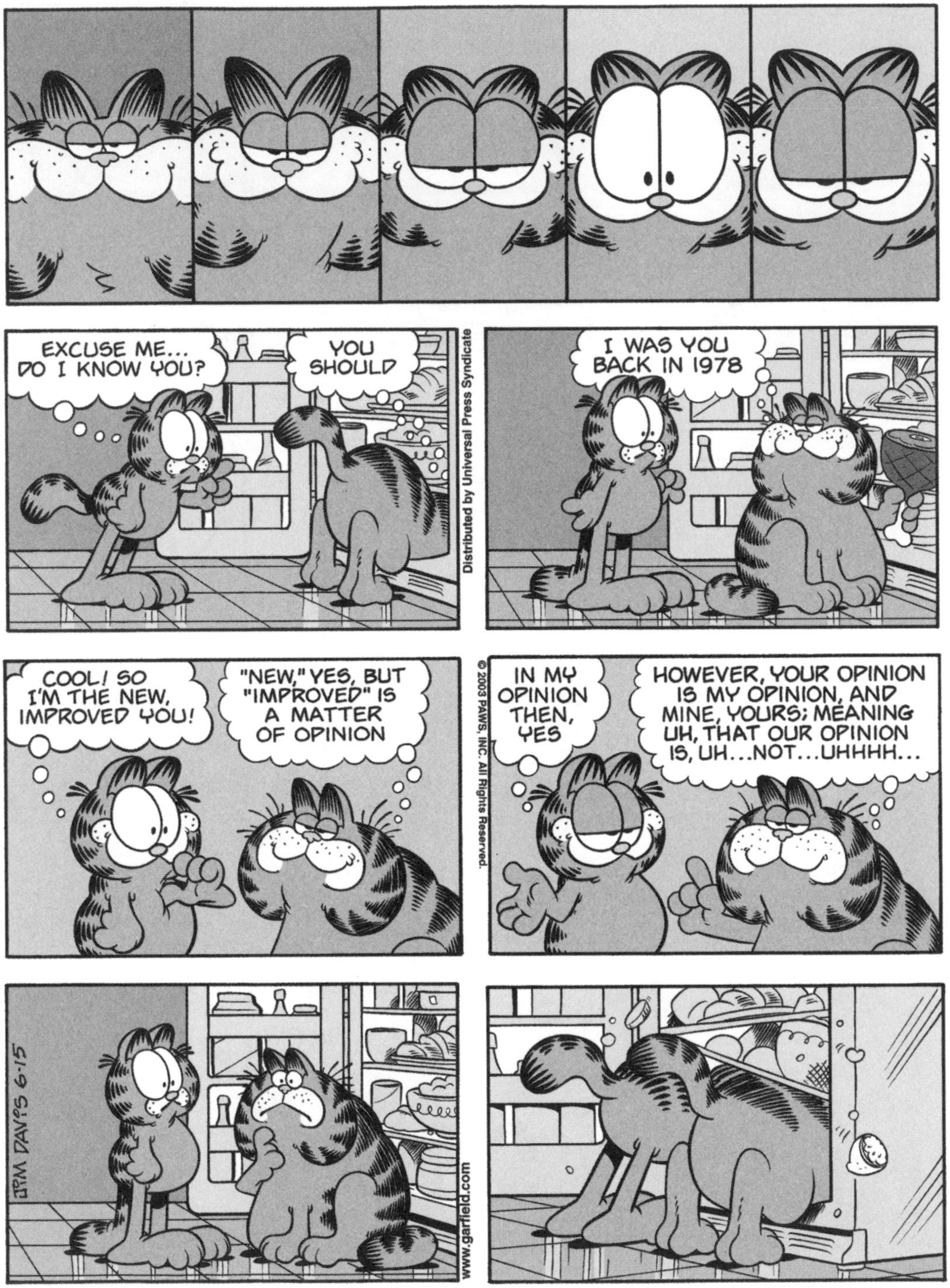

EXCUSE ME... DO I KNOW YOU?
YOU SHOULD
I WAS YOU BACK IN 1978
COOL! SO I'M THE NEW, IMPROVED YOU!
"NEW," YES, BUT "IMPROVED" IS A MATTER OF OPINION
IN MY OPINION THEN, YES
HOWEVER, YOUR OPINION IS MY OPINION, AND MINE, YOURS; MEANING UH, THAT OUR OPINION IS, UH...NOT...UHHHH...
Distributed by Universal Press Syndicate
© 2003 PAWS, INC. All Rights Reserved.
JPM DAVIS 6-15
www.garfield.com

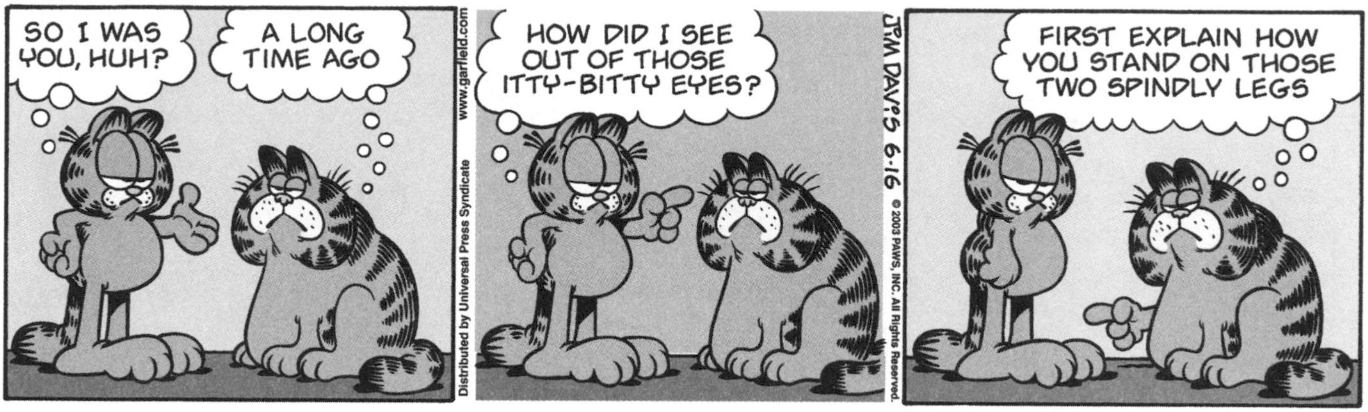
SO I WAS YOU, HUH?
A LONG TIME AGO
www.garfield.com
Distributed by Universal Press Syndicate
HOW DID I SEE OUT OF THOSE ITTY-BITTY EYES?
JIM DAVIS 6-16
© 2003 PAWS, INC. All Rights Reserved.
FIRST EXPLAIN HOW YOU STAND ON THOSE TWO SPINDLY LEGS

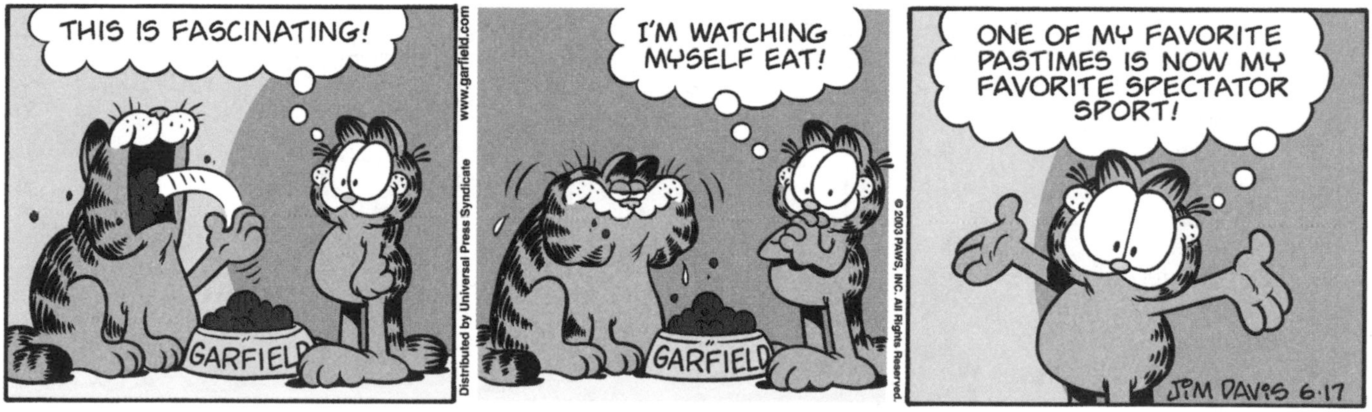
THIS IS FASCINATING!
GARFIELD
www.garfield.com
Distributed by Universal Press Syndicate
I'M WATCHING MYSELF EAT!
GARFIELD
© 2003 PAWS, INC. All Rights Reserved.
ONE OF MY FAVORITE PASTIMES IS NOW MY FAVORITE SPECTATOR SPORT!
JIM DAVIS 6-17

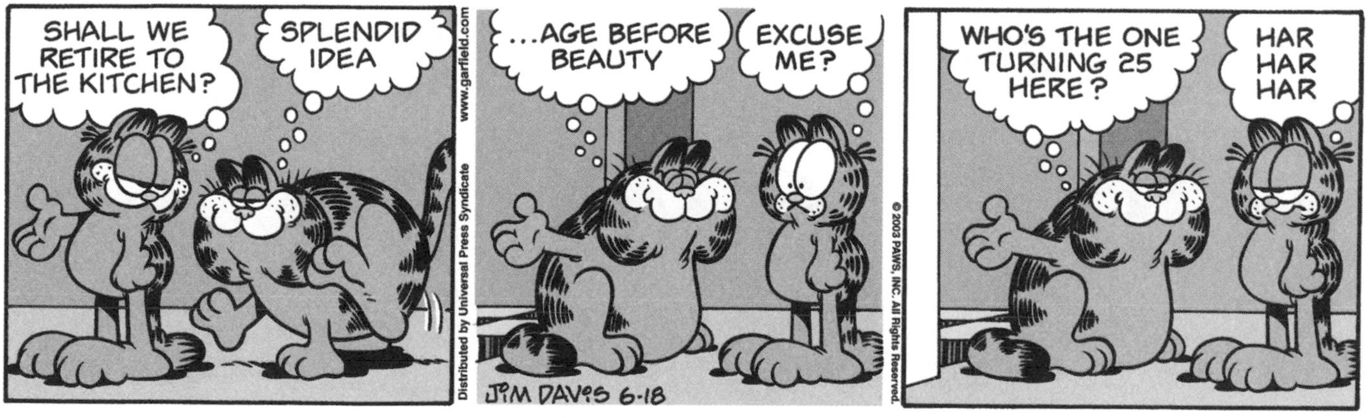
SHALL WE RETIRE TO THE KITCHEN?
SPLENDID IDEA
www.garfield.com
Distributed by Universal Press Syndicate
...AGE BEFORE BEAUTY
EXCUSE ME?
JIM DAVIS 6-18
© 2003 PAWS, INC. All Rights Reserved.
WHO'S THE ONE TURNING 25 HERE?
HAR HAR HAR

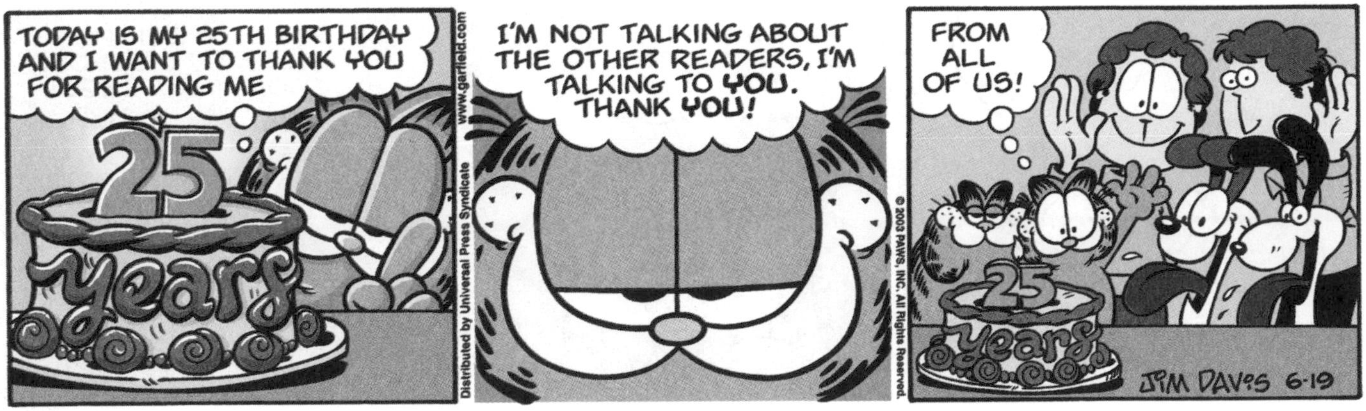
TODAY IS MY 25TH BIRTHDAY AND I WANT TO THANK YOU FOR READING ME
25 years
www.garfield.com
Distributed by Universal Press Syndicate
I'M NOT TALKING ABOUT THE OTHER READERS, I'M TALKING TO YOU. THANK YOU!
© 2003 PAWS, INC. All Rights Reserved.
FROM ALL OF US!
25 years
JIM DAVIS 6-19

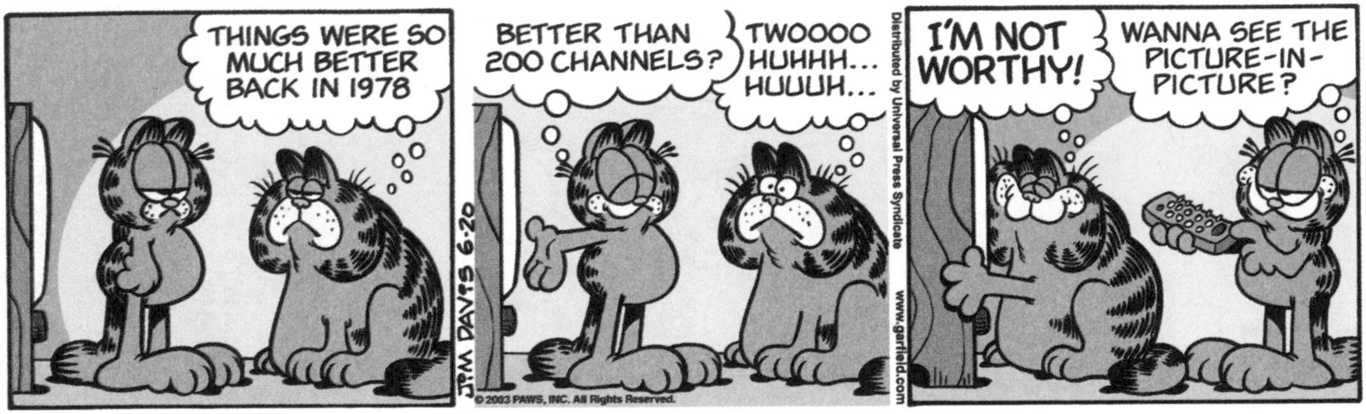
THINGS WERE SO MUCH BETTER BACK IN 1978
JIM DAVIS 6-20
BETTER THAN 200 CHANNELS?
TWOOOO HUHHH... HUUUH...
© 2003 PAWS, INC. All Rights Reserved.
Distributed by Universal Press Syndicate
www.garfield.com
I'M NOT WORTHY!
WANNA SEE THE PICTURE-IN-PICTURE?

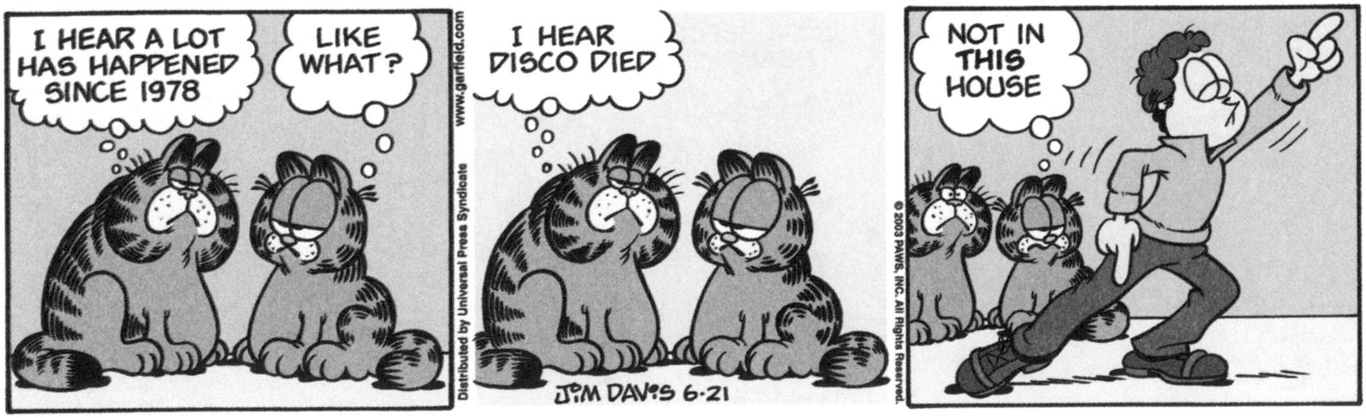
I HEAR A LOT HAS HAPPENED SINCE 1978
LIKE WHAT?
www.garfield.com
Distributed by Universal Press Syndicate
I HEAR DISCO DIED
JIM DAVIS 6-21
© 2003 PAWS, INC. All Rights Reserved.
NOT IN THIS HOUSE

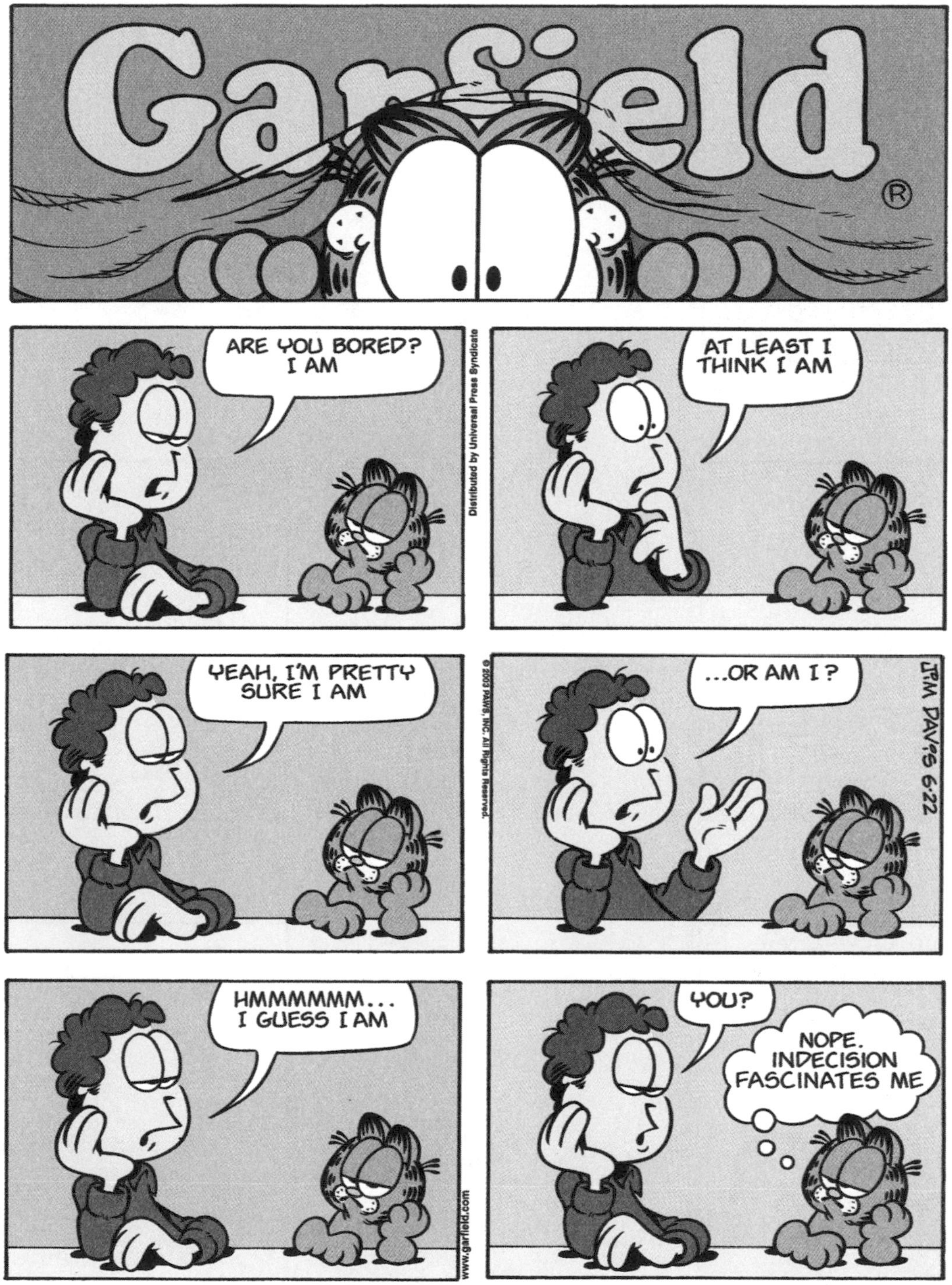
Garfield®
ARE YOU BORED? I AM
Distributed by Universal Press Syndicate
AT LEAST I THINK I AM
YEAH, I'M PRETTY SURE I AM
© 2003 PAWS, INC. All Rights Reserved.
...OR AM I?
JIM DAVIS 6-22
HMMMMMM... I GUESS I AM
www.garfield.com
YOU?
NOPE. INDECISION FASCINATES ME

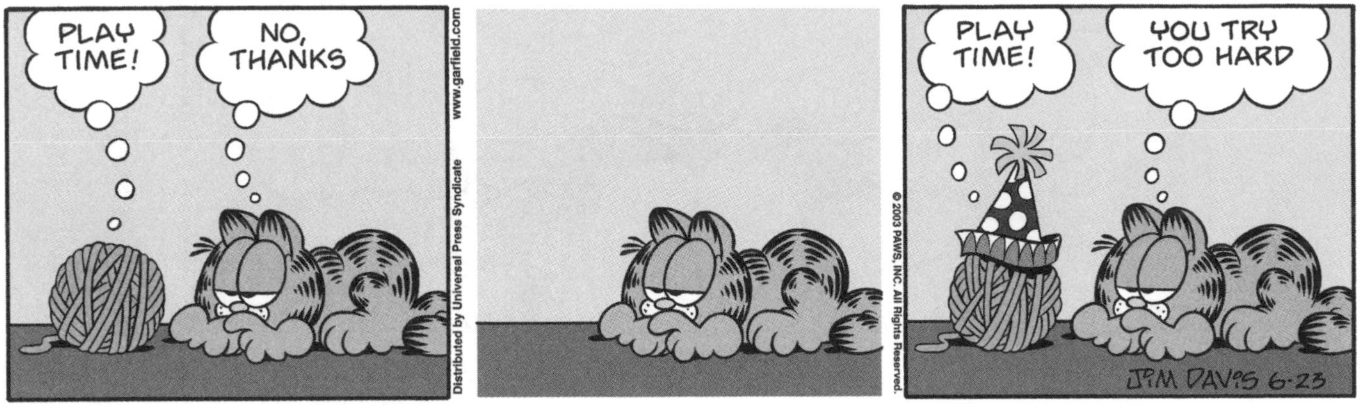
PLAY TIME!
NO, THANKS
PLAY TIME!
YOU TRY TOO HARD
JIM DAVIS 6-23
www.garfield.com
Distributed by Universal Press Syndicate
© 2003 PAWS, INC. All Rights Reserved.

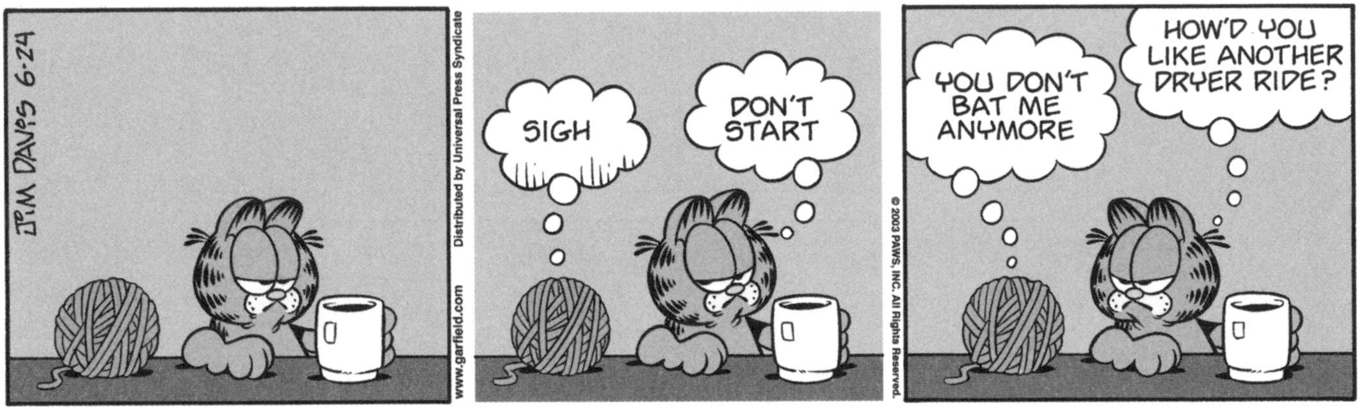
JIM DAVIS 6-24
SIGH
DON'T START
YOU DON'T BAT ME ANYMORE
HOW'D YOU LIKE ANOTHER DRYER RIDE?
Distributed by Universal Press Syndicate
www.garfield.com
© 2003 PAWS, INC. All Rights Reserved.

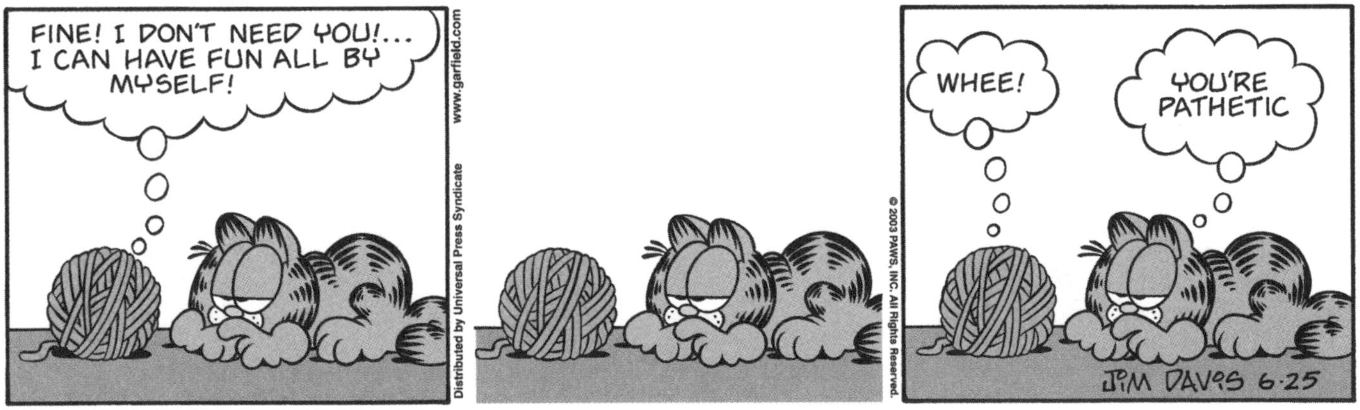
FINE! I DON'T NEED YOU!... I CAN HAVE FUN ALL BY MYSELF!
WHEE!
YOU'RE PATHETIC
JIM DAVIS 6-25
www.garfield.com
Distributed by Universal Press Syndicate
© 2003 PAWS, INC. All Rights Reserved.

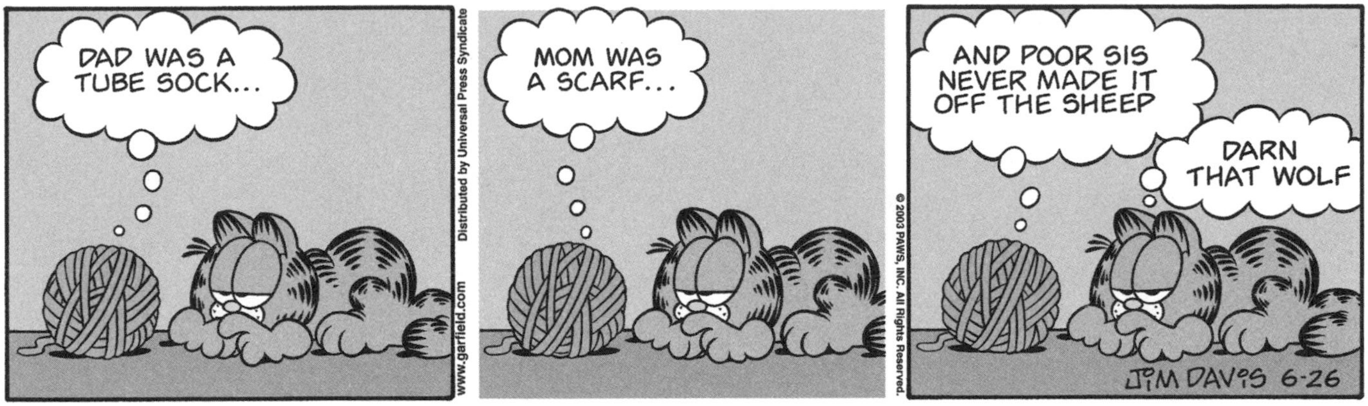
DAD WAS A TUBE SOCK...
Distributed by Universal Press Syndicate
www.garfield.com
MOM WAS A SCARF...
© 2003 PAWS, INC. All Rights Reserved.
AND POOR SIS NEVER MADE IT OFF THE SHEEP
DARN THAT WOLF
JIM DAVIS 6-26

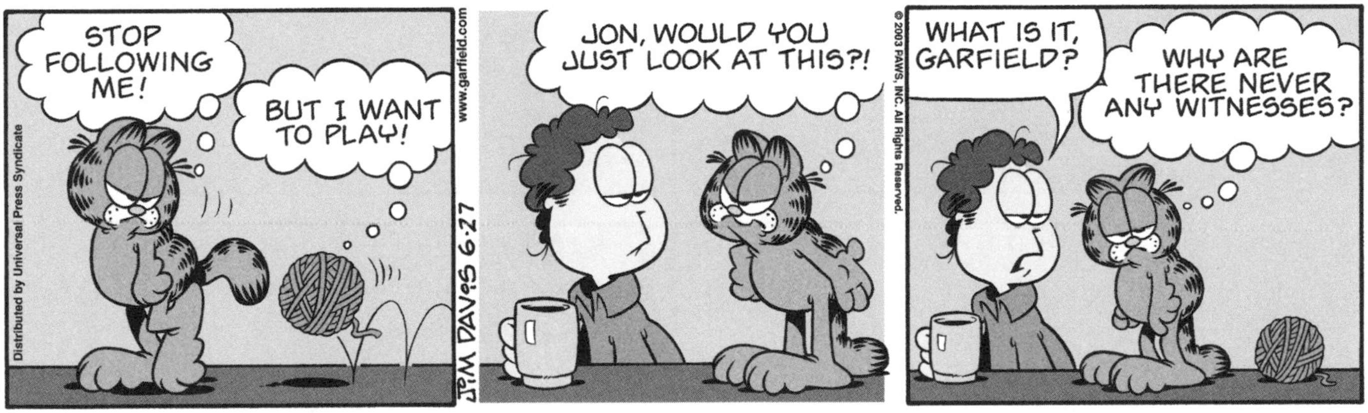
STOP FOLLOWING ME!
BUT I WANT TO PLAY!
Distributed by Universal Press Syndicate
www.garfield.com
JIM DAVIS 6-27
JON, WOULD YOU JUST LOOK AT THIS?!
© 2003 PAWS, INC. All Rights Reserved.
WHAT IS IT, GARFIELD?
WHY ARE THERE NEVER ANY WITNESSES?

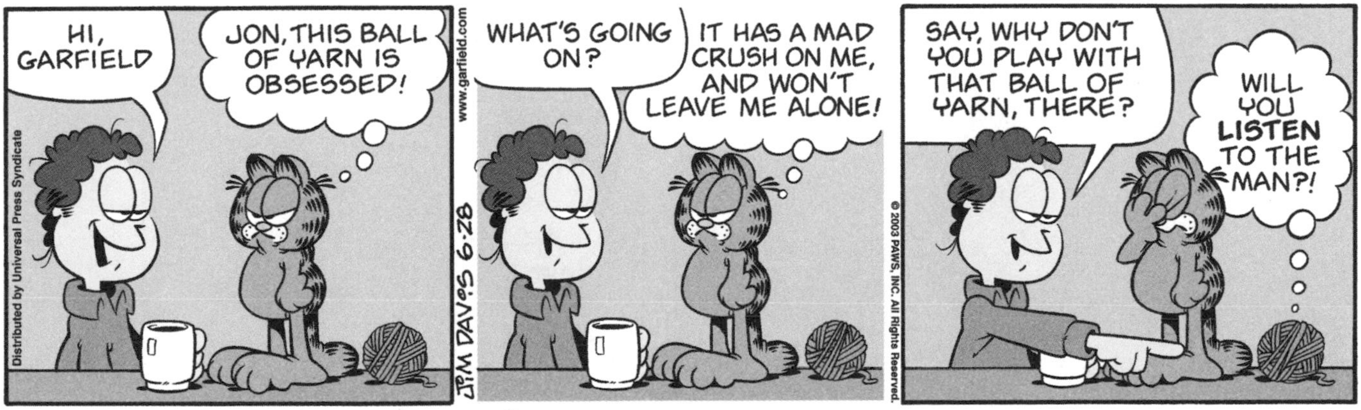
HI, GARFIELD
JON, THIS BALL OF YARN IS OBSESSED!
Distributed by Universal Press Syndicate
www.garfield.com
JIM DAVIS 6-28
WHAT'S GOING ON?
IT HAS A MAD CRUSH ON ME, AND WON'T LEAVE ME ALONE!
© 2003 PAWS, INC. All Rights Reserved.
SAY, WHY DON'T YOU PLAY WITH THAT BALL OF YARN, THERE?
WILL YOU **LISTEN** TO THE MAN?!

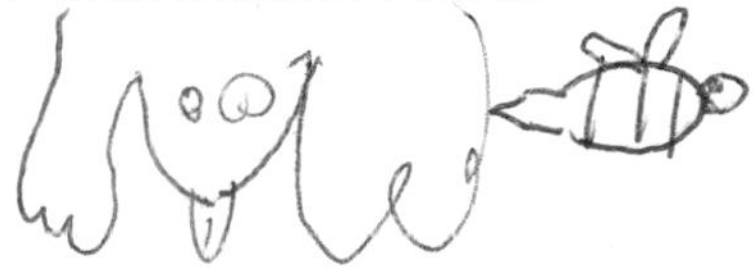

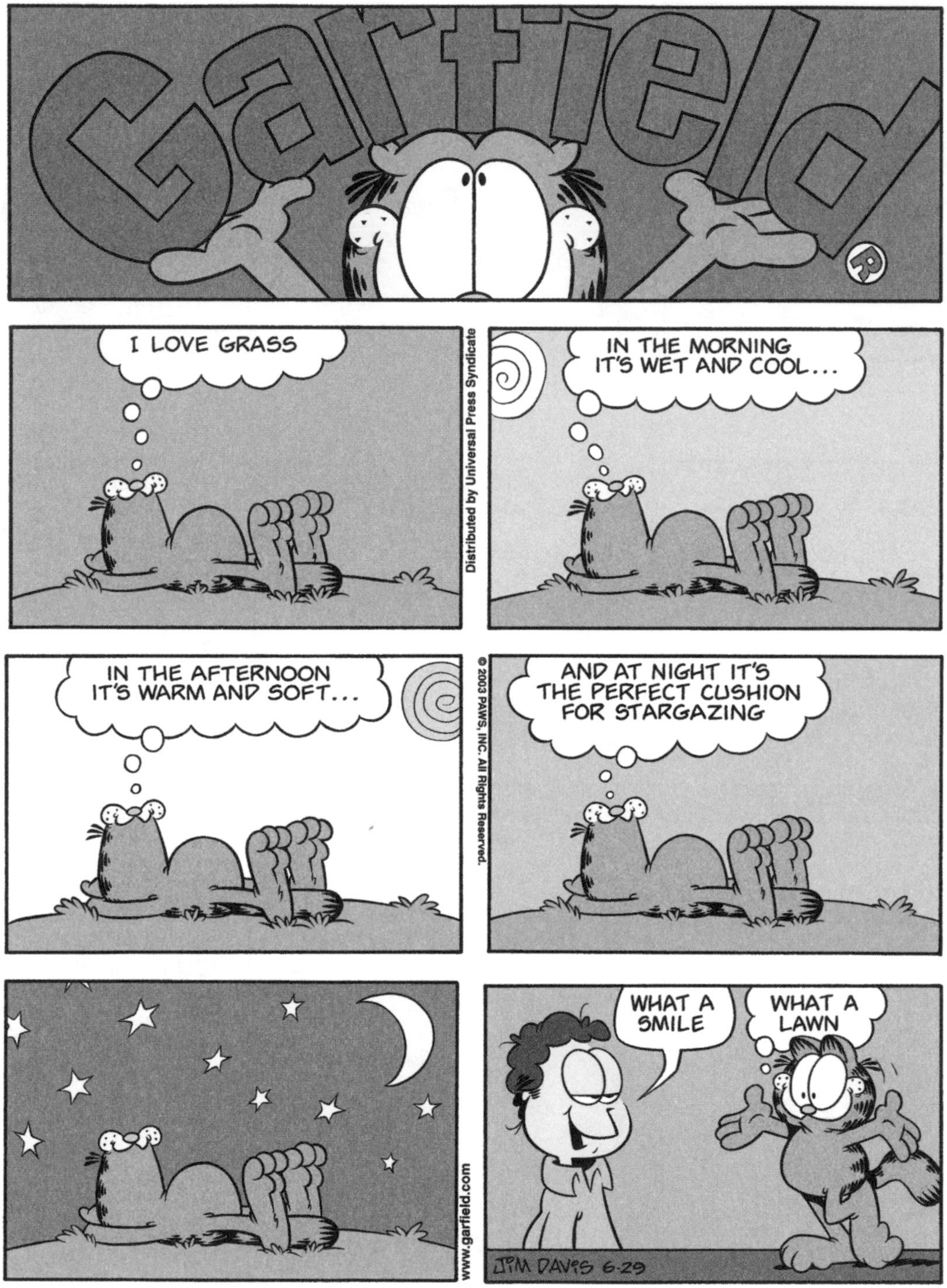
Garfield
I LOVE GRASS
IN THE MORNING IT'S WET AND COOL...
IN THE AFTERNOON IT'S WARM AND SOFT...
AND AT NIGHT IT'S THE PERFECT CUSHION FOR STARGAZING
WHAT A SMILE
WHAT A LAWN
Distributed by Universal Press Syndicate
© 2003 PAWS, INC. All Rights Reserved.
www.garfield.com
JIM DAVIS 6-29

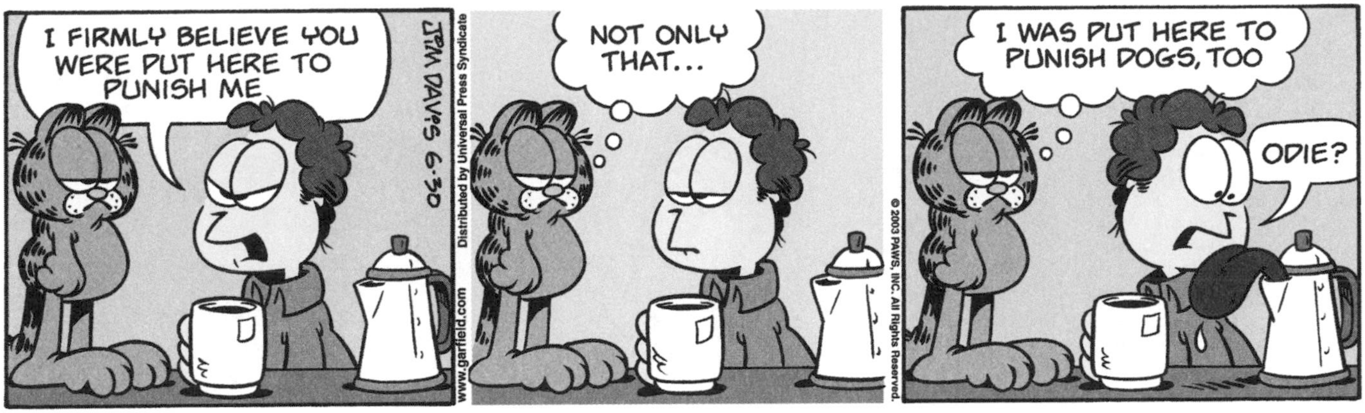
I FIRMLY BELIEVE YOU WERE PUT HERE TO PUNISH ME
JIM DAVIS 6-30
Distributed by Universal Press Syndicate
www.garfield.com
NOT ONLY THAT...
© 2003 PAWS, INC. All Rights Reserved.
I WAS PUT HERE TO PUNISH DOGS, TOO
ODIE?

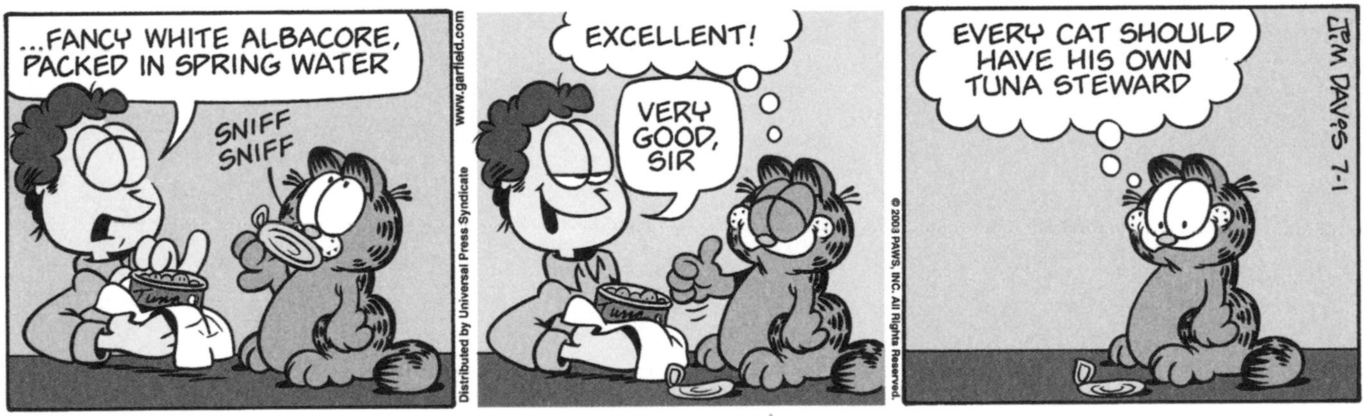
...FANCY WHITE ALBACORE, PACKED IN SPRING WATER
SNIFF SNIFF
www.garfield.com
Distributed by Universal Press Syndicate
EXCELLENT!
VERY GOOD, SIR
© 2003 PAWS, INC. All Rights Reserved.
EVERY CAT SHOULD HAVE HIS OWN TUNA STEWARD
JIM DAVIS 7-1

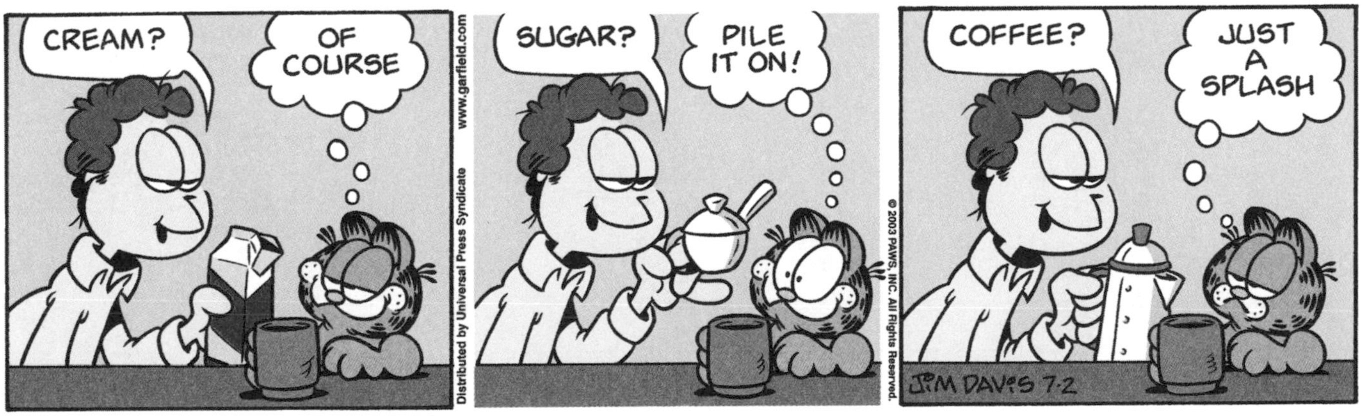
CREAM?
OF COURSE
www.garfield.com
Distributed by Universal Press Syndicate
SUGAR?
PILE IT ON!
© 2003 PAWS, INC. All Rights Reserved.
COFFEE?
JUST A SPLASH
JIM DAVIS 7-2

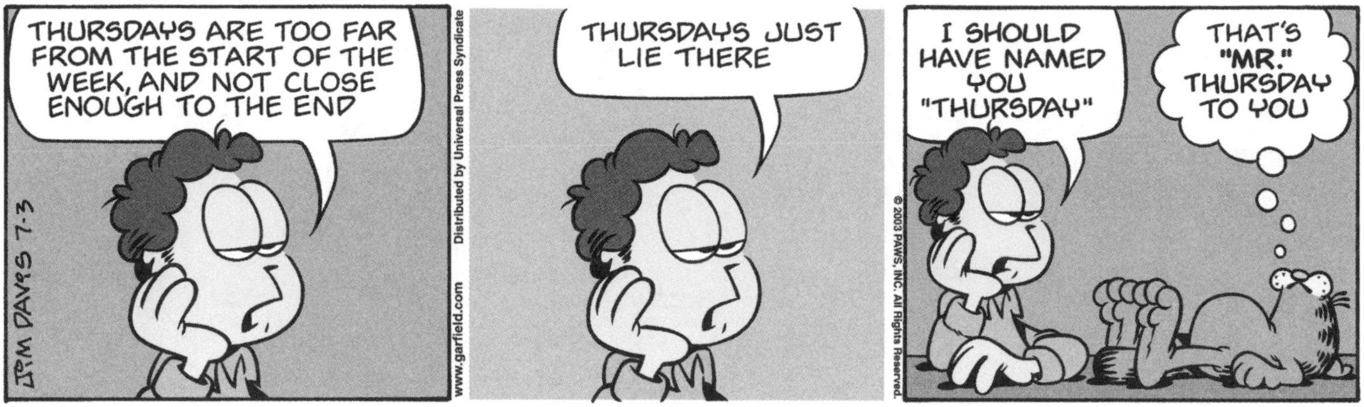
THURSDAYS ARE TOO FAR FROM THE START OF THE WEEK, AND NOT CLOSE ENOUGH TO THE END
JIM DAVIS 7-3
Distributed by Universal Press Syndicate
www.garfield.com
THURSDAYS JUST LIE THERE
I SHOULD HAVE NAMED YOU "THURSDAY"
THAT'S "MR." THURSDAY TO YOU
© 2003 PAWS, INC. All Rights Reserved.

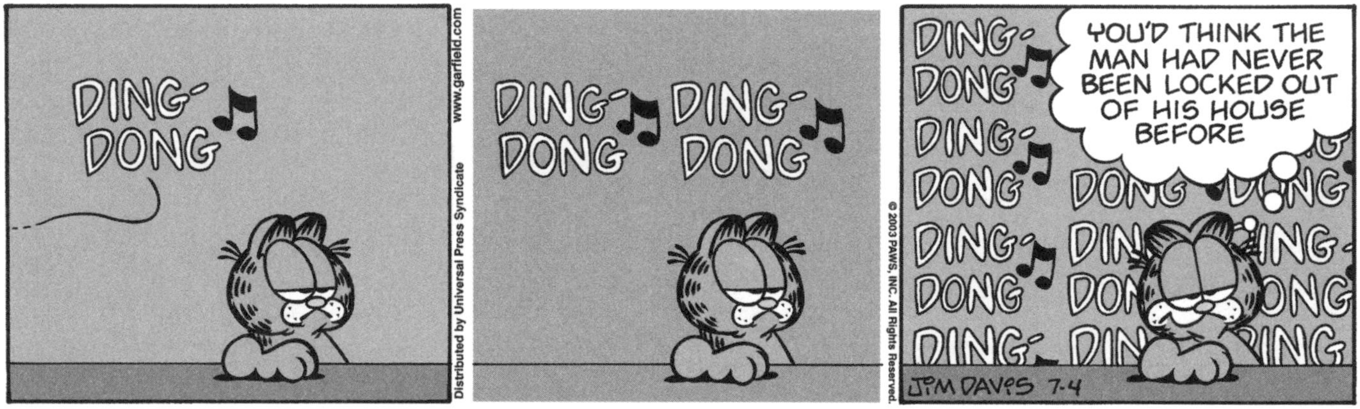
DING-DONG
www.garfield.com
Distributed by Universal Press Syndicate
DING-DONG DING-DONG
© 2003 PAWS, INC. All Rights Reserved.
YOU'D THINK THE MAN HAD NEVER BEEN LOCKED OUT OF HIS HOUSE BEFORE
JIM DAVIS 7-4

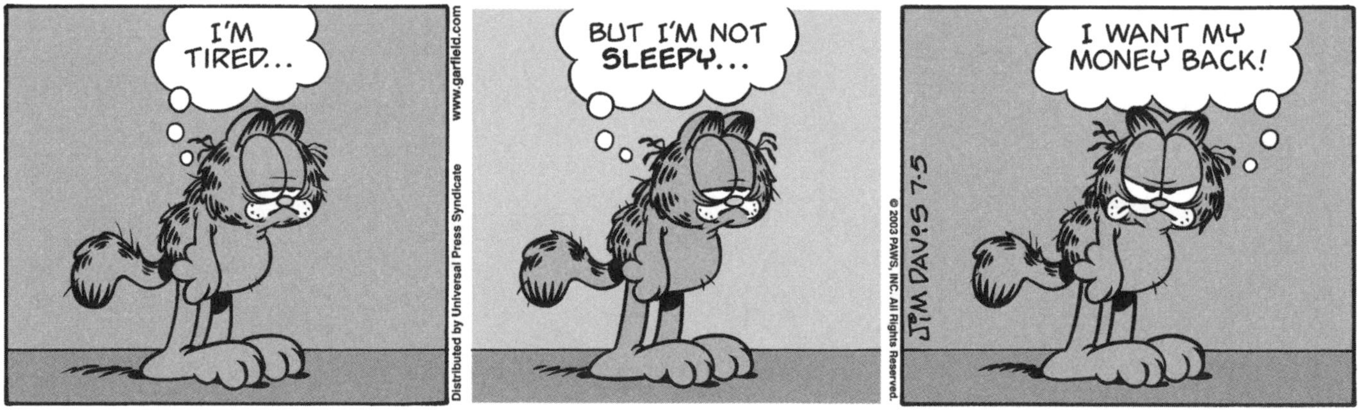
I'M TIRED...
www.garfield.com
Distributed by Universal Press Syndicate
BUT I'M NOT SLEEPY...
© 2003 PAWS, INC. All Rights Reserved.
JIM DAVIS 7-5
I WANT MY MONEY BACK!

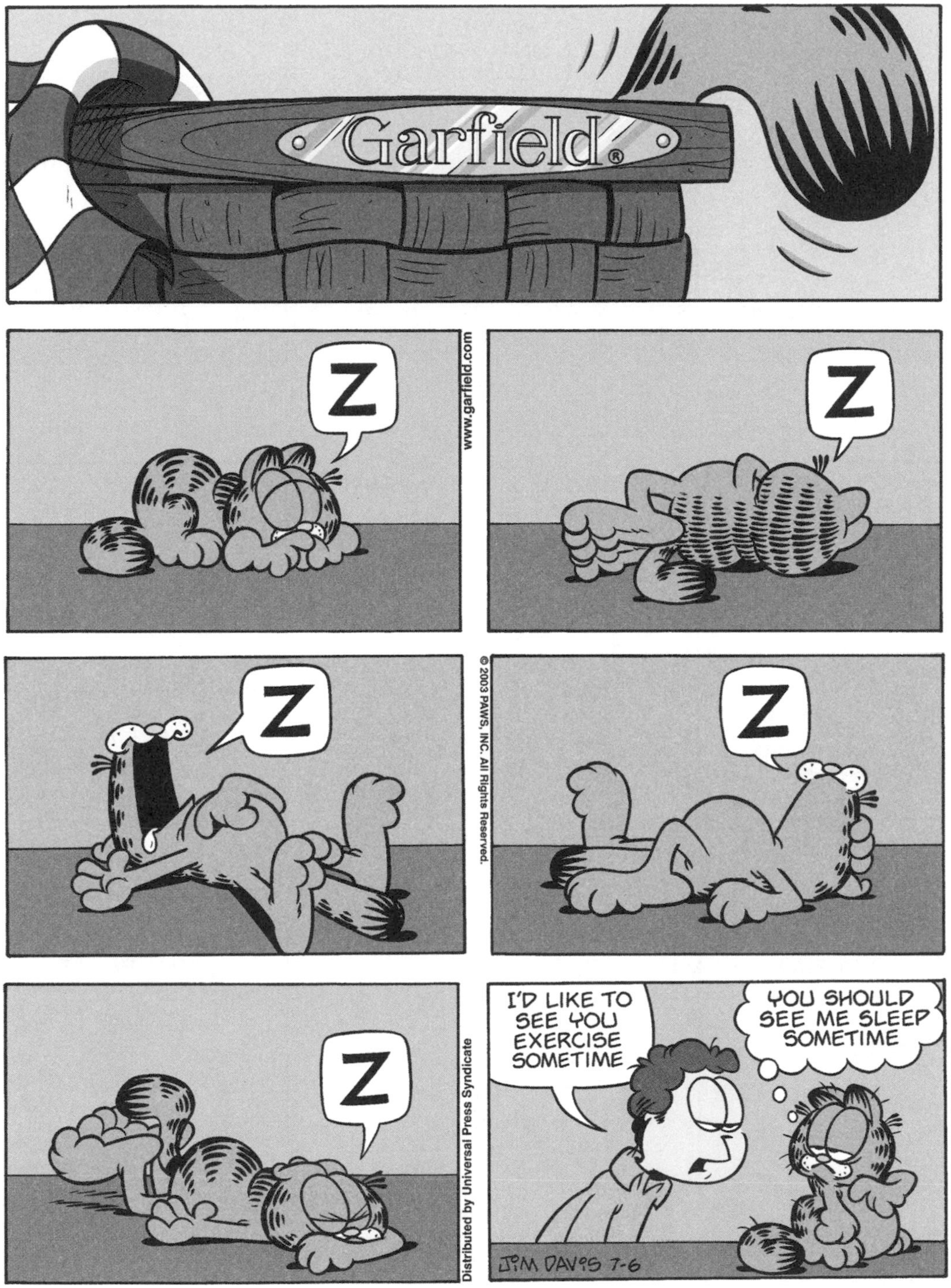
Garfield®
www.garfield.com
Z
Z
© 2003 PAWS, INC. All Rights Reserved.
Z
Z
Distributed by Universal Press Syndicate
Z
I'D LIKE TO SEE YOU EXERCISE SOMETIME
YOU SHOULD SEE ME SLEEP SOMETIME
JIM DAVIS 7-6

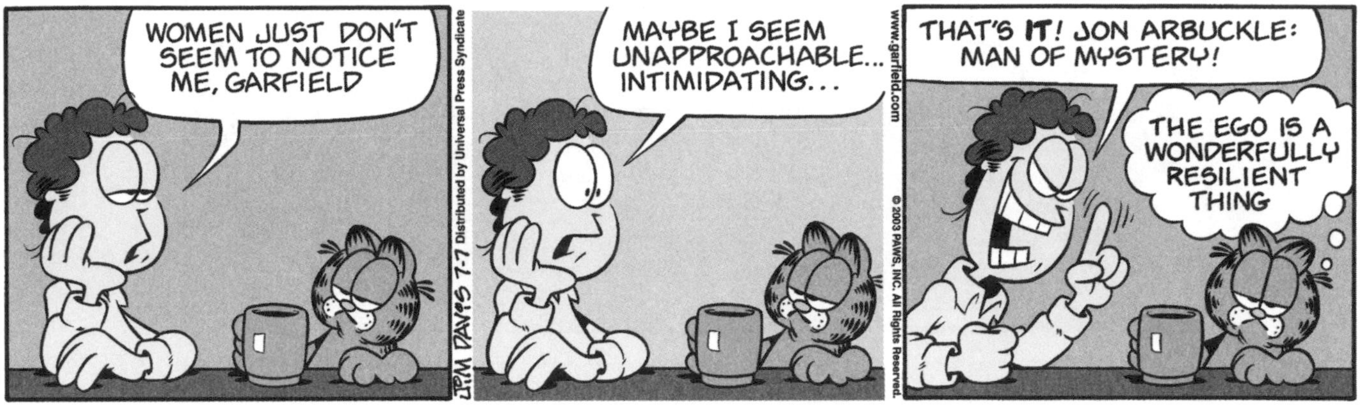
WOMEN JUST DON'T SEEM TO NOTICE ME, GARFIELD
JIM DAVIS 7-7
Distributed by Universal Press Syndicate
MAYBE I SEEM UNAPPROACHABLE... INTIMIDATING...
www.garfield.com
© 2003 PAWS, INC. All Rights Reserved.
THAT'S IT! JON ARBUCKLE: MAN OF MYSTERY!
THE EGO IS A WONDERFULLY RESILIENT THING

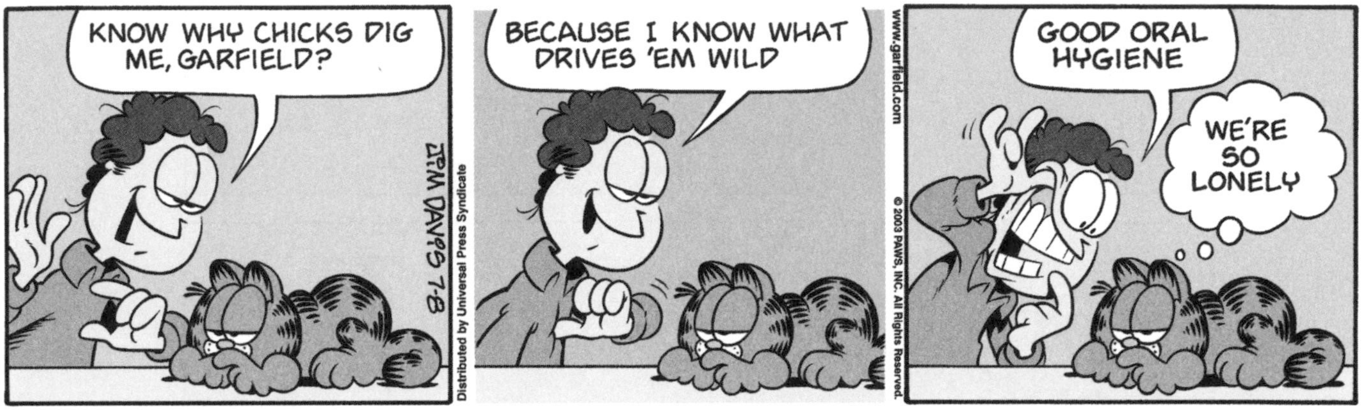
KNOW WHY CHICKS DIG ME, GARFIELD?
JIM DAVIS 7-8
Distributed by Universal Press Syndicate
BECAUSE I KNOW WHAT DRIVES 'EM WILD
www.garfield.com
© 2003 PAWS, INC. All Rights Reserved.
GOOD ORAL HYGIENE
WE'RE SO LONELY

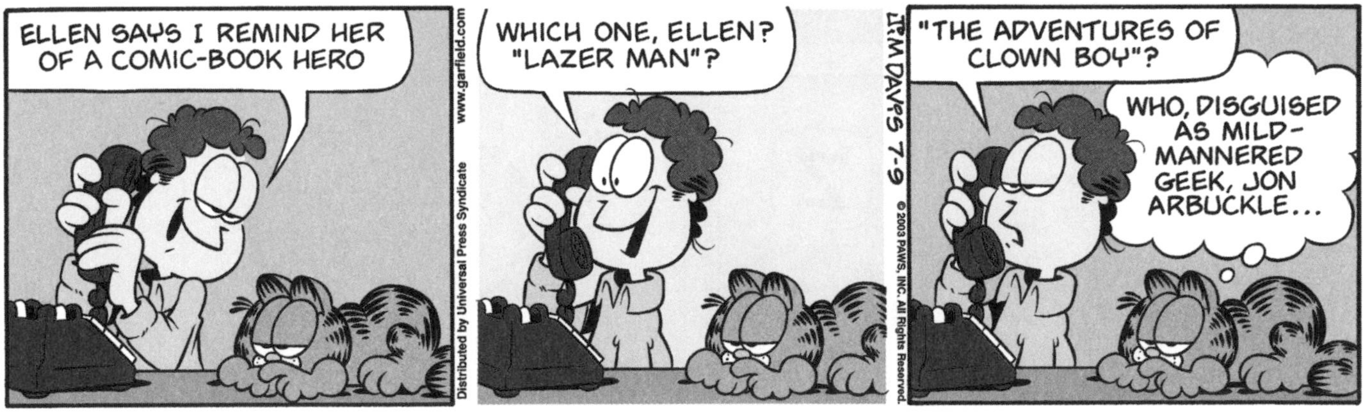
ELLEN SAYS I REMIND HER OF A COMIC-BOOK HERO
www.garfield.com
Distributed by Universal Press Syndicate
WHICH ONE, ELLEN? "LAZER MAN"?
JIM DAVIS 7-9
© 2003 PAWS, INC. All Rights Reserved.
"THE ADVENTURES OF CLOWN BOY"?
WHO, DISGUISED AS MILD-MANNERED GEEK, JON ARBUCKLE...

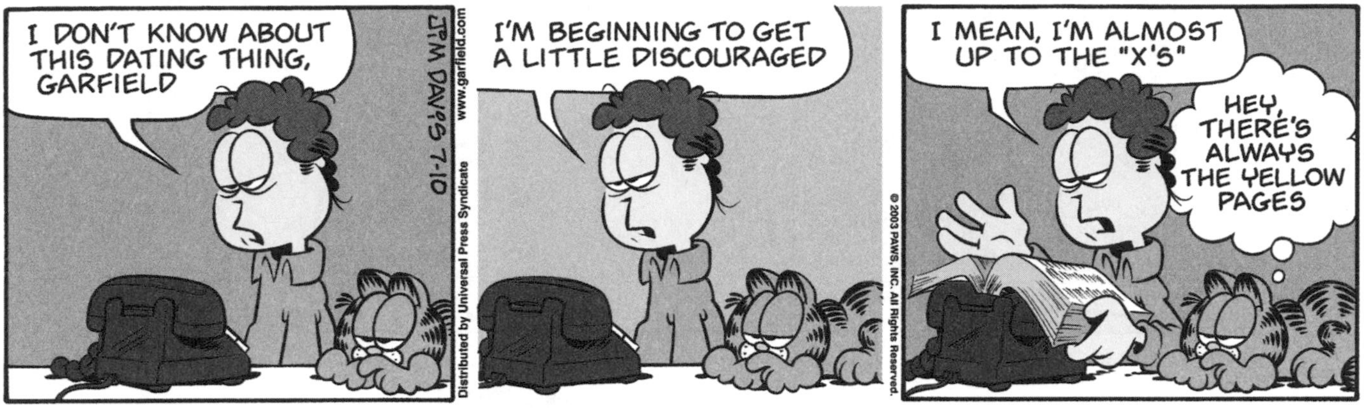
I DON'T KNOW ABOUT THIS DATING THING, GARFIELD
JIM DAVIS 7-10
www.garfield.com
Distributed by Universal Press Syndicate
I'M BEGINNING TO GET A LITTLE DISCOURAGED
© 2003 PAWS, INC. All Rights Reserved.
I MEAN, I'M ALMOST UP TO THE "X'S"
HEY, THERE'S ALWAYS THE YELLOW PAGES

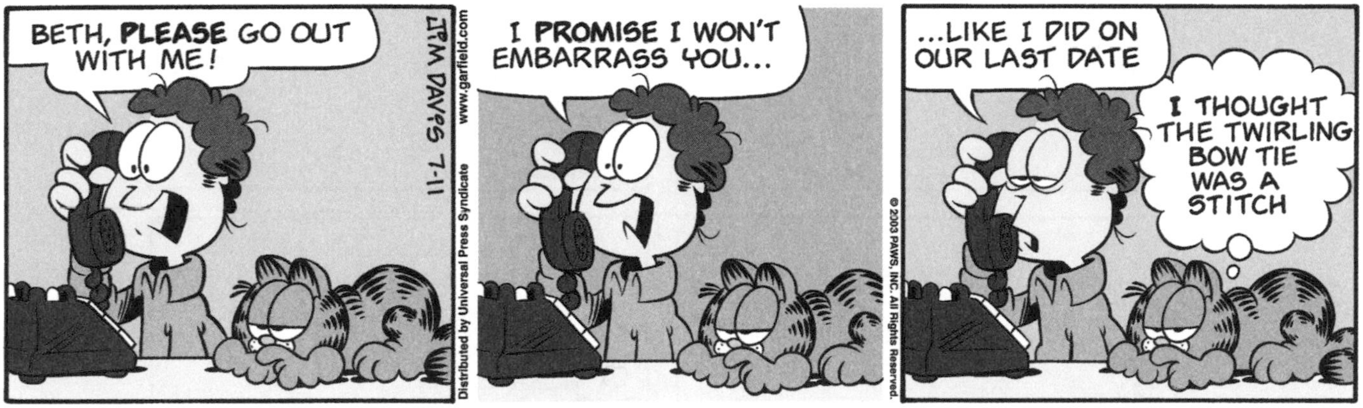
BETH, PLEASE GO OUT WITH ME!
JIM DAVIS 7-11
www.garfield.com
Distributed by Universal Press Syndicate
I PROMISE I WON'T EMBARRASS YOU...
© 2003 PAWS, INC. All Rights Reserved.
...LIKE I DID ON OUR LAST DATE
I THOUGHT THE TWIRLING BOW TIE WAS A STITCH

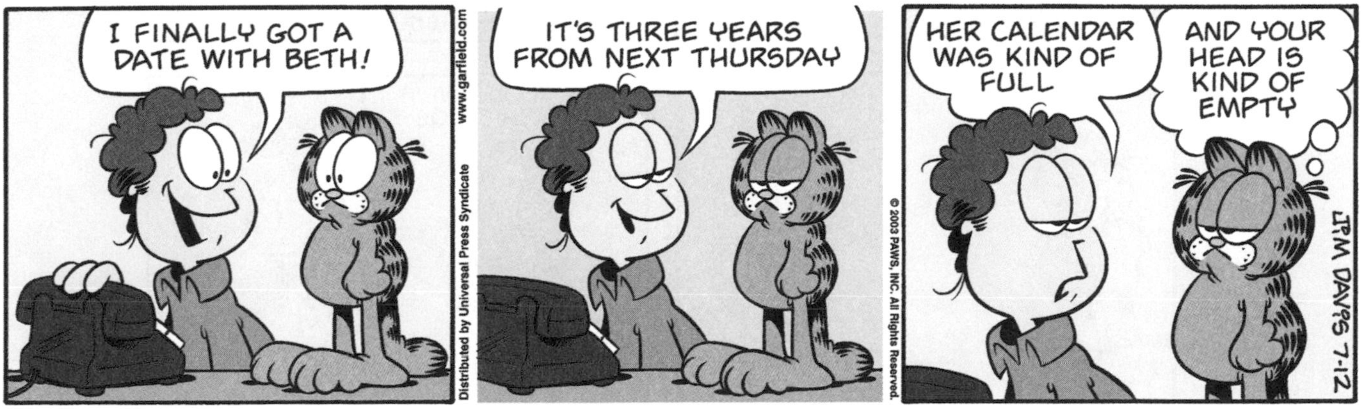
I FINALLY GOT A DATE WITH BETH!
www.garfield.com
Distributed by Universal Press Syndicate
IT'S THREE YEARS FROM NEXT THURSDAY
© 2003 PAWS, INC. All Rights Reserved.
HER CALENDAR WAS KIND OF FULL
AND YOUR HEAD IS KIND OF EMPTY
JIM DAVIS 7-12

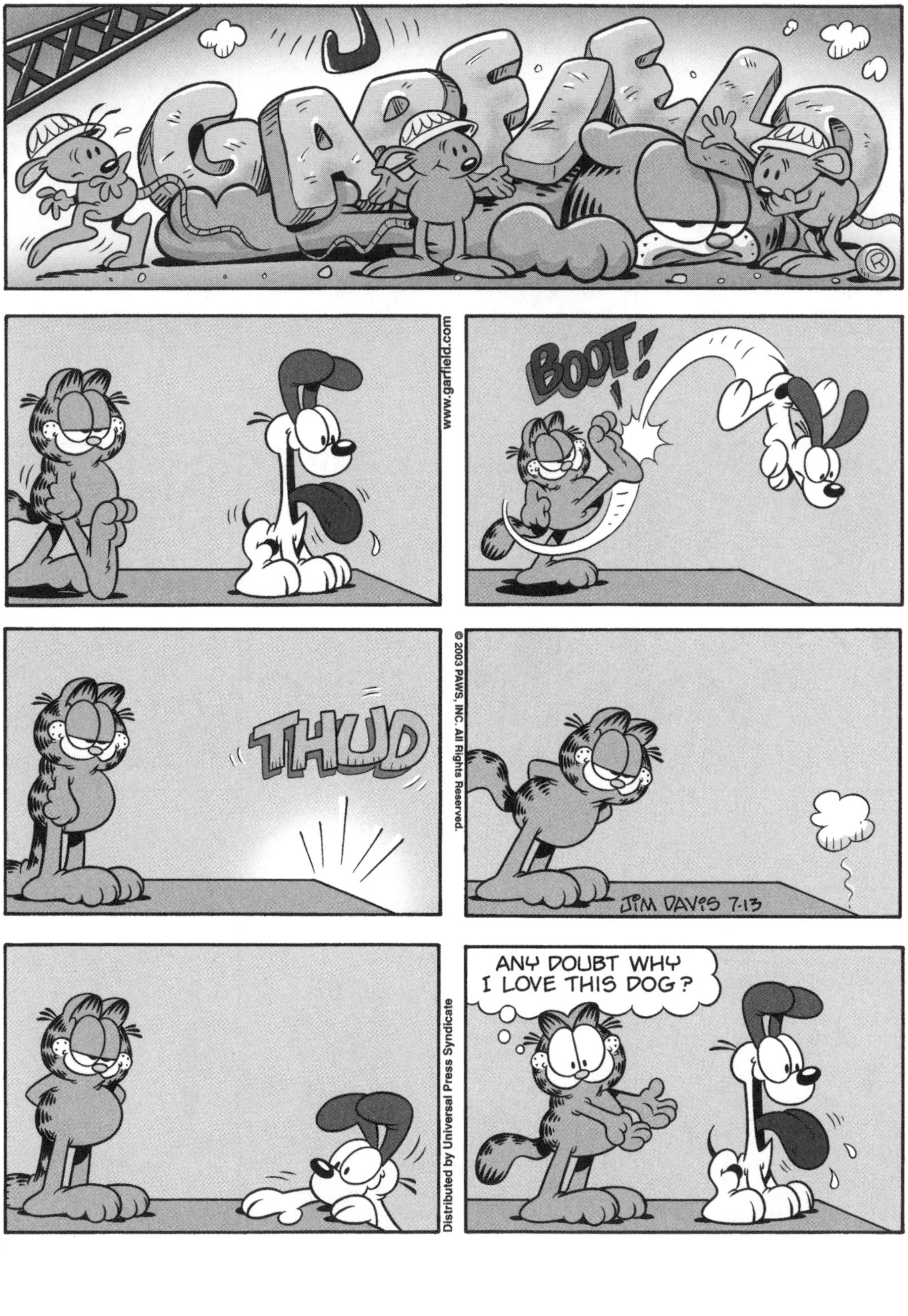
GARFIELD
www.garfield.com
BOOT!
THUD
© 2003 PAWS, INC. All Rights Reserved.
JIM DAVIS 7-13
Distributed by Universal Press Syndicate
ANY DOUBT WHY I LOVE THIS DOG?

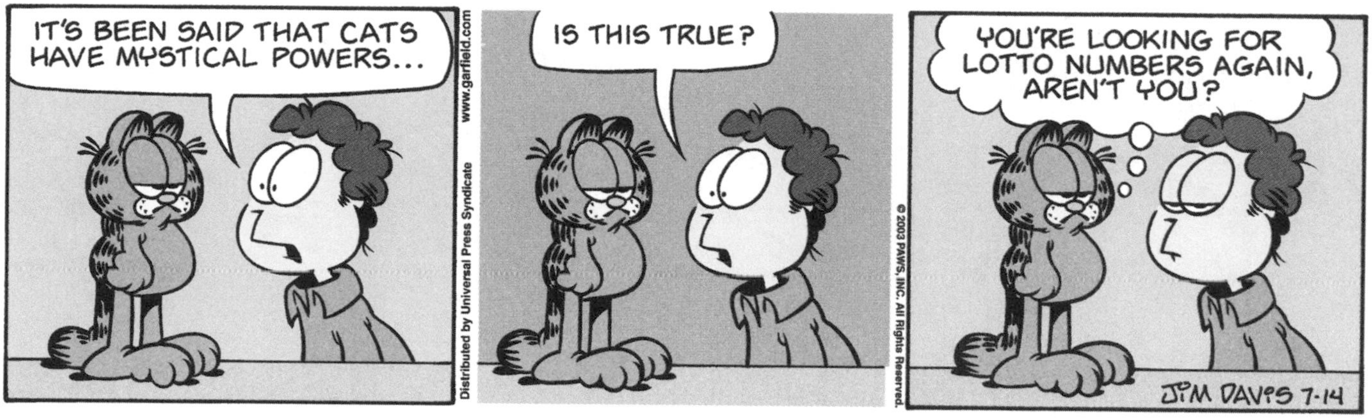
IT'S BEEN SAID THAT CATS HAVE MYSTICAL POWERS...
IS THIS TRUE?
YOU'RE LOOKING FOR LOTTO NUMBERS AGAIN, AREN'T YOU?
JIM DAVIS 7-14
www.garfield.com
Distributed by Universal Press Syndicate
© 2003 PAWS, INC. All Rights Reserved.

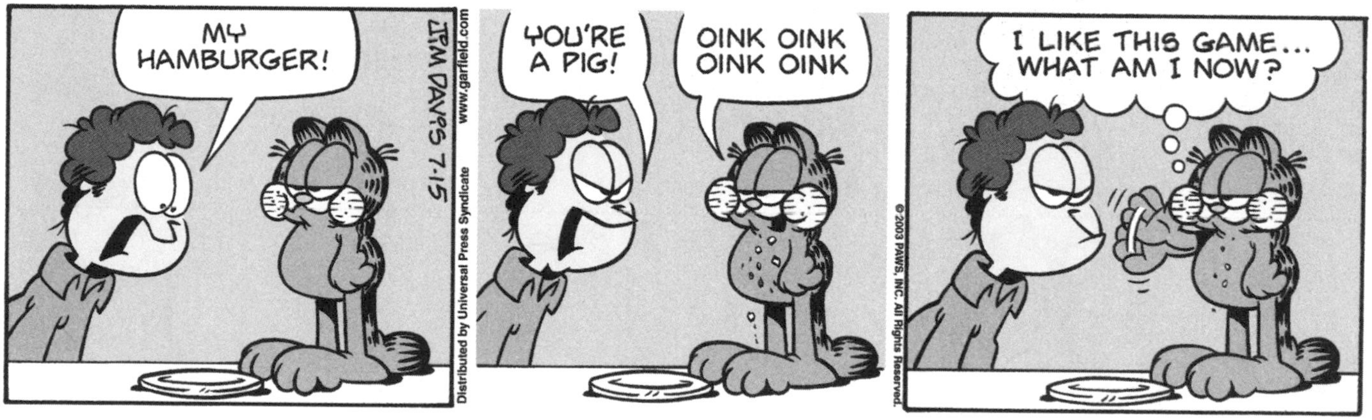
MY HAMBURGER!
YOU'RE A PIG!
OINK OINK OINK OINK
I LIKE THIS GAME... WHAT AM I NOW?
JIM DAVIS 7-15
www.garfield.com
Distributed by Universal Press Syndicate
© 2003 PAWS, INC. All Rights Reserved.

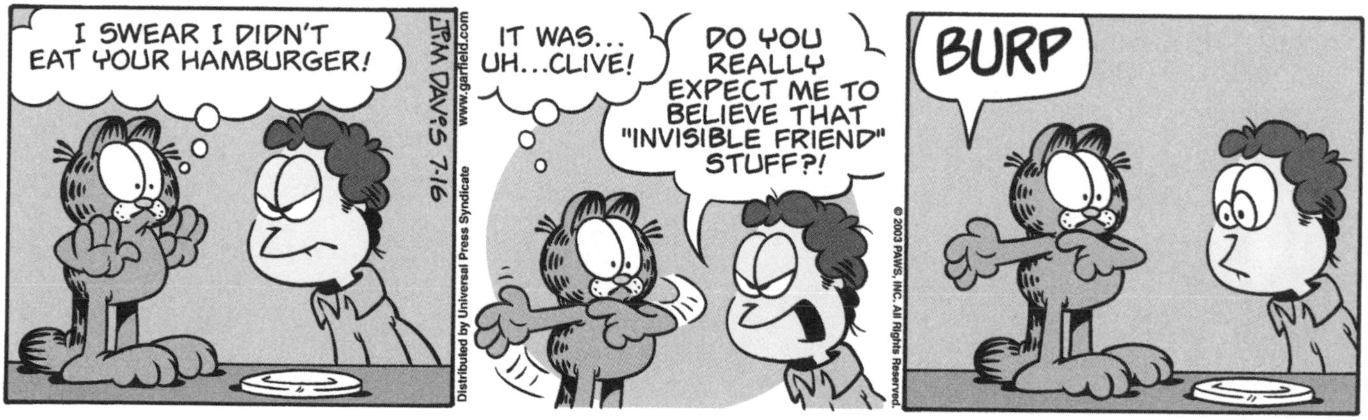
I SWEAR I DIDN'T EAT YOUR HAMBURGER!
IT WAS... UH...CLIVE!
DO YOU REALLY EXPECT ME TO BELIEVE THAT "INVISIBLE FRIEND" STUFF?!
BURP
JIM DAVIS 7-16
www.garfield.com
Distributed by Universal Press Syndicate
© 2003 PAWS, INC. All Rights Reserved.

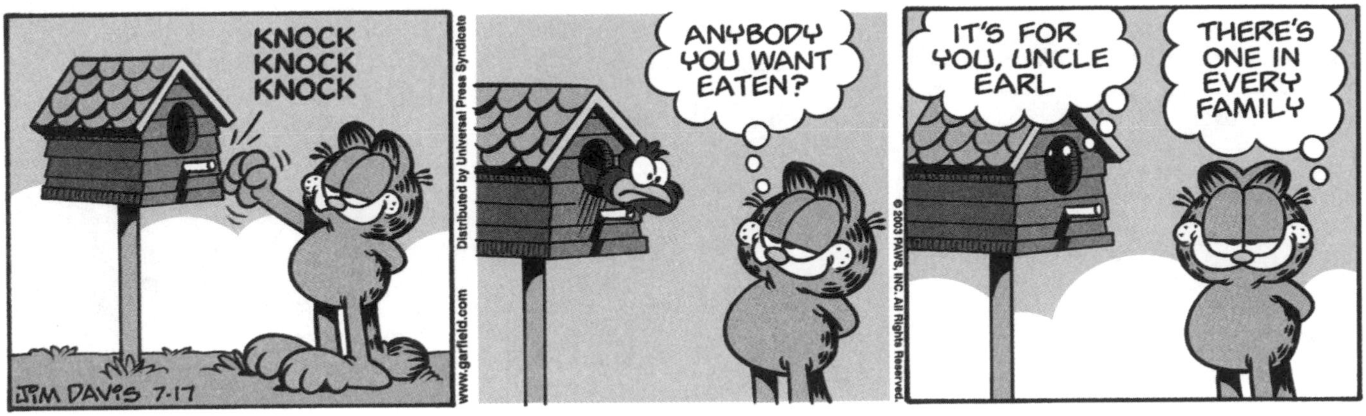
KNOCK KNOCK KNOCK
JIM DAVIS 7-17
www.garfield.com Distributed by Universal Press Syndicate
ANYBODY YOU WANT EATEN?
© 2003 PAWS, INC. All Rights Reserved.
IT'S FOR YOU, UNCLE EARL
THERE'S ONE IN EVERY FAMILY

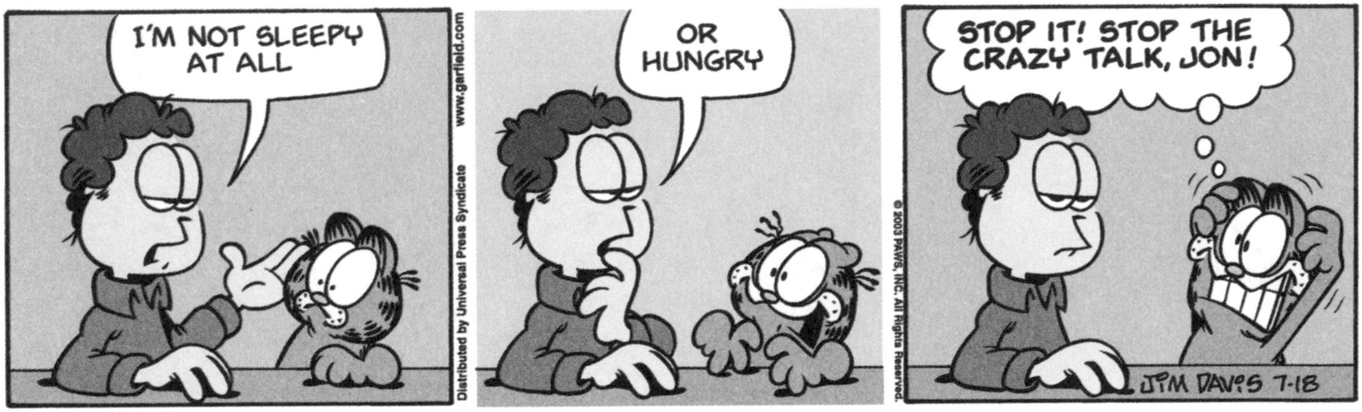
I'M NOT SLEEPY AT ALL
Distributed by Universal Press Syndicate www.garfield.com
OR HUNGRY
© 2003 PAWS, INC. All Rights Reserved.
STOP IT! STOP THE CRAZY TALK, JON!
JIM DAVIS 7-18

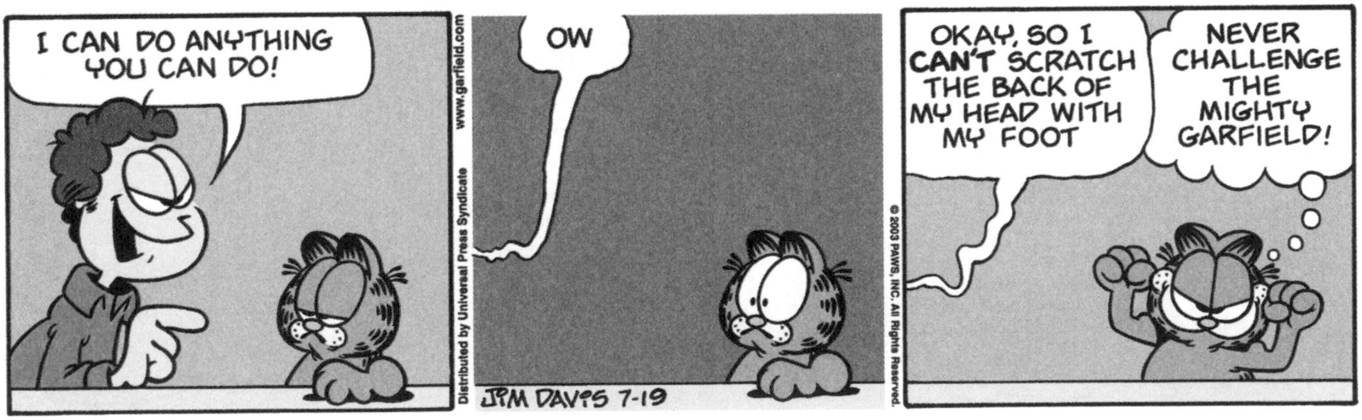
I CAN DO ANYTHING YOU CAN DO!
Distributed by Universal Press Syndicate www.garfield.com
OW
JIM DAVIS 7-19
© 2003 PAWS, INC. All Rights Reserved.
OKAY, SO I **CAN'T** SCRATCH THE BACK OF MY HEAD WITH MY FOOT
NEVER CHALLENGE THE MIGHTY GARFIELD!

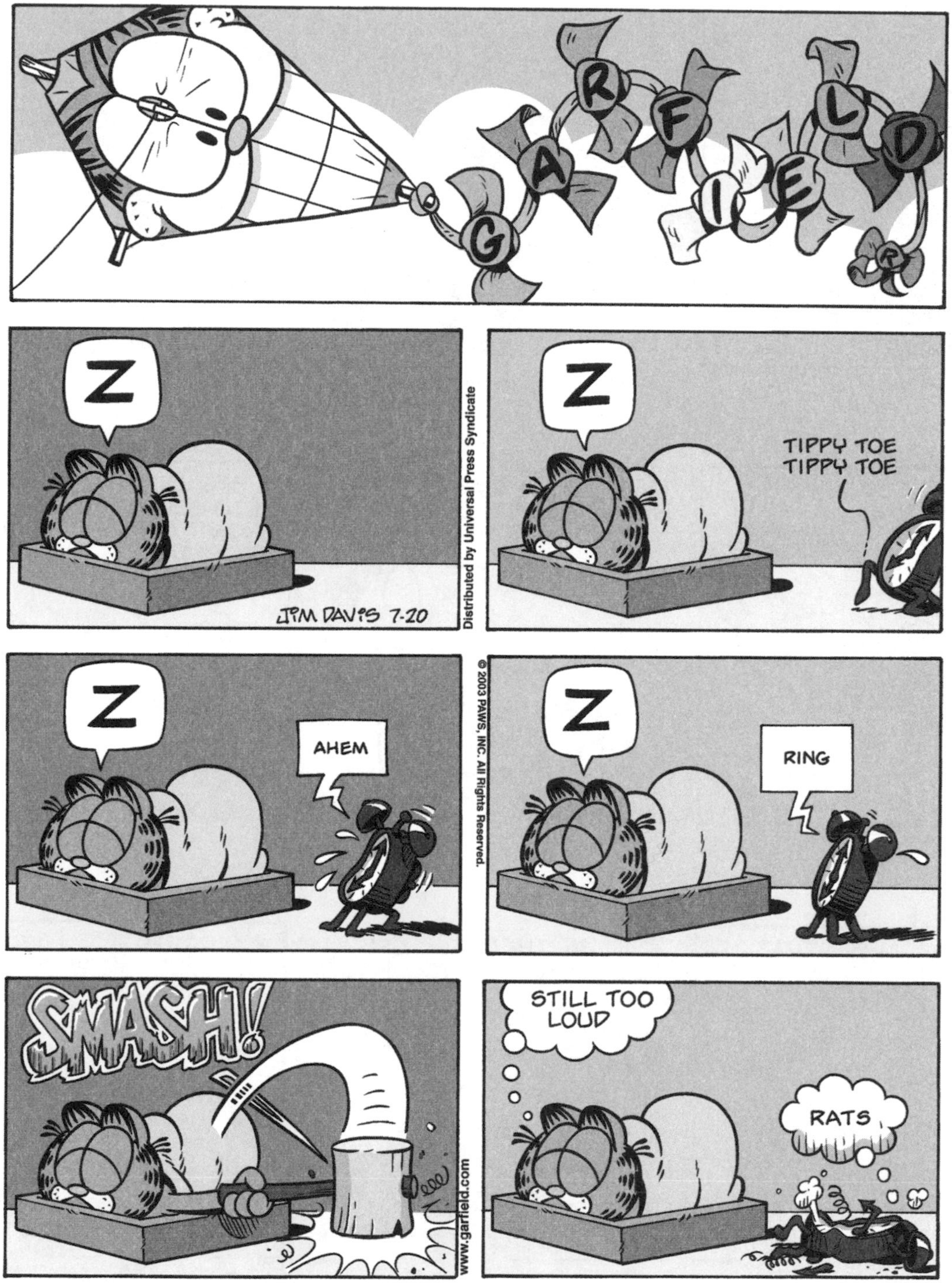
GARFIELD
Z
JIM DAVIS 7-20
Distributed by Universal Press Syndicate
Z
TIPPY TOE
TIPPY TOE
© 2003 PAWS, INC. All Rights Reserved.
Z
AHEM
Z
RING
SMASH!
www.garfield.com
STILL TOO LOUD
RATS

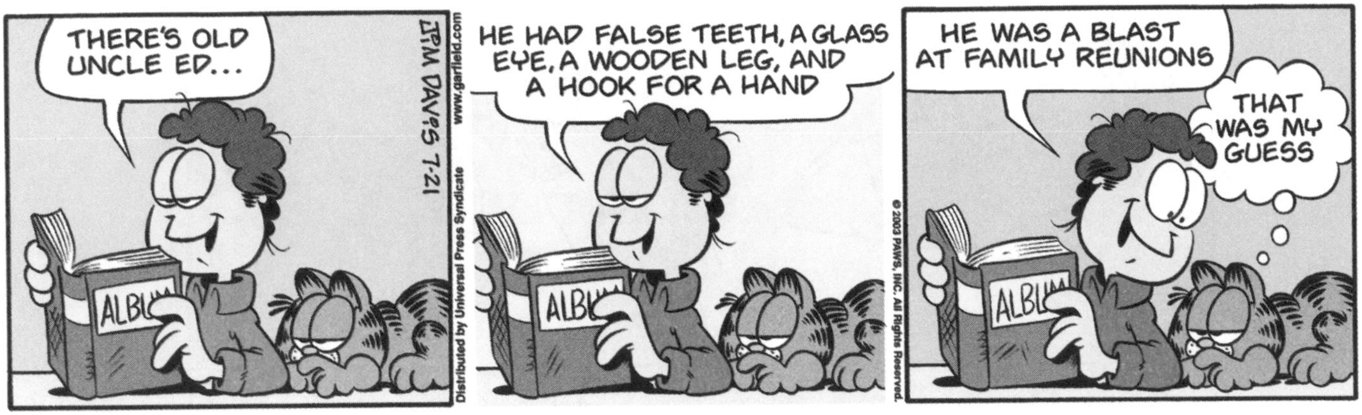
THERE'S OLD UNCLE ED...
HE HAD FALSE TEETH, A GLASS EYE, A WOODEN LEG, AND A HOOK FOR A HAND
HE WAS A BLAST AT FAMILY REUNIONS
THAT WAS MY GUESS
ALBUM
JIM DAVIS 7-21
www.garfield.com
Distributed by Universal Press Syndicate
© 2003 PAWS, INC. All Rights Reserved.

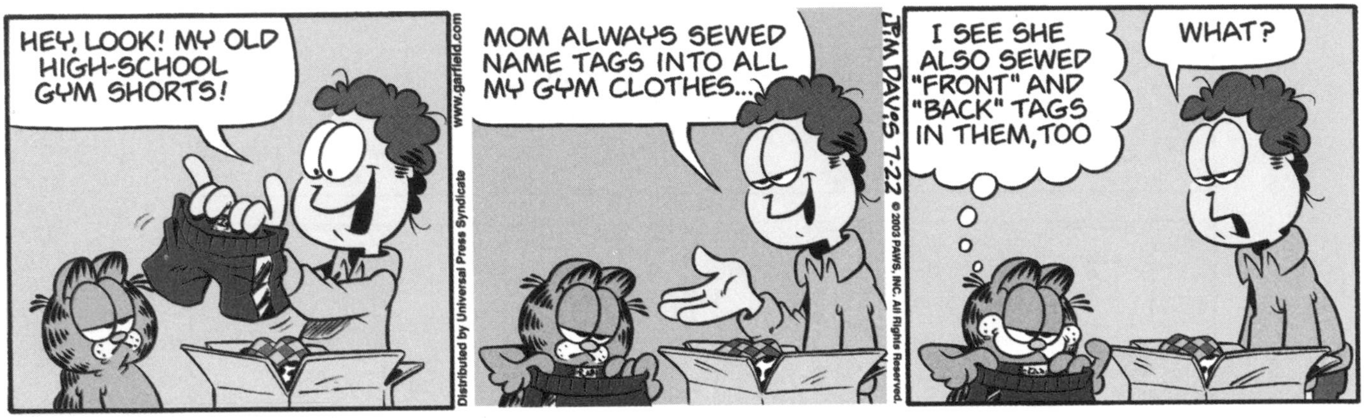
HEY, LOOK! MY OLD HIGH-SCHOOL GYM SHORTS!
MOM ALWAYS SEWED NAME TAGS INTO ALL MY GYM CLOTHES...
I SEE SHE ALSO SEWED "FRONT" AND "BACK" TAGS IN THEM, TOO
WHAT?
JIM DAVIS 7-22
www.garfield.com
Distributed by Universal Press Syndicate
© 2003 PAWS, INC. All Rights Reserved.

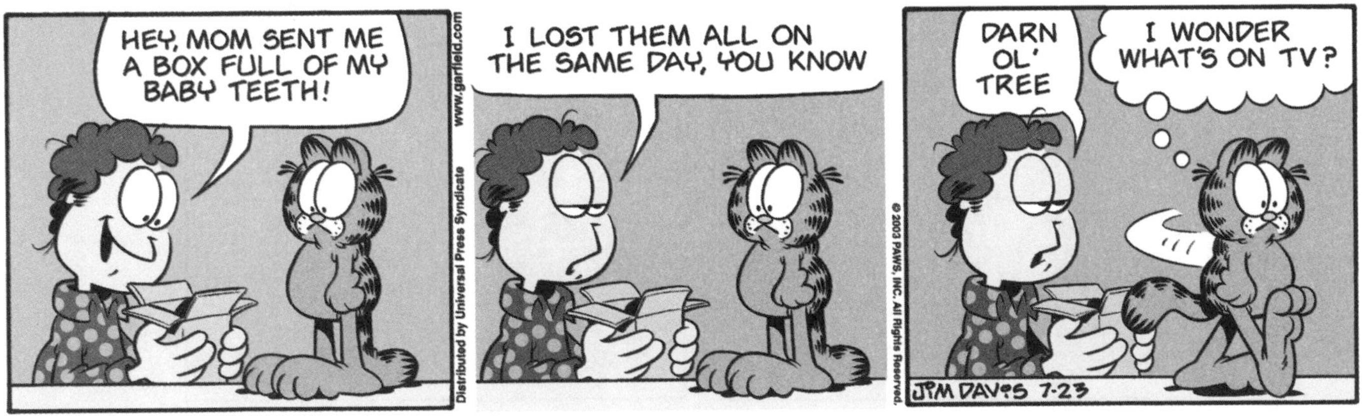
HEY, MOM SENT ME A BOX FULL OF MY BABY TEETH!
I LOST THEM ALL ON THE SAME DAY, YOU KNOW
DARN OL' TREE
I WONDER WHAT'S ON TV?
JIM DAVIS 7-23
www.garfield.com
Distributed by Universal Press Syndicate
© 2003 PAWS, INC. All Rights Reserved.

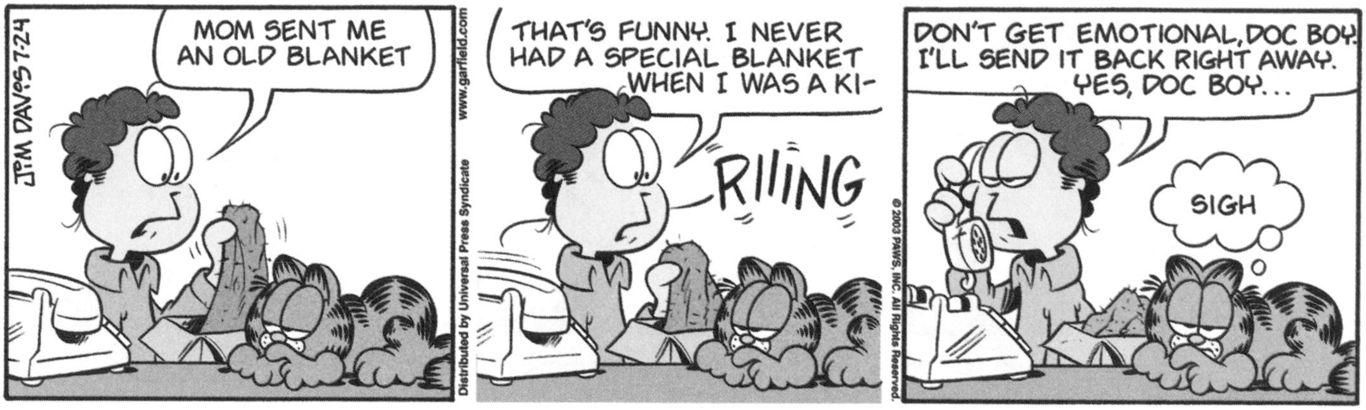
JIM DAVIS 7-24
MOM SENT ME AN OLD BLANKET
Distributed by Universal Press Syndicate www.garfield.com
THAT'S FUNNY. I NEVER HAD A SPECIAL BLANKET WHEN I WAS A KI-
RIIING
© 2003 PAWS, INC. All Rights Reserved.
DON'T GET EMOTIONAL, DOC BOY. I'LL SEND IT BACK RIGHT AWAY. YES, DOC BOY...
SIGH

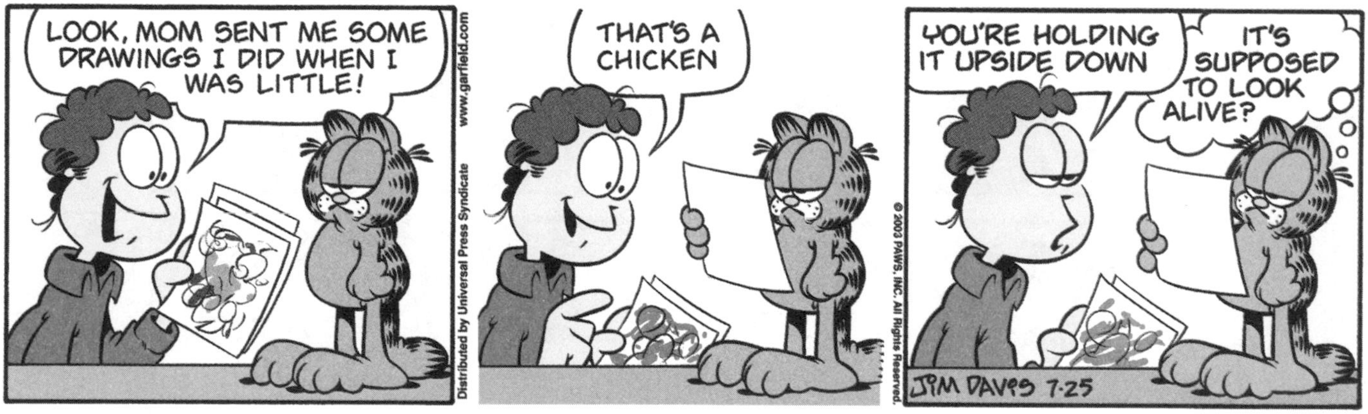
LOOK, MOM SENT ME SOME DRAWINGS I DID WHEN I WAS LITTLE!
Distributed by Universal Press Syndicate www.garfield.com
THAT'S A CHICKEN
© 2003 PAWS, INC. All Rights Reserved.
YOU'RE HOLDING IT UPSIDE DOWN
IT'S SUPPOSED TO LOOK ALIVE?
JIM DAVIS 7-25

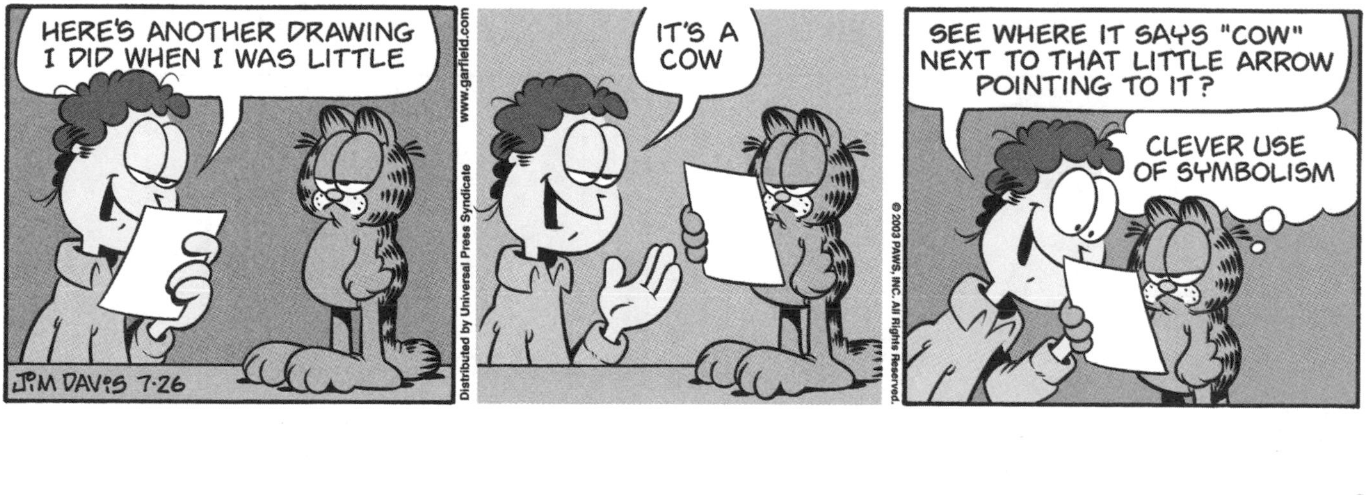
HERE'S ANOTHER DRAWING I DID WHEN I WAS LITTLE
JIM DAVIS 7-26
Distributed by Universal Press Syndicate www.garfield.com
IT'S A COW
© 2003 PAWS, INC. All Rights Reserved.
SEE WHERE IT SAYS "COW" NEXT TO THAT LITTLE ARROW POINTING TO IT?
CLEVER USE OF SYMBOLISM

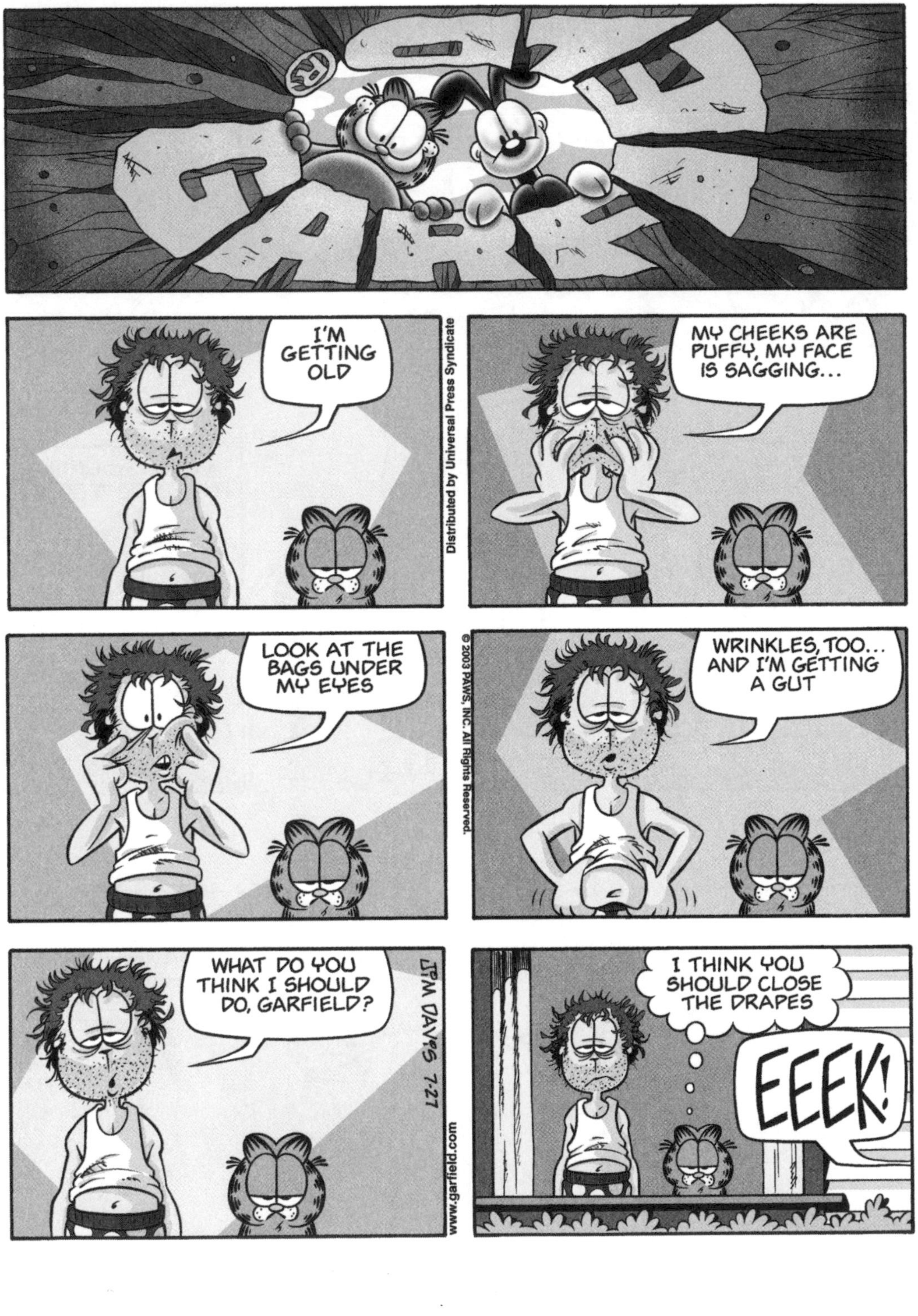
I'M GETTING OLD
MY CHEEKS ARE PUFFY, MY FACE IS SAGGING...
LOOK AT THE BAGS UNDER MY EYES
WRINKLES, TOO... AND I'M GETTING A GUT
WHAT DO YOU THINK I SHOULD DO, GARFIELD?
I THINK YOU SHOULD CLOSE THE DRAPES
EEEK!
Distributed by Universal Press Syndicate
© 2003 PAWS, INC. All Rights Reserved.
JIM DAVIS 7-27
www.garfield.com

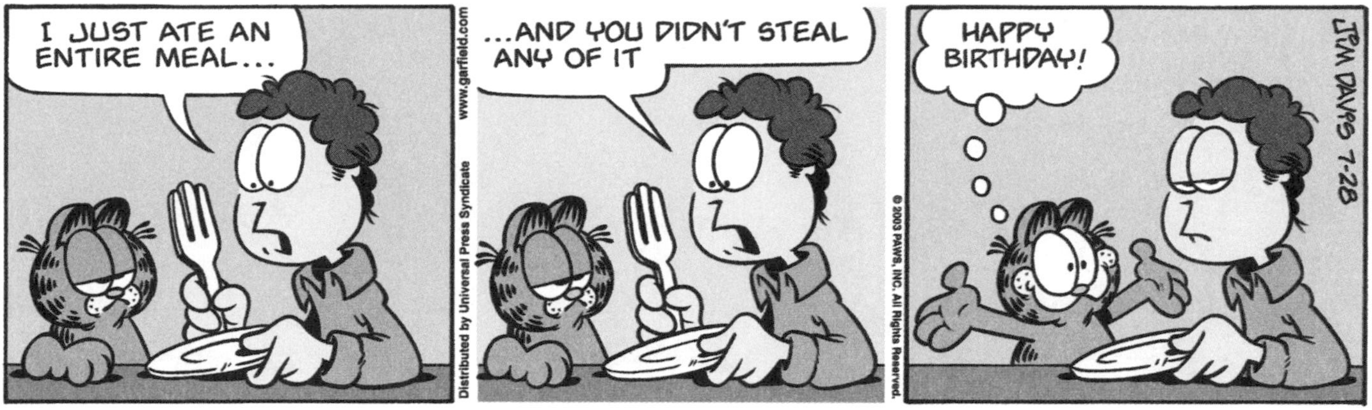
I JUST ATE AN ENTIRE MEAL...
...AND YOU DIDN'T STEAL ANY OF IT
HAPPY BIRTHDAY!
JIM DAVIS 7-28
www.garfield.com Distributed by Universal Press Syndicate
© 2003 PAWS, INC. All Rights Reserved.

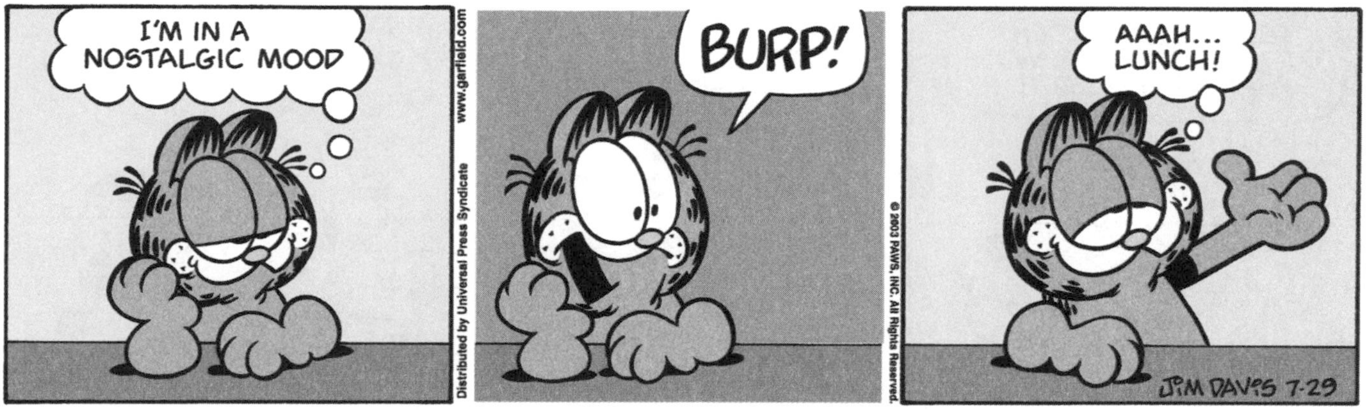
I'M IN A NOSTALGIC MOOD
BURP!
AAAH... LUNCH!
JIM DAVIS 7-29
www.garfield.com Distributed by Universal Press Syndicate
© 2003 PAWS, INC. All Rights Reserved.

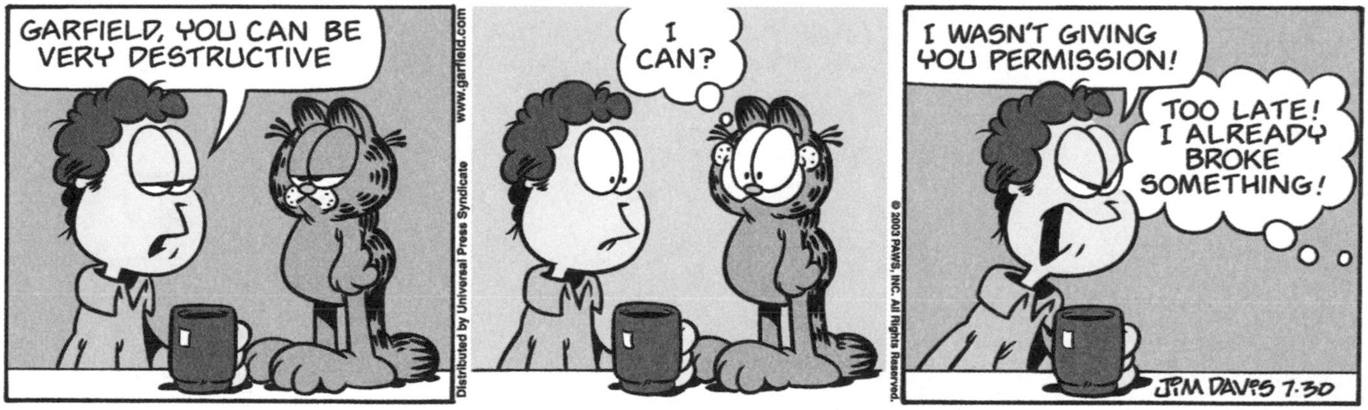
GARFIELD, YOU CAN BE VERY DESTRUCTIVE
I CAN?
I WASN'T GIVING YOU PERMISSION!
TOO LATE! I ALREADY BROKE SOMETHING!
JIM DAVIS 7-30
www.garfield.com Distributed by Universal Press Syndicate
© 2003 PAWS, INC. All Rights Reserved.

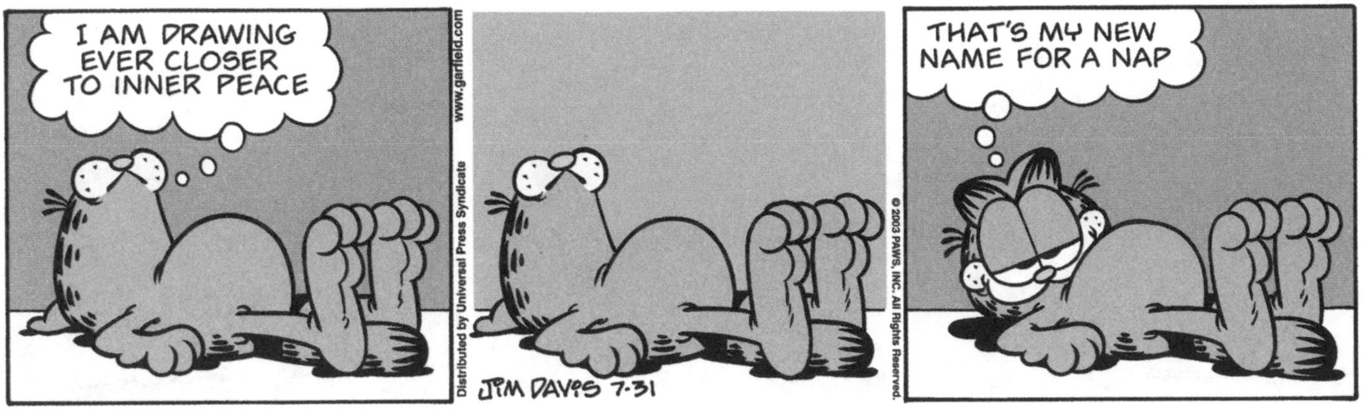
I AM DRAWING EVER CLOSER TO INNER PEACE
www.garfield.com
Distributed by Universal Press Syndicate
JIM DAVIS 7-31
© 2003 PAWS, INC. All Rights Reserved.
THAT'S MY NEW NAME FOR A NAP

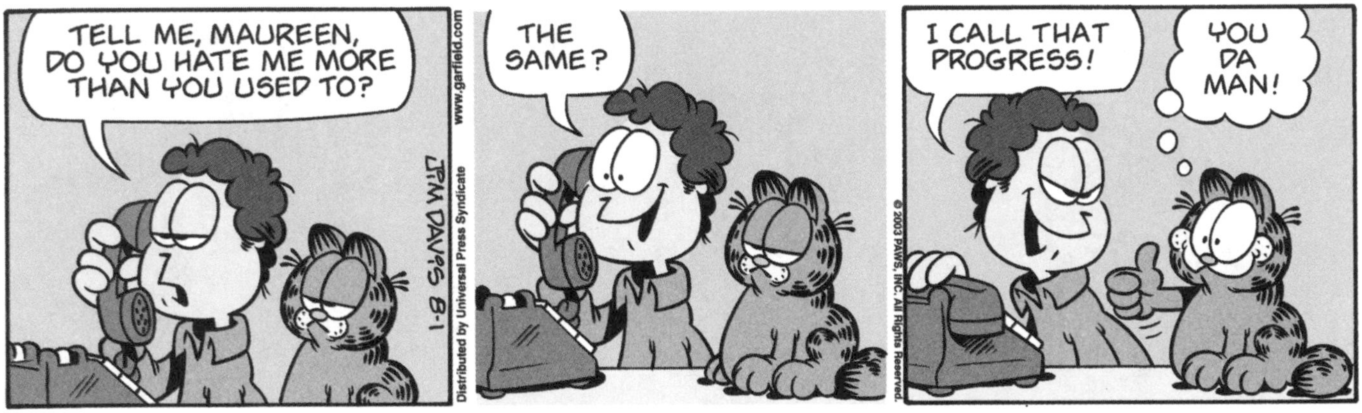
TELL ME, MAUREEN, DO YOU HATE ME MORE THAN YOU USED TO?
JIM DAVIS 8-1
www.garfield.com
Distributed by Universal Press Syndicate
THE SAME?
© 2003 PAWS, INC. All Rights Reserved.
I CALL THAT PROGRESS!
YOU DA MAN!

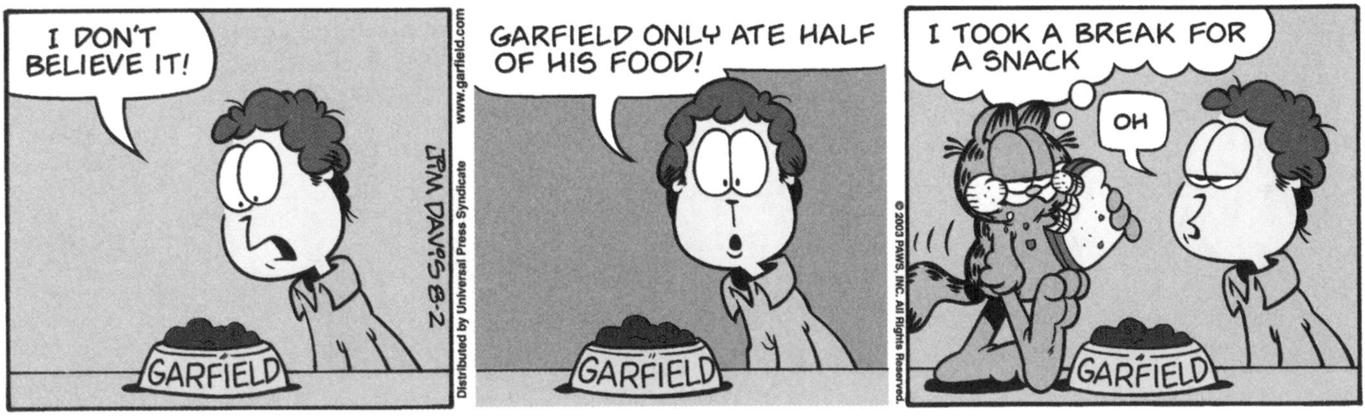
I DON'T BELIEVE IT!
GARFIELD
JIM DAVIS 8-2
www.garfield.com
Distributed by Universal Press Syndicate
GARFIELD ONLY ATE HALF OF HIS FOOD!
GARFIELD
© 2003 PAWS, INC. All Rights Reserved.
I TOOK A BREAK FOR A SNACK
OH
GARFIELD

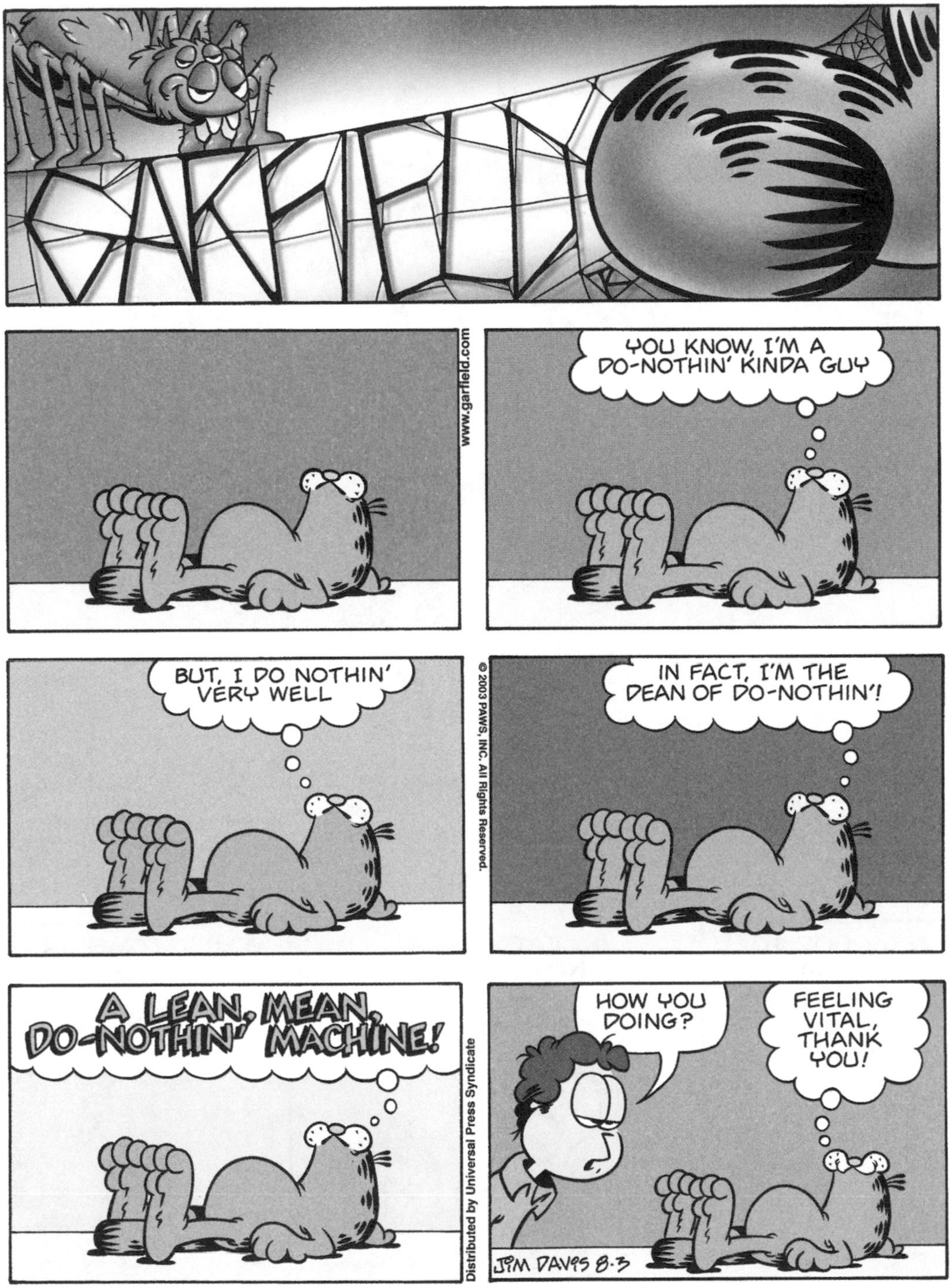

www.garfield.com
YOU KNOW, I'M A DO-NOTHIN' KINDA GUY
BUT, I DO NOTHIN' VERY WELL
© 2003 PAWS, INC. All Rights Reserved.
IN FACT, I'M THE DEAN OF DO-NOTHIN'!
A LEAN, MEAN, DO-NOTHIN' MACHINE!
Distributed by Universal Press Syndicate
HOW YOU DOING?
FEELING VITAL, THANK YOU!
JIM DAVIS 8-3

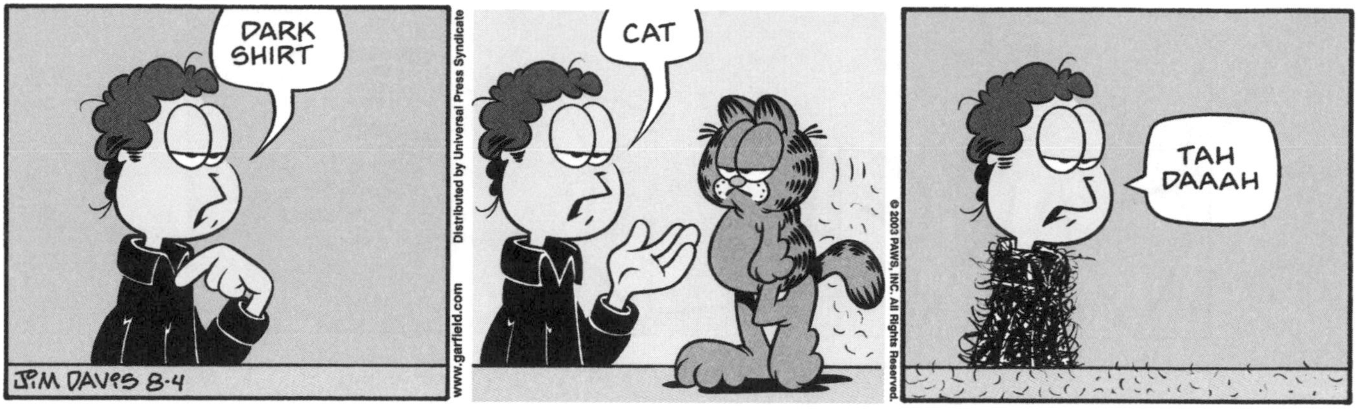
DARK SHIRT
JIM DAVIS 8-4
www.garfield.com
Distributed by Universal Press Syndicate
CAT
© 2003 PAWS, INC. All Rights Reserved.
TAH DAAAH

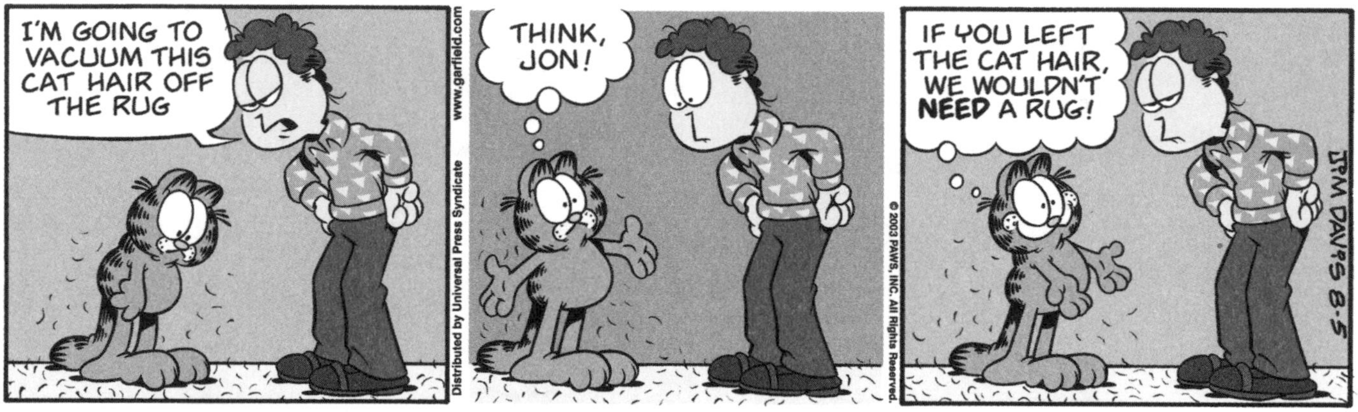
I'M GOING TO VACUUM THIS CAT HAIR OFF THE RUG
www.garfield.com
Distributed by Universal Press Syndicate
THINK, JON!
© 2003 PAWS, INC. All Rights Reserved.
IF YOU LEFT THE CAT HAIR, WE WOULDN'T **NEED** A RUG!
JIM DAVIS 8-5

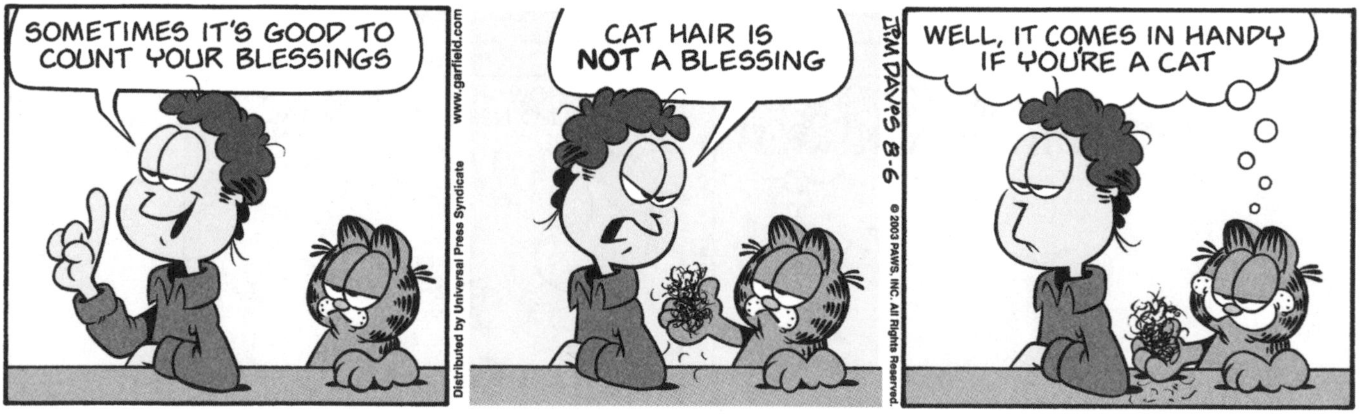
SOMETIMES IT'S GOOD TO COUNT YOUR BLESSINGS
www.garfield.com
Distributed by Universal Press Syndicate
CAT HAIR IS **NOT** A BLESSING
JIM DAVIS 8-6
© 2003 PAWS, INC. All Rights Reserved.
WELL, IT COMES IN HANDY IF YOU'RE A CAT

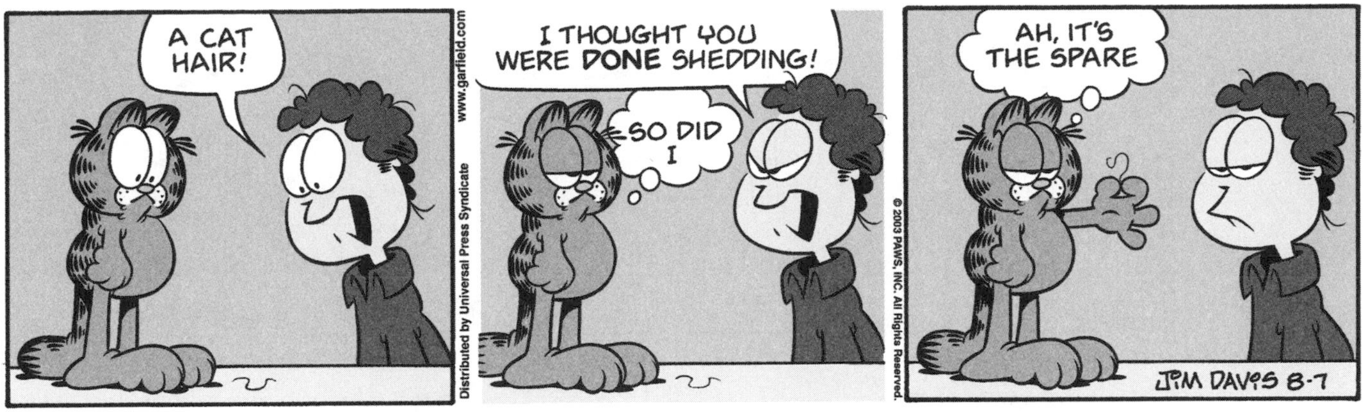
A CAT HAIR!
I THOUGHT YOU WERE DONE SHEDDING!
SO DID I
AH, IT'S THE SPARE
JIM DAVIS 8-7
www.garfield.com
Distributed by Universal Press Syndicate
© 2003 PAWS, INC. All Rights Reserved.

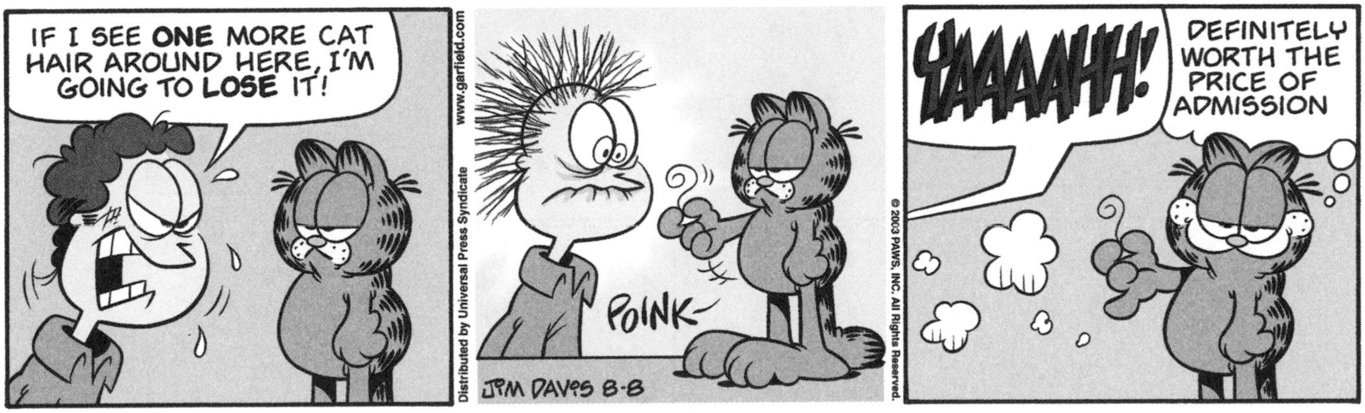
IF I SEE ONE MORE CAT HAIR AROUND HERE, I'M GOING TO LOSE IT!
POINK
JIM DAVIS 8-8
YAAAAHH!
DEFINITELY WORTH THE PRICE OF ADMISSION
www.garfield.com
Distributed by Universal Press Syndicate
© 2003 PAWS, INC. All Rights Reserved.

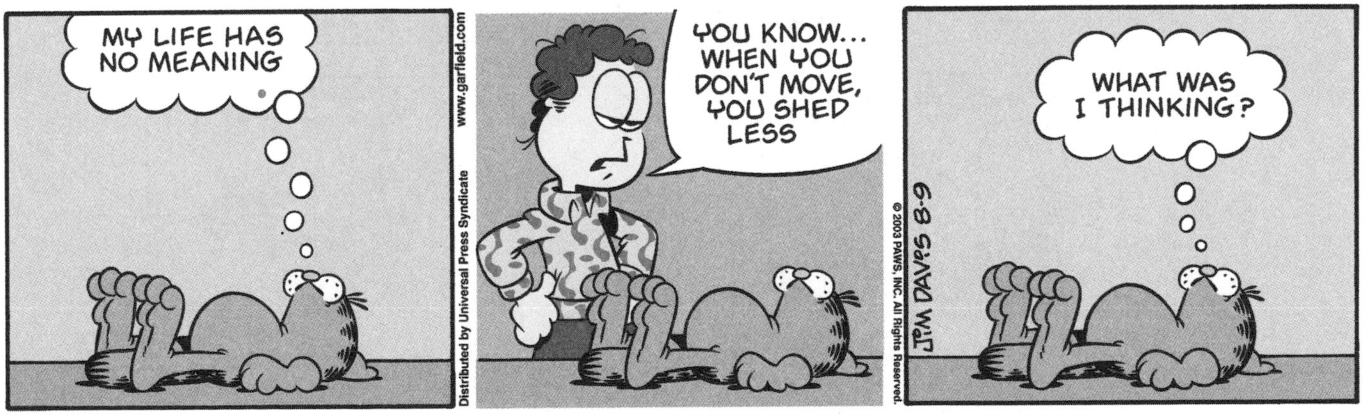
MY LIFE HAS NO MEANING
YOU KNOW... WHEN YOU DON'T MOVE, YOU SHED LESS
WHAT WAS I THINKING?
JIM DAVIS 8-9
www.garfield.com
Distributed by Universal Press Syndicate
© 2003 PAWS, INC. All Rights Reserved.

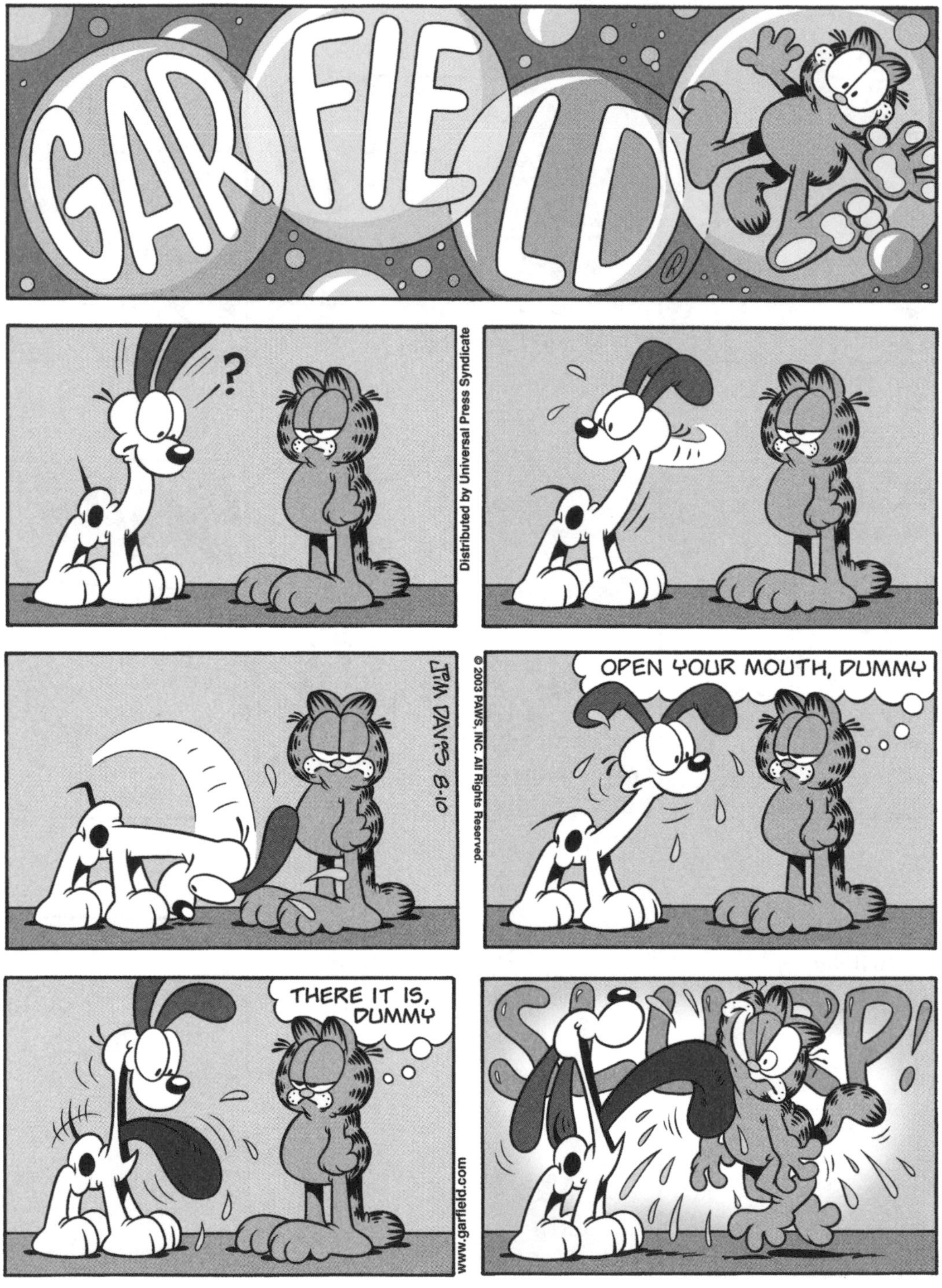
GARFIELD®
?
Distributed by Universal Press Syndicate
JIM DAVIS 8-10
© 2003 PAWS, INC. All Rights Reserved.
OPEN YOUR MOUTH, DUMMY
THERE IT IS, DUMMY
www.garfield.com

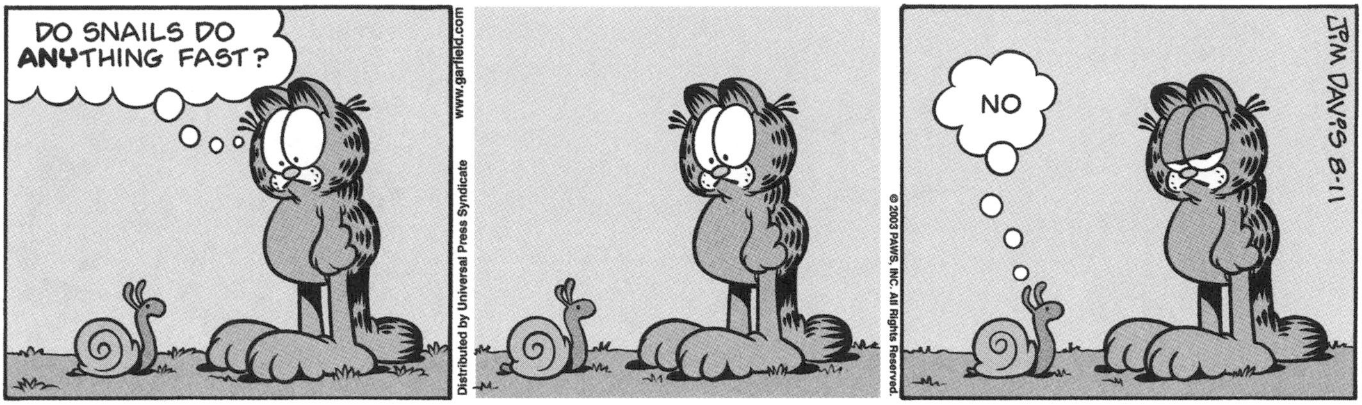
DO SNAILS DO ANYTHING FAST?
NO
JIM DAVIS 8-11
Distributed by Universal Press Syndicate www.garfield.com
© 2003 PAWS, INC. All Rights Reserved.

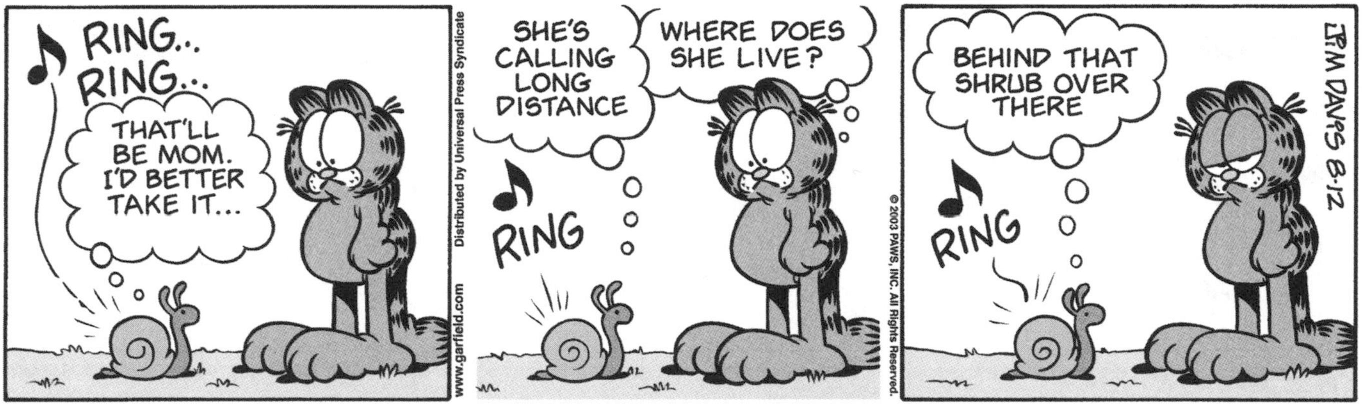
RING.. RING..
THAT'LL BE MOM. I'D BETTER TAKE IT...
RING
SHE'S CALLING LONG DISTANCE
WHERE DOES SHE LIVE?
RING
BEHIND THAT SHRUB OVER THERE
JIM DAVIS 8-12
www.garfield.com Distributed by Universal Press Syndicate
© 2003 PAWS, INC. All Rights Reserved.

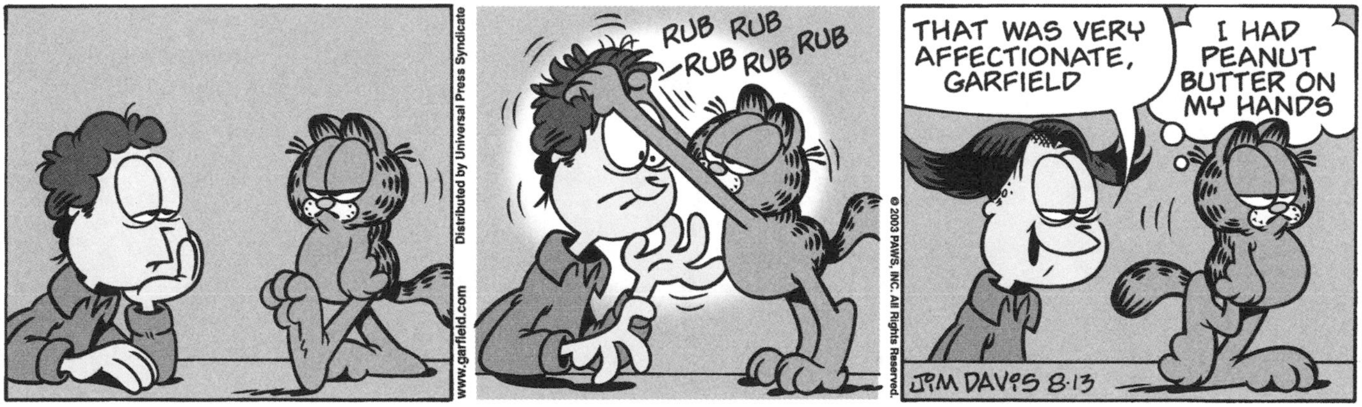
RUB RUB RUB RUB RUB
THAT WAS VERY AFFECTIONATE, GARFIELD
I HAD PEANUT BUTTER ON MY HANDS
JIM DAVIS 8-13
www.garfield.com Distributed by Universal Press Syndicate
© 2003 PAWS, INC. All Rights Reserved.

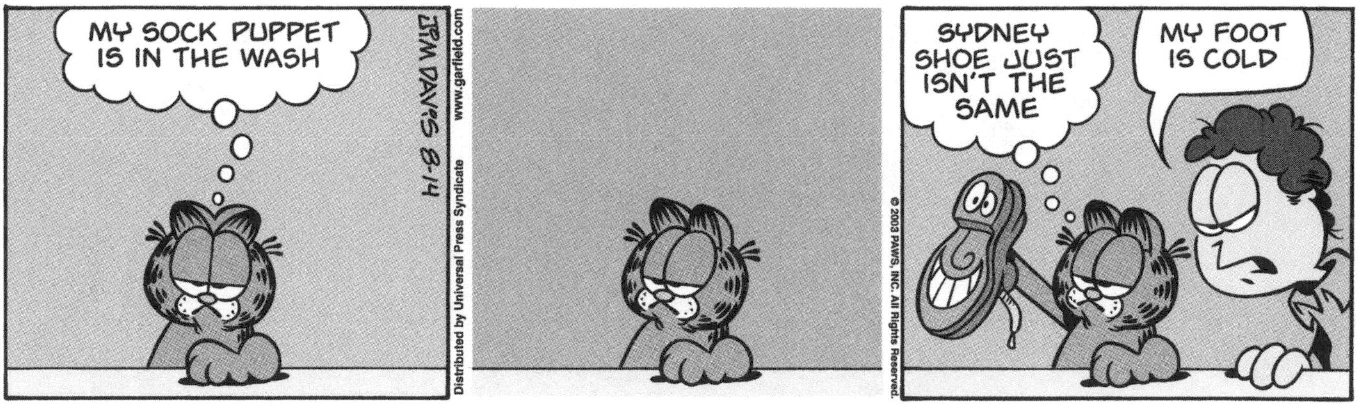
MY SOCK PUPPET IS IN THE WASH
JIM DAVIS 8-14
www.garfield.com
Distributed by Universal Press Syndicate
SYDNEY SHOE JUST ISN'T THE SAME
MY FOOT IS COLD
© 2003 PAWS, INC. All Rights Reserved.

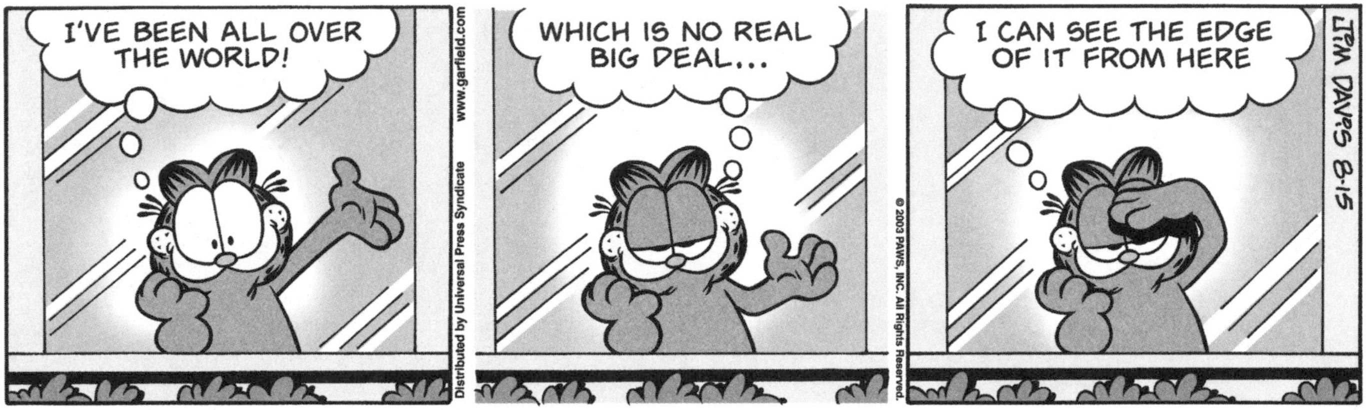
I'VE BEEN ALL OVER THE WORLD!
www.garfield.com
Distributed by Universal Press Syndicate
WHICH IS NO REAL BIG DEAL...
© 2003 PAWS, INC. All Rights Reserved.
I CAN SEE THE EDGE OF IT FROM HERE
JIM DAVIS 8-15

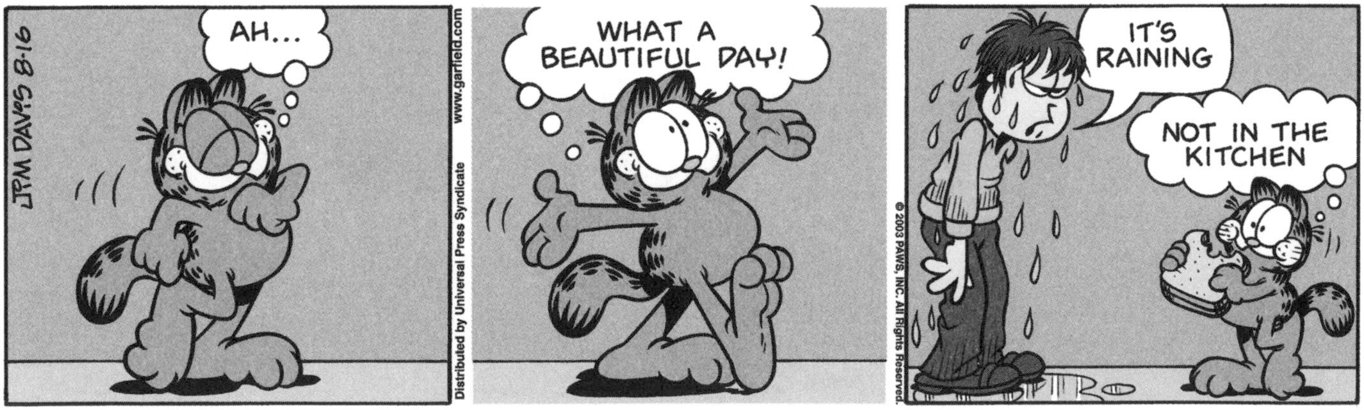
JIM DAVIS 8-16
AH...
www.garfield.com
Distributed by Universal Press Syndicate
WHAT A BEAUTIFUL DAY!
© 2003 PAWS, INC. All Rights Reserved.
IT'S RAINING
NOT IN THE KITCHEN

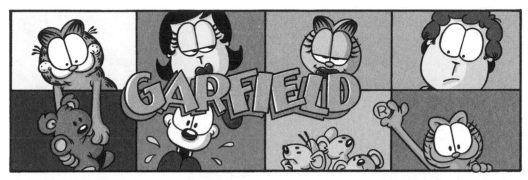

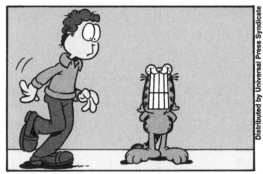

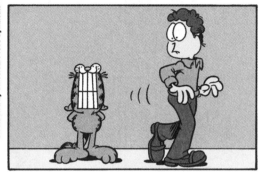

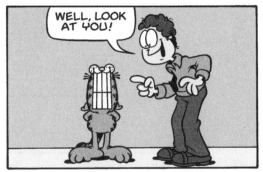

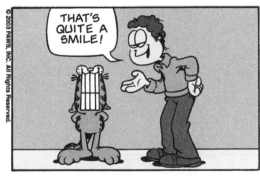

GARFIELD
Distributed by Universal Press Syndicate
WELL, LOOK AT YOU!
© 2003 PAWS, INC. All Rights Reserved.
THAT'S QUITE A SMILE!
IT'S NICE TO SEE YOU IN A GOOD MOOD FOR A CHANGE
www.garfield.com
I SAT ON A MOUSETRAP
JIM DAVIS 8-17

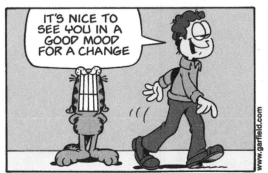

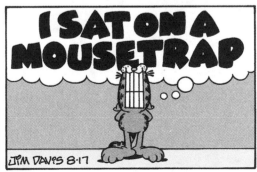

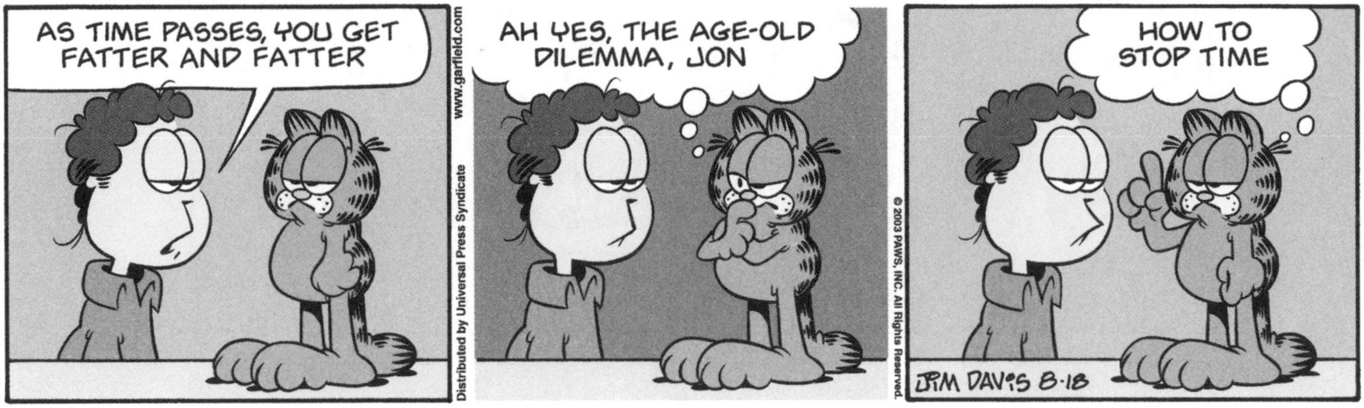
AS TIME PASSES, YOU GET FATTER AND FATTER
AH YES, THE AGE-OLD DILEMMA, JON
HOW TO STOP TIME
JIM DAVIS 8-18
www.garfield.com
Distributed by Universal Press Syndicate
© 2003 PAWS, INC. All Rights Reserved.

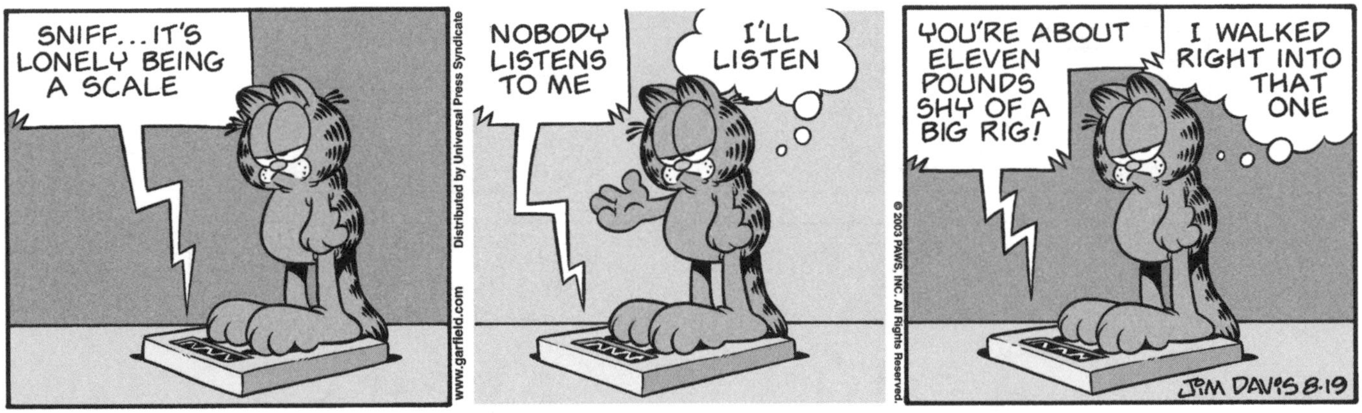
SNIFF... IT'S LONELY BEING A SCALE
NOBODY LISTENS TO ME
I'LL LISTEN
YOU'RE ABOUT ELEVEN POUNDS SHY OF A BIG RIG!
I WALKED RIGHT INTO THAT ONE
JIM DAVIS 8-19
Distributed by Universal Press Syndicate
www.garfield.com
© 2003 PAWS, INC. All Rights Reserved.

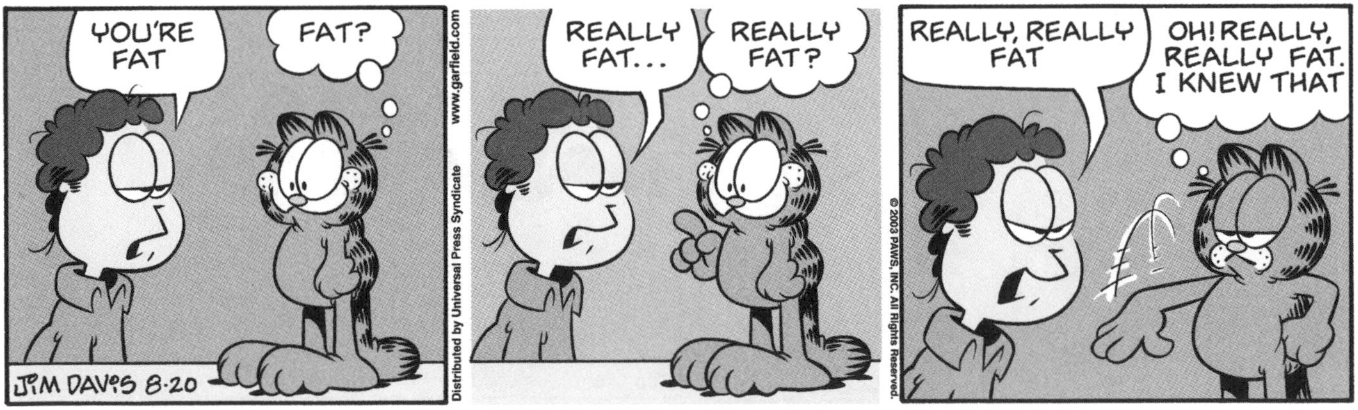
YOU'RE FAT
FAT?
REALLY FAT...
REALLY FAT?
REALLY, REALLY FAT
OH! REALLY, REALLY FAT. I KNEW THAT
JIM DAVIS 8-20
www.garfield.com
Distributed by Universal Press Syndicate
© 2003 PAWS, INC. All Rights Reserved.

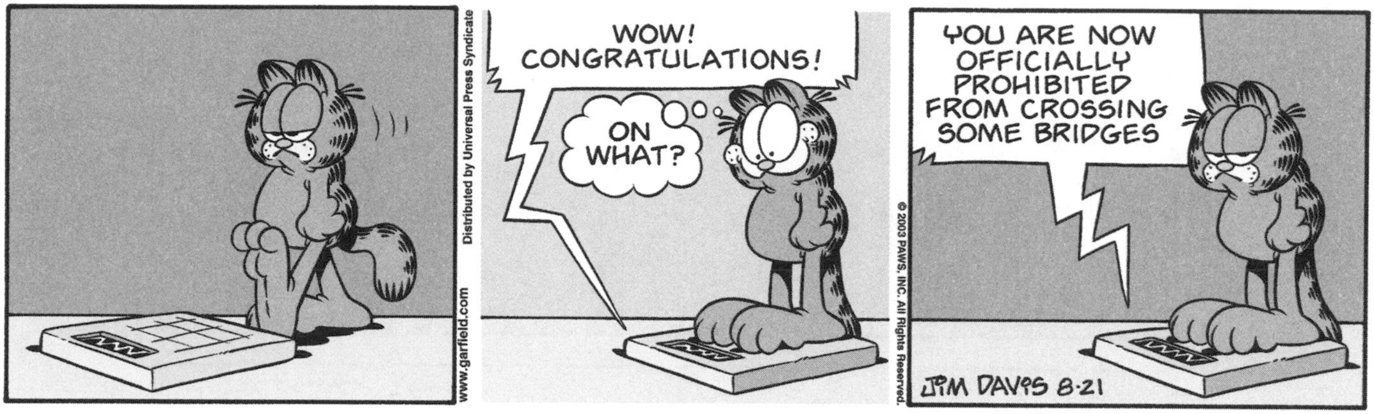
www.garfield.com
Distributed by Universal Press Syndicate
WOW! CONGRATULATIONS!
ON WHAT?
© 2003 PAWS, INC. All Rights Reserved.
YOU ARE NOW OFFICIALLY PROHIBITED FROM CROSSING SOME BRIDGES
JIM DAVIS 8-21

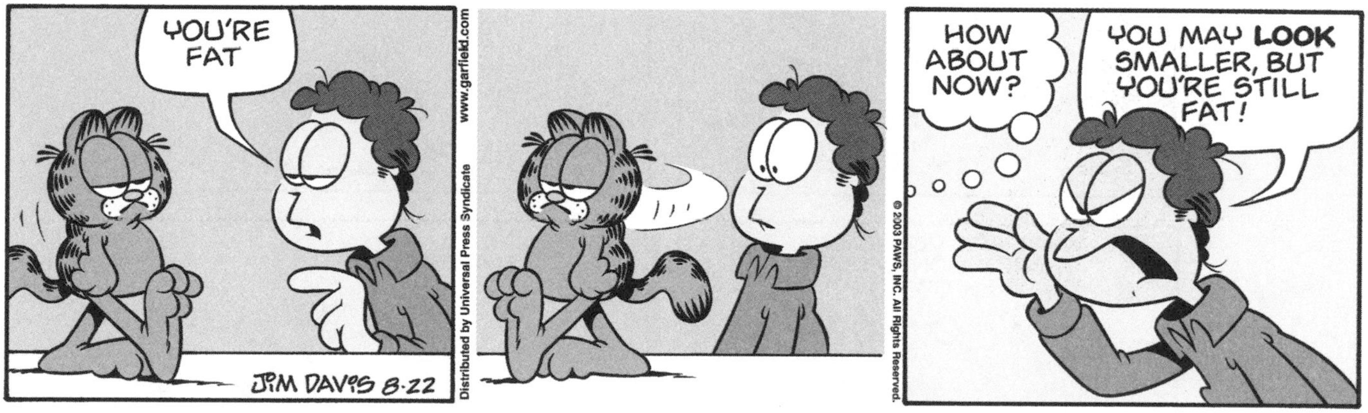
YOU'RE FAT
JIM DAVIS 8-22
Distributed by Universal Press Syndicate www.garfield.com
© 2003 PAWS, INC. All Rights Reserved.
HOW ABOUT NOW?
YOU MAY **LOOK** SMALLER, BUT YOU'RE STILL FAT!

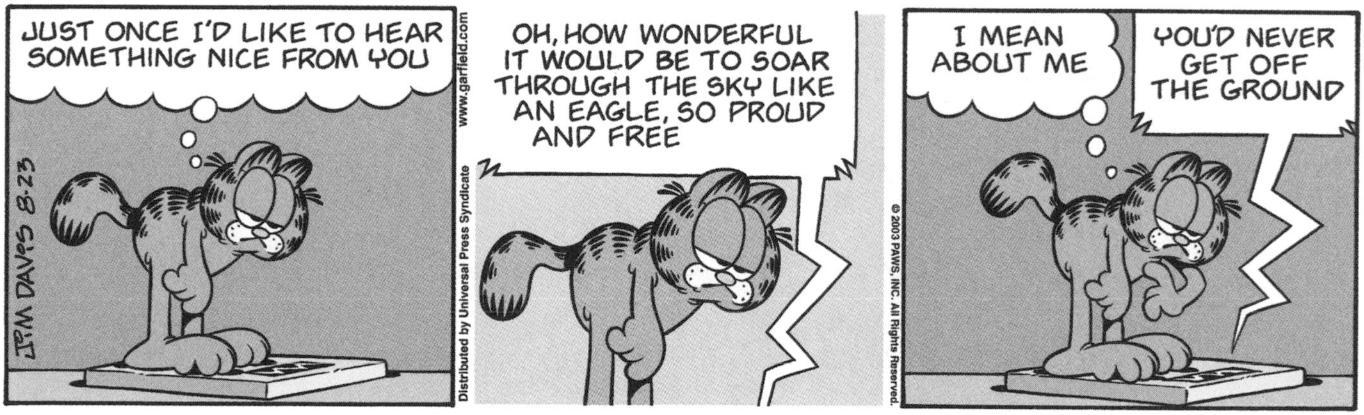
JUST ONCE I'D LIKE TO HEAR SOMETHING NICE FROM YOU
JIM DAVIS 8-23
Distributed by Universal Press Syndicate www.garfield.com
OH, HOW WONDERFUL IT WOULD BE TO SOAR THROUGH THE SKY LIKE AN EAGLE, SO PROUD AND FREE
© 2003 PAWS, INC. All Rights Reserved.
I MEAN ABOUT ME
YOU'D NEVER GET OFF THE GROUND

Garfield®
HEY, PAL!
HEY, HALLUCINATION
Distributed by Universal Press Syndicate
WAIT A MINUTE!
WHAT ARE YOU DOING HERE? I ONLY SEE YOU WHEN I'M ON A DIET
© 2003 PAWS, INC. All Rights Reserved.
WELL, SURPRISE!
JIM DAVIS 8-24
I JUST HEARD YOUR OWNER ON THE PHONE WITH THE VET, AND YOU'RE GOING ON ONE NOW!
I AM NOT!
www.garfield.com
I'LL VOUCH FOR HIM
OH, NO! PIZZAS NEVER LIE!
SLAP

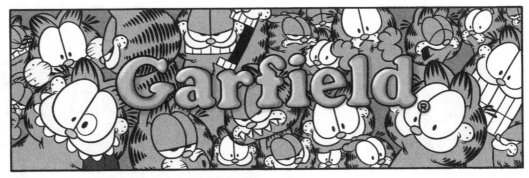

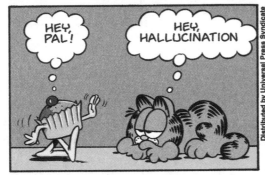

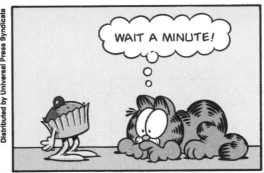

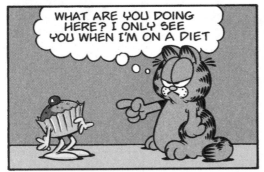

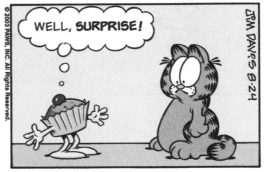

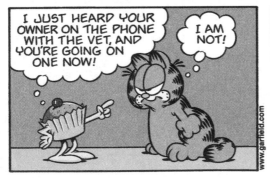

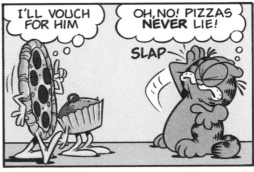

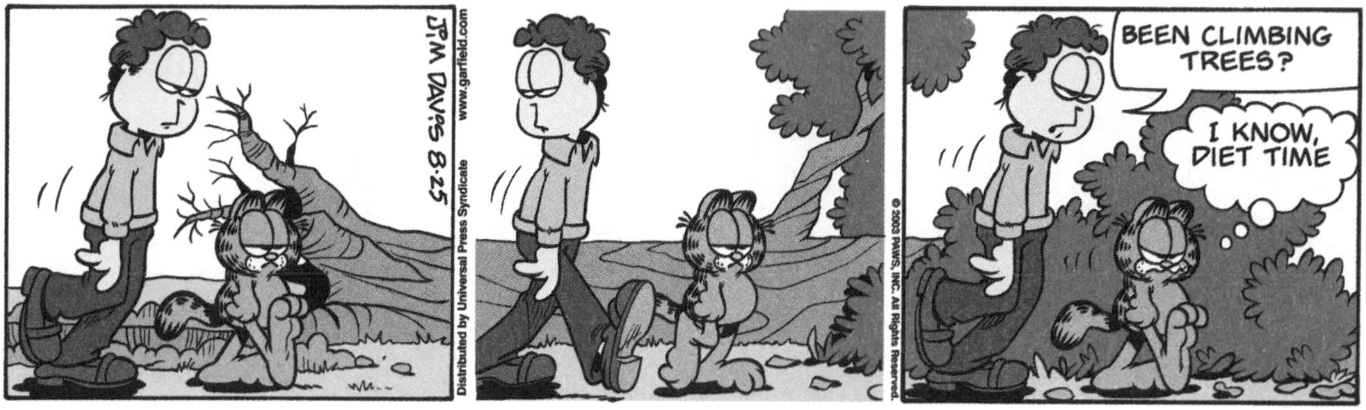
JIM DAVIS 8-25
www.garfield.com
Distributed by Universal Press Syndicate
© 2003 PAWS, INC. All Rights Reserved.
BEEN CLIMBING TREES?
I KNOW, DIET TIME

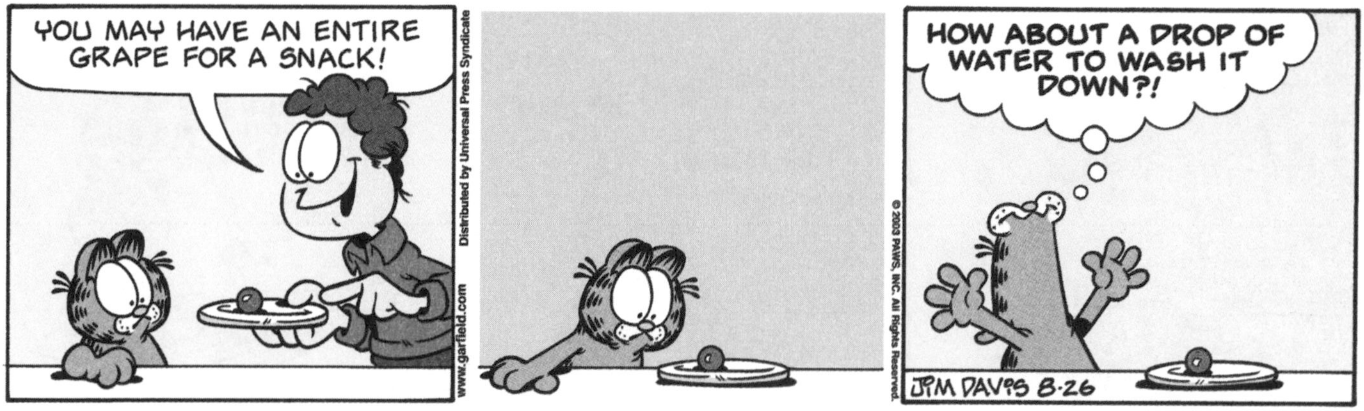
YOU MAY HAVE AN ENTIRE GRAPE FOR A SNACK!
Distributed by Universal Press Syndicate
www.garfield.com
© 2003 PAWS, INC. All Rights Reserved.
HOW ABOUT A DROP OF WATER TO WASH IT DOWN?!
JIM DAVIS 8-26

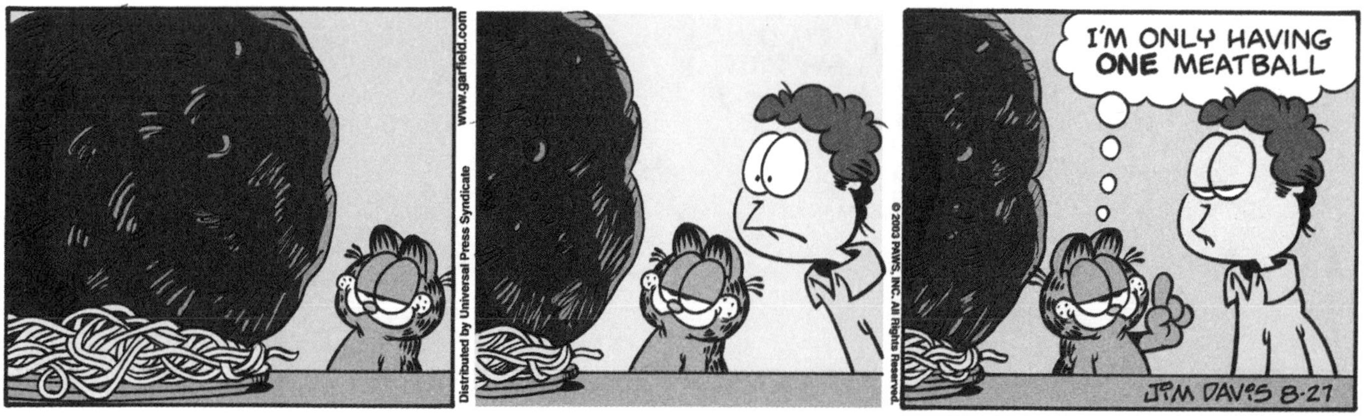
www.garfield.com
Distributed by Universal Press Syndicate
© 2003 PAWS, INC. All Rights Reserved.
I'M ONLY HAVING **ONE** MEATBALL
JIM DAVIS 8-27

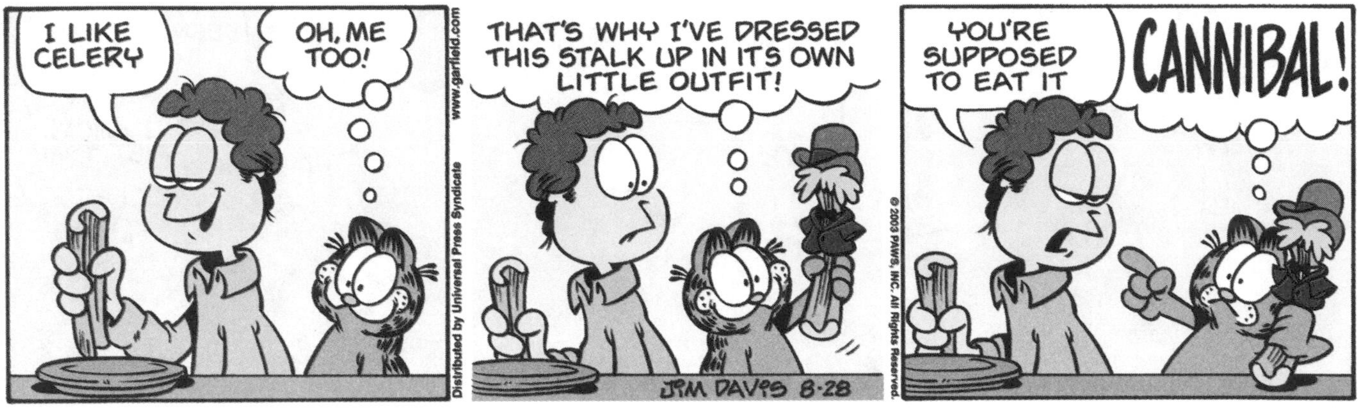
I LIKE CELERY
OH, ME TOO!
www.garfield.com
Distributed by Universal Press Syndicate
THAT'S WHY I'VE DRESSED THIS STALK UP IN ITS OWN LITTLE OUTFIT!
JIM DAVIS 8-28
© 2003 PAWS, INC. All Rights Reserved.
YOU'RE SUPPOSED TO EAT IT
CANNIBAL!

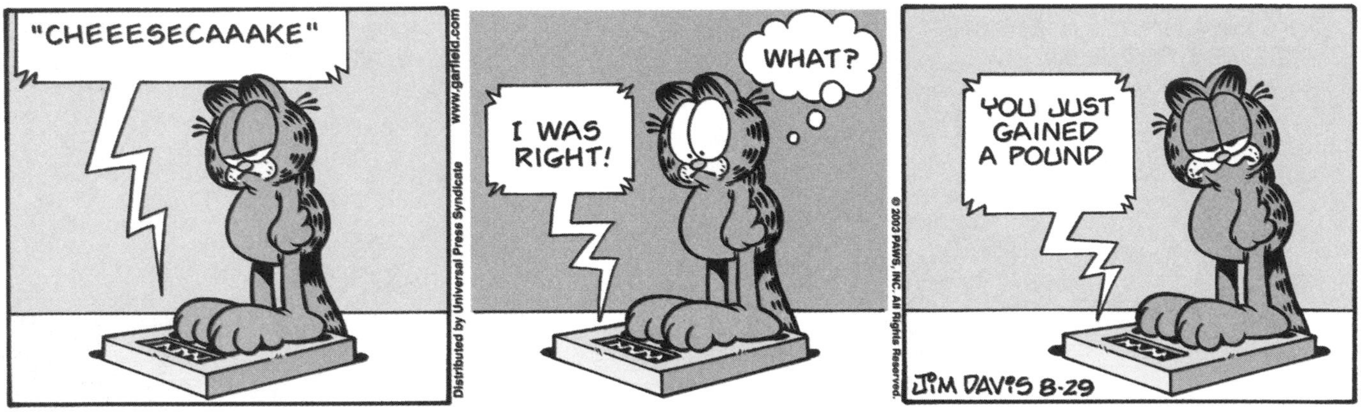
"CHEEESECAAAKE"
www.garfield.com
Distributed by Universal Press Syndicate
I WAS RIGHT!
WHAT?
© 2003 PAWS, INC. All Rights Reserved.
YOU JUST GAINED A POUND
JIM DAVIS 8-29

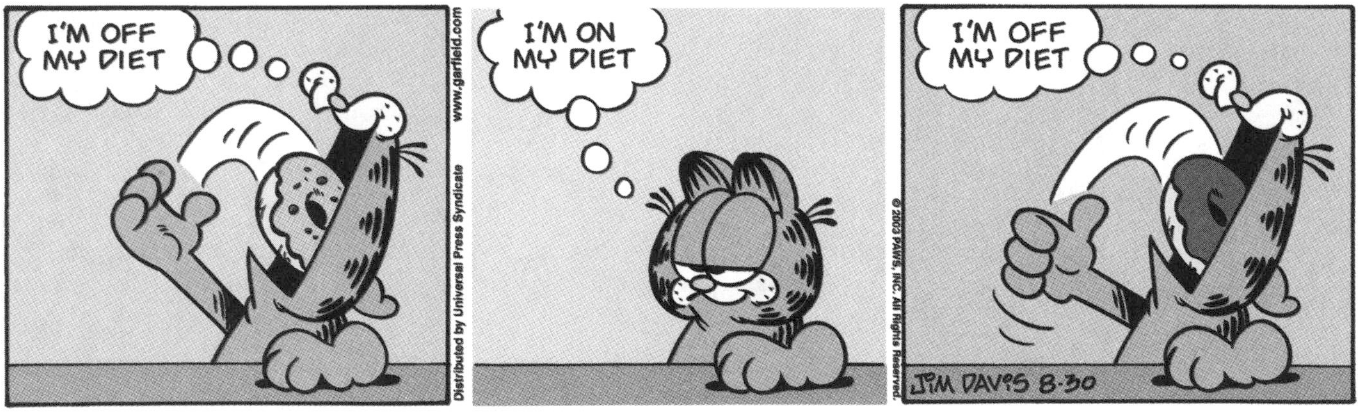
I'M OFF MY DIET
www.garfield.com
Distributed by Universal Press Syndicate
I'M ON MY DIET
© 2003 PAWS, INC. All Rights Reserved.
I'M OFF MY DIET
JIM DAVIS 8-30

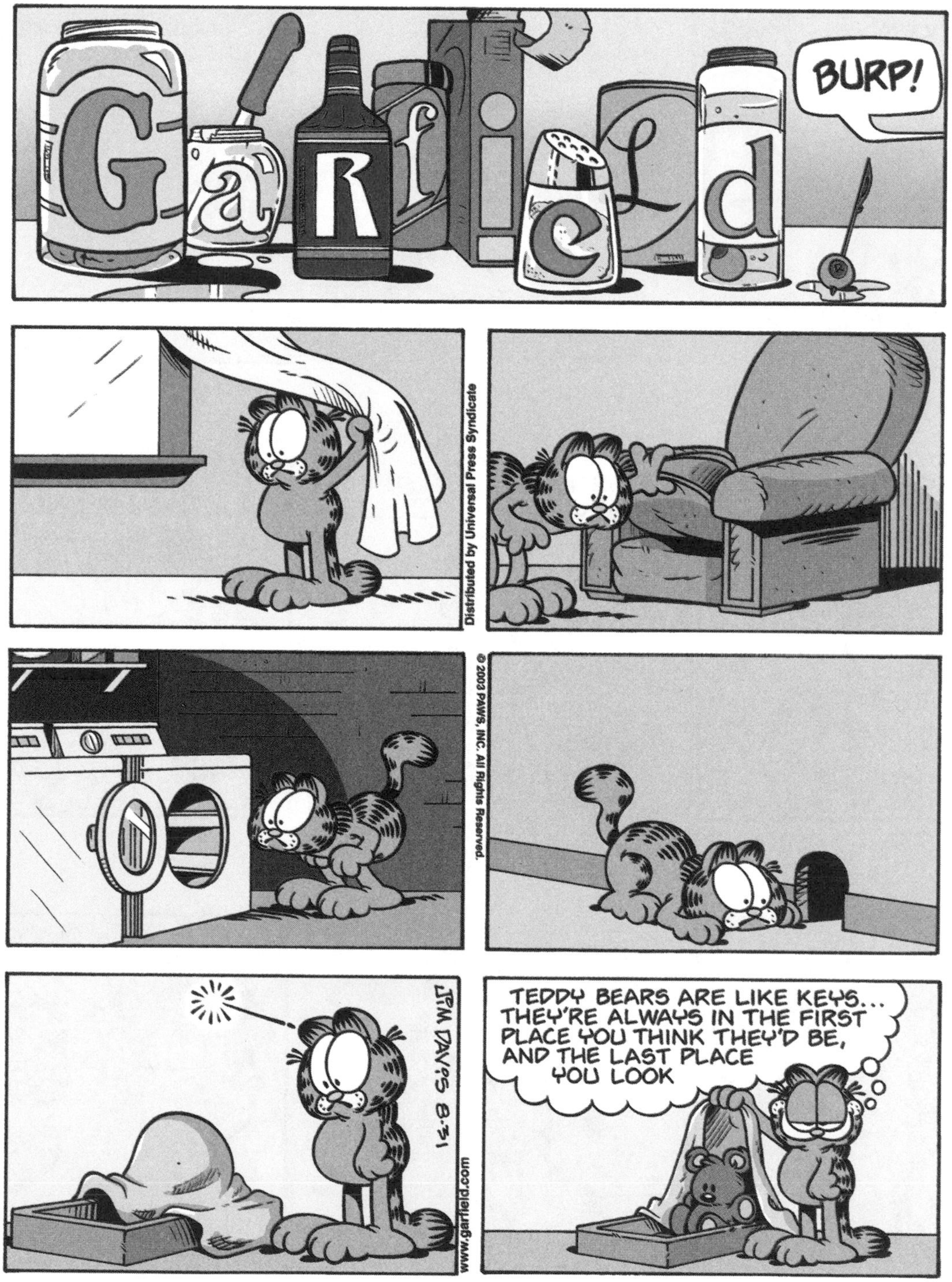
GARFIELD
BURP!
Distributed by Universal Press Syndicate
© 2003 PAWS, INC. All Rights Reserved.
JPM DAVIS 8-31
www.garfield.com
TEDDY BEARS ARE LIKE KEYS... THEY'RE ALWAYS IN THE FIRST PLACE YOU THINK THEY'D BE, AND THE LAST PLACE YOU LOOK

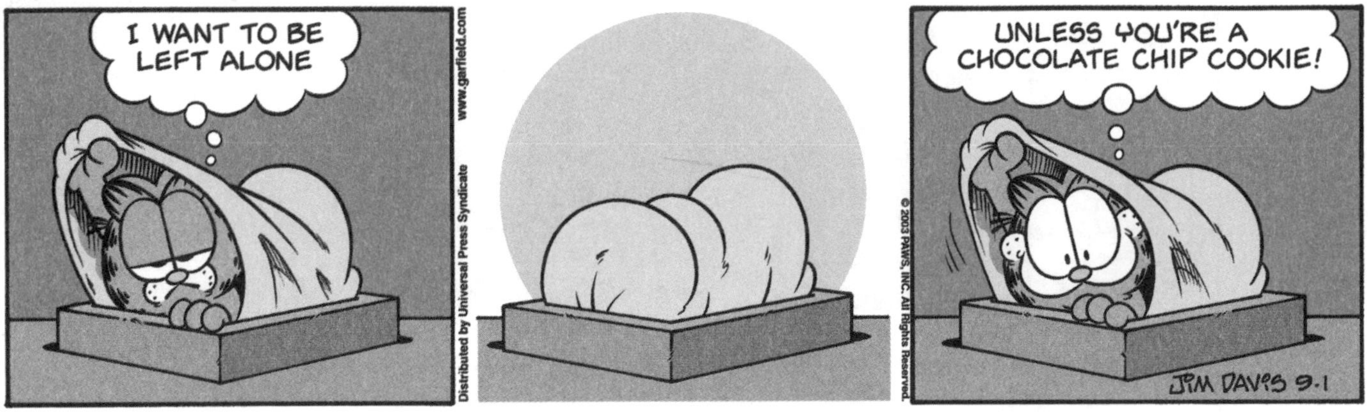
I WANT TO BE LEFT ALONE
UNLESS YOU'RE A CHOCOLATE CHIP COOKIE!
JIM DAVIS 9-1
www.garfield.com
Distributed by Universal Press Syndicate
© 2003 PAWS, INC. All Rights Reserved.

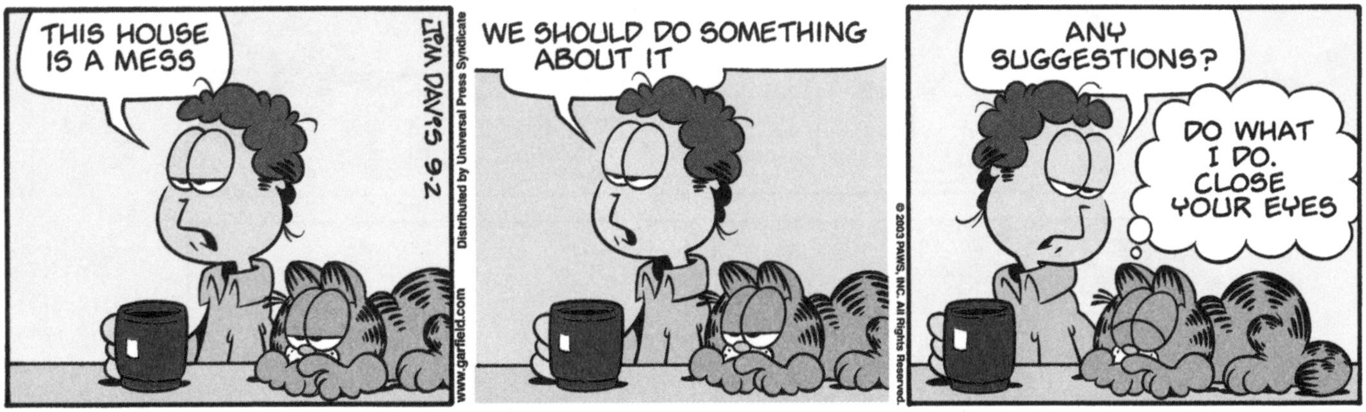
THIS HOUSE IS A MESS
WE SHOULD DO SOMETHING ABOUT IT
ANY SUGGESTIONS?
DO WHAT I DO. CLOSE YOUR EYES
JIM DAVIS 9-2
www.garfield.com
Distributed by Universal Press Syndicate
© 2003 PAWS, INC. All Rights Reserved.

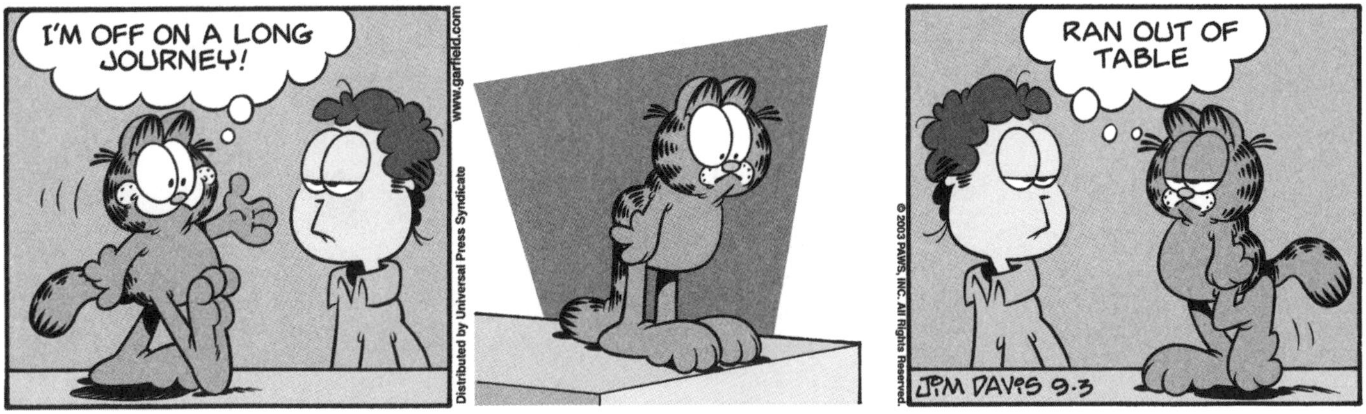
I'M OFF ON A LONG JOURNEY!
RAN OUT OF TABLE
JIM DAVIS 9-3
www.garfield.com
Distributed by Universal Press Syndicate
© 2003 PAWS, INC. All Rights Reserved.

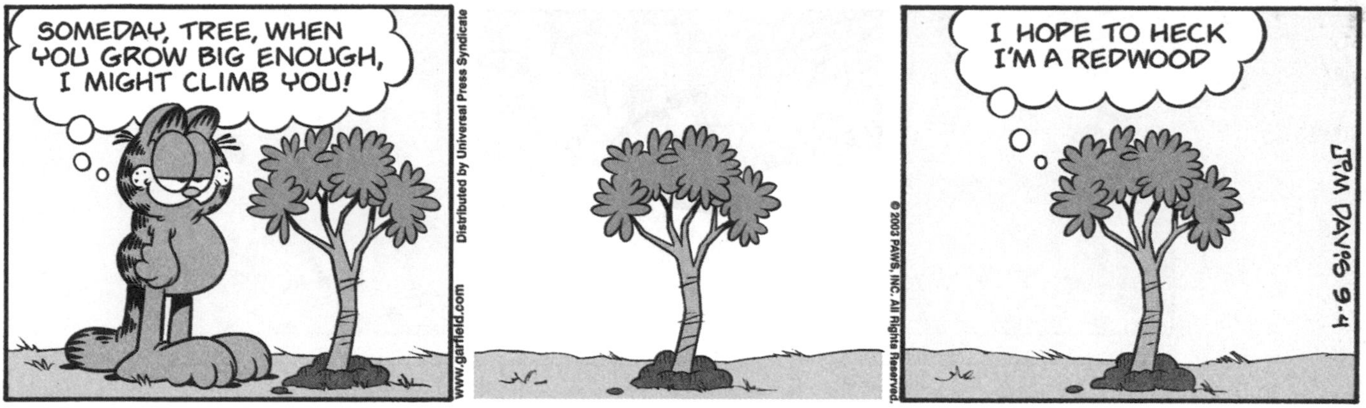
SOMEDAY, TREE, WHEN YOU GROW BIG ENOUGH, I MIGHT CLIMB YOU!
www.garfield.com Distributed by Universal Press Syndicate
© 2003 PAWS, INC. All Rights Reserved.
I HOPE TO HECK I'M A REDWOOD
JIM DAVIS 9-4

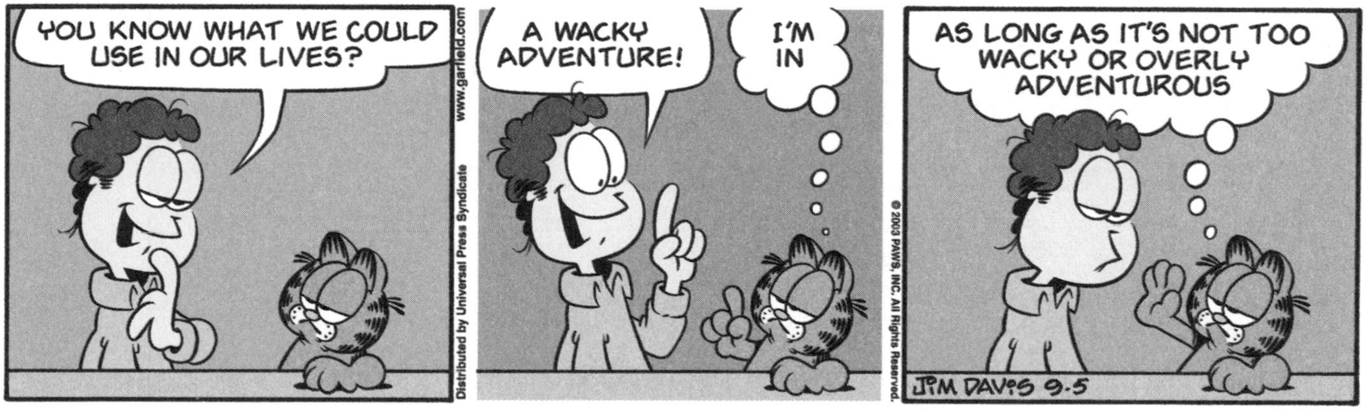
YOU KNOW WHAT WE COULD USE IN OUR LIVES?
Distributed by Universal Press Syndicate www.garfield.com
A WACKY ADVENTURE!
I'M IN
© 2003 PAWS, INC. All Rights Reserved.
AS LONG AS IT'S NOT TOO WACKY OR OVERLY ADVENTUROUS
JIM DAVIS 9-5

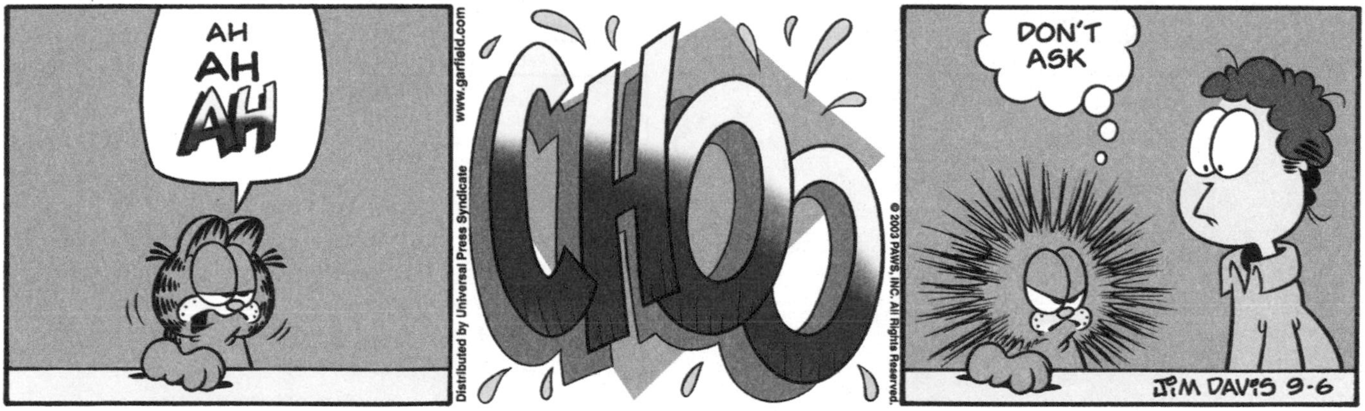
AH
AH
AH
Distributed by Universal Press Syndicate www.garfield.com
CHOO
© 2003 PAWS, INC. All Rights Reserved.
DON'T ASK
JIM DAVIS 9-6

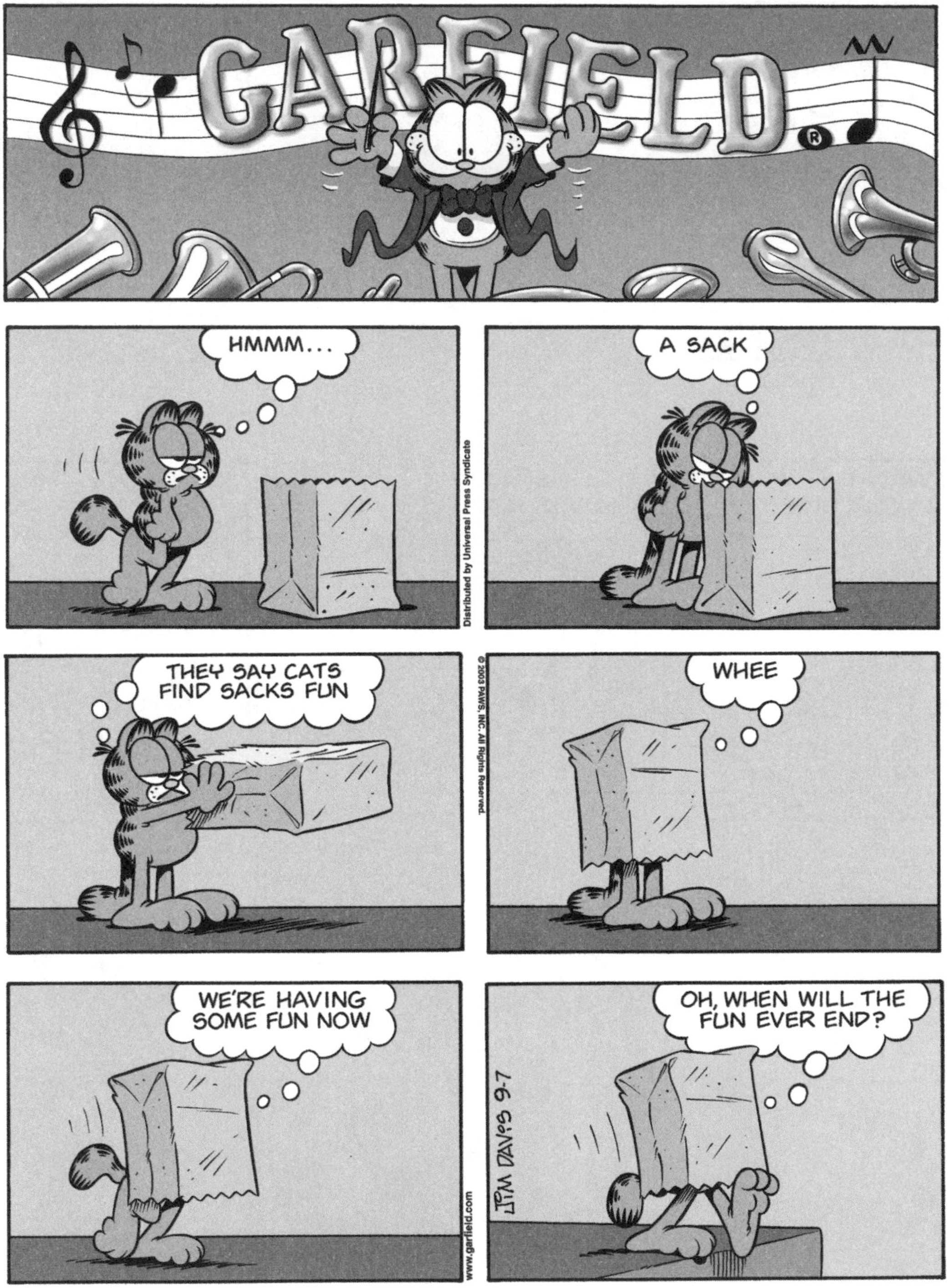
GARFIELD®
HMMM...
A SACK
THEY SAY CATS FIND SACKS FUN
WHEE
WE'RE HAVING SOME FUN NOW
OH, WHEN WILL THE FUN EVER END?
Distributed by Universal Press Syndicate
© 2003 PAWS, INC. All Rights Reserved.
www.garfield.com
JIM DAVIS 9-7

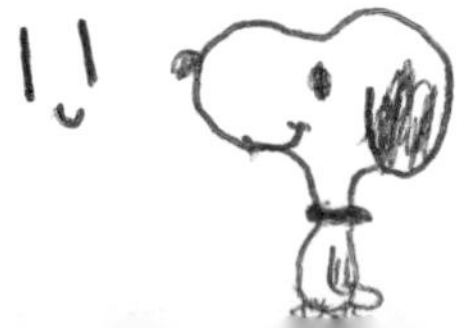

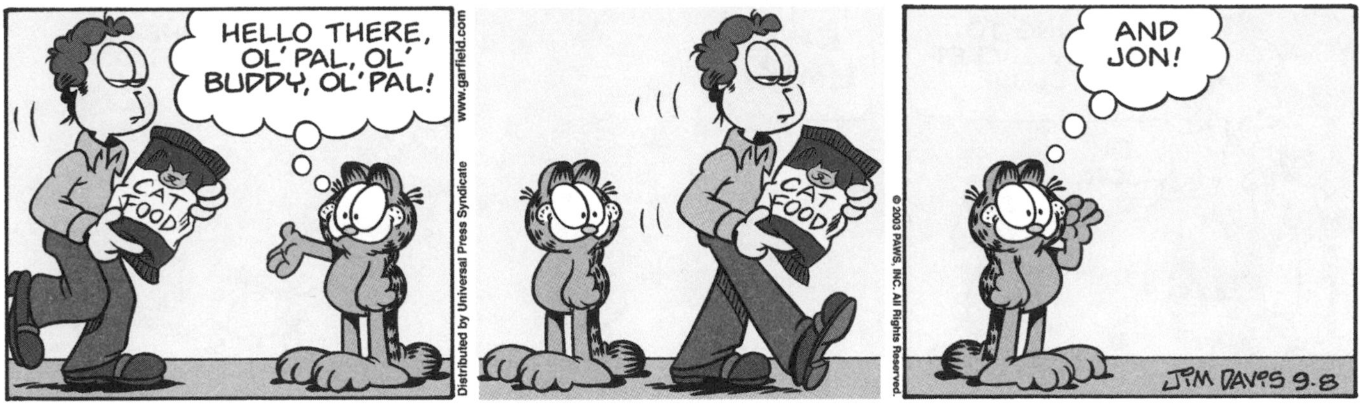
HELLO THERE, OL' PAL, OL' BUDDY, OL' PAL!
CAT FOOD
www.garfield.com
Distributed by Universal Press Syndicate
CAT FOOD
© 2003 PAWS, INC. All Rights Reserved.
AND JON!
JIM DAVIS 9.8

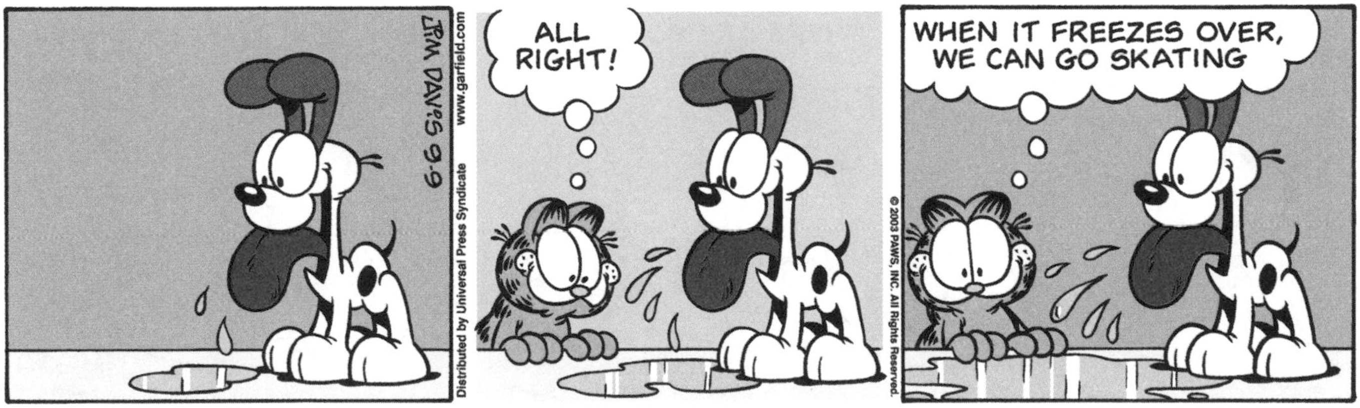
JIM DAVIS 9.9
www.garfield.com
Distributed by Universal Press Syndicate
ALL RIGHT!
© 2003 PAWS, INC. All Rights Reserved.
WHEN IT FREEZES OVER, WE CAN GO SKATING

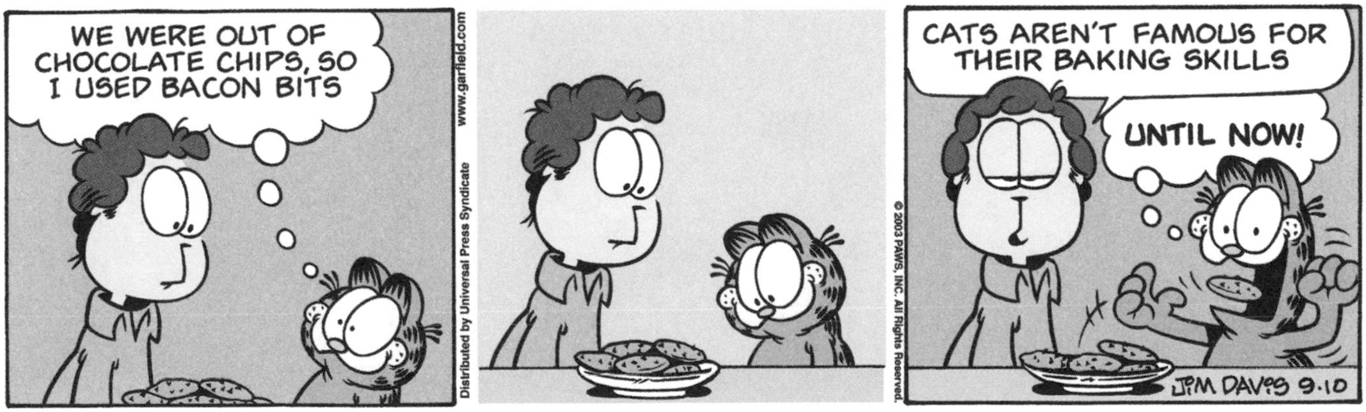
WE WERE OUT OF CHOCOLATE CHIPS, SO I USED BACON BITS
www.garfield.com
Distributed by Universal Press Syndicate
© 2003 PAWS, INC. All Rights Reserved.
CATS AREN'T FAMOUS FOR THEIR BAKING SKILLS
UNTIL NOW!
JIM DAVIS 9.10

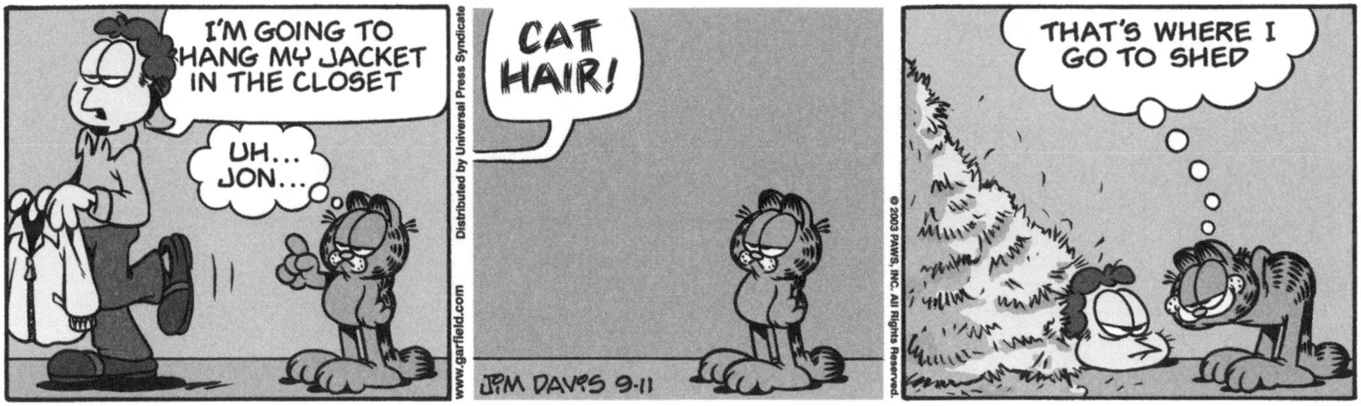
I'M GOING TO HANG MY JACKET IN THE CLOSET
UH... JON...
Distributed by Universal Press Syndicate
www.garfield.com
CAT HAIR!
JIM DAVIS 9-11
THAT'S WHERE I GO TO SHED
© 2003 PAWS, INC. All Rights Reserved.

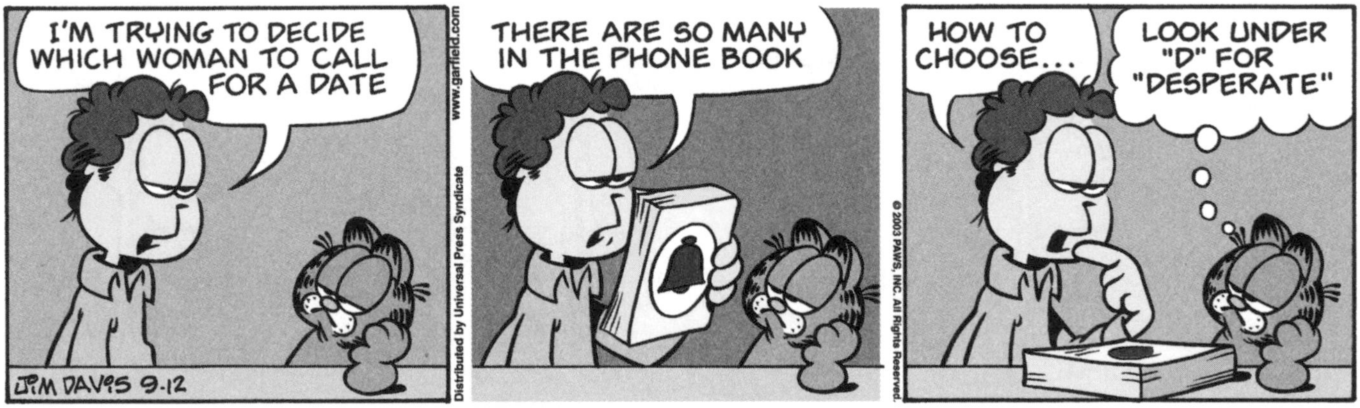
I'M TRYING TO DECIDE WHICH WOMAN TO CALL FOR A DATE
JIM DAVIS 9-12
www.garfield.com
Distributed by Universal Press Syndicate
THERE ARE SO MANY IN THE PHONE BOOK
© 2003 PAWS, INC. All Rights Reserved.
HOW TO CHOOSE...
LOOK UNDER "D" FOR "DESPERATE"

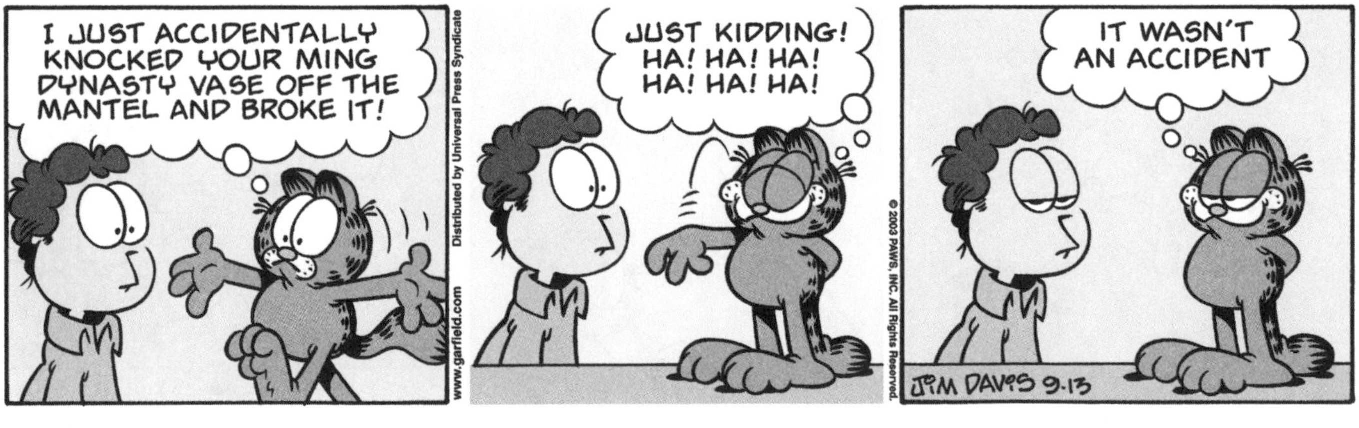
I JUST ACCIDENTALLY KNOCKED YOUR MING DYNASTY VASE OFF THE MANTEL AND BROKE IT!
Distributed by Universal Press Syndicate
www.garfield.com
JUST KIDDING! HA! HA! HA! HA! HA! HA!
© 2003 PAWS, INC. All Rights Reserved.
IT WASN'T AN ACCIDENT
JIM DAVIS 9-13

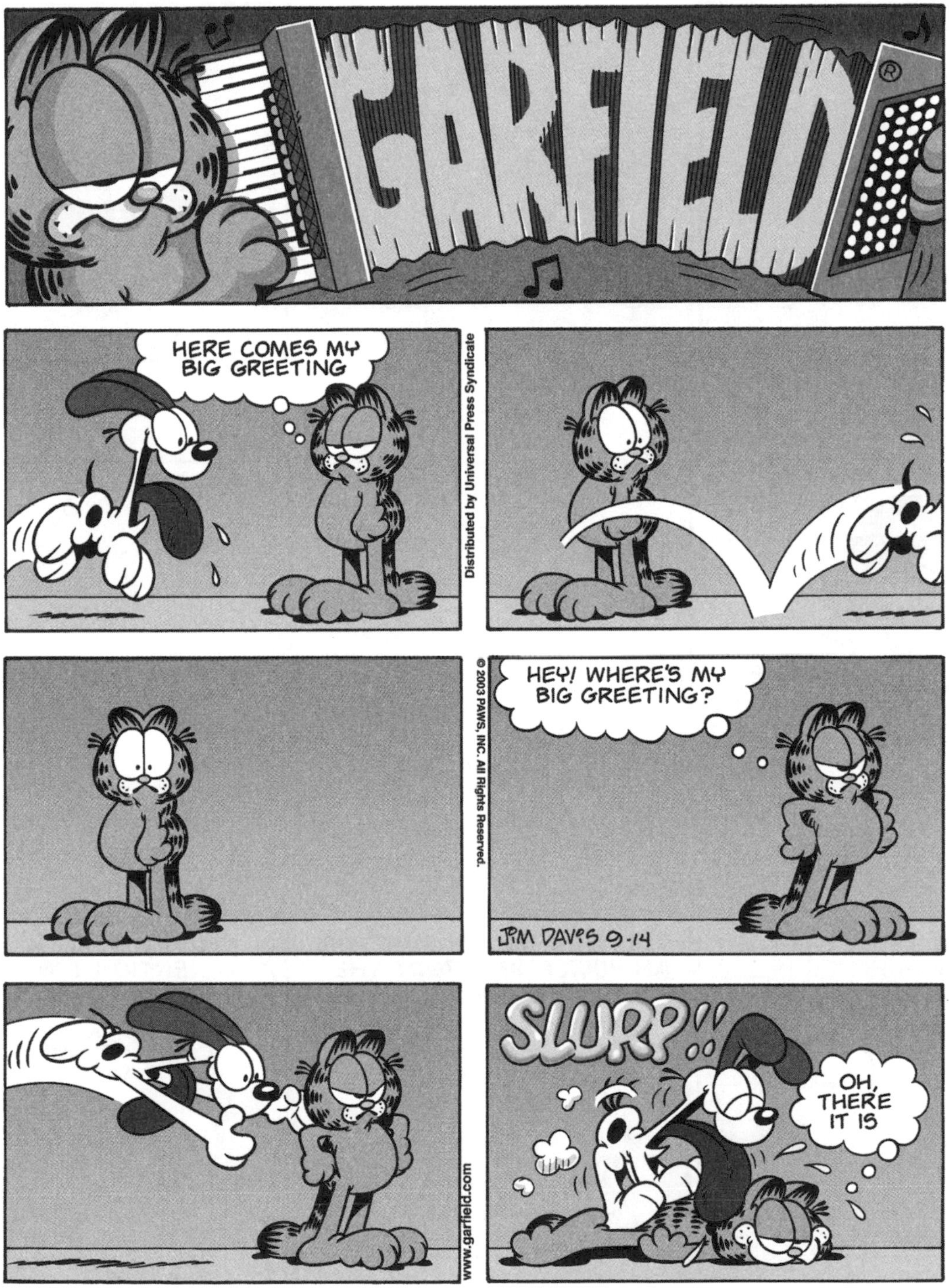

GARFIELD®
HERE COMES MY BIG GREETING
Distributed by Universal Press Syndicate
© 2003 PAWS, INC. All Rights Reserved.
HEY! WHERE'S MY BIG GREETING?
JIM DAVIS 9-14
www.garfield.com
SLURP!!
OH, THERE IT IS

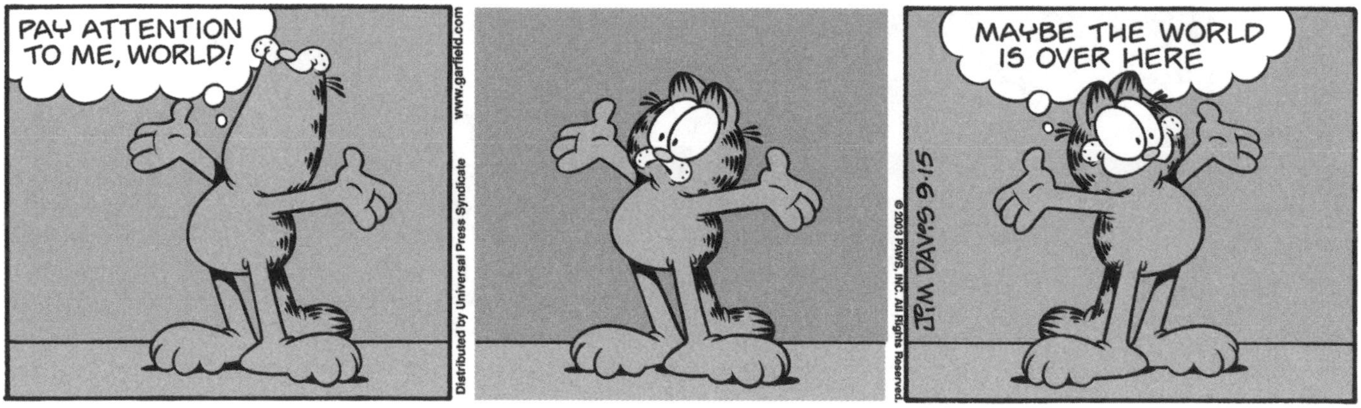
PAY ATTENTION TO ME, WORLD!
www.garfield.com
Distributed by Universal Press Syndicate
MAYBE THE WORLD IS OVER HERE
JIM DAVIS 9.15
© 2003 PAWS, INC. All Rights Reserved.

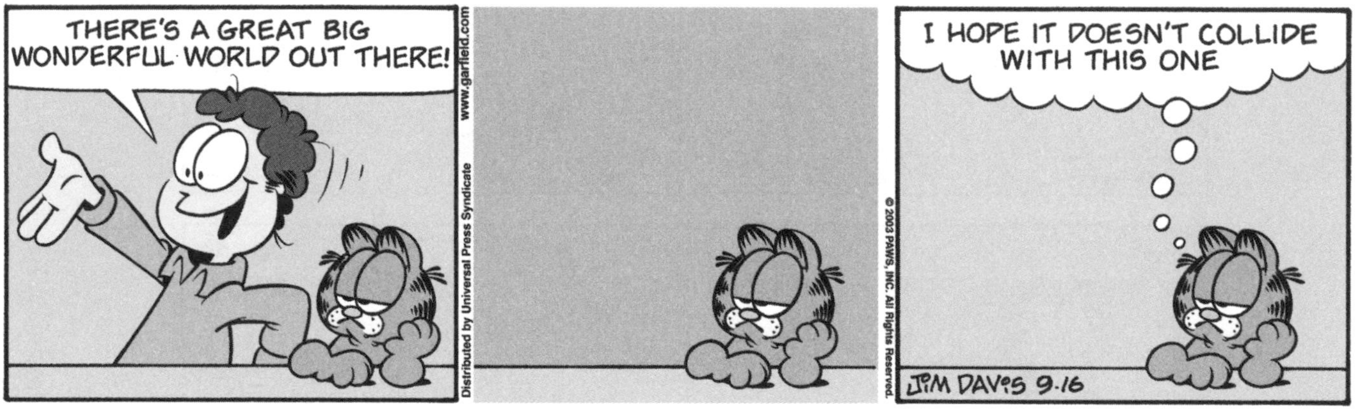
THERE'S A GREAT BIG WONDERFUL WORLD OUT THERE!
www.garfield.com
Distributed by Universal Press Syndicate
I HOPE IT DOESN'T COLLIDE WITH THIS ONE
© 2003 PAWS, INC. All Rights Reserved.
JIM DAVIS 9.16

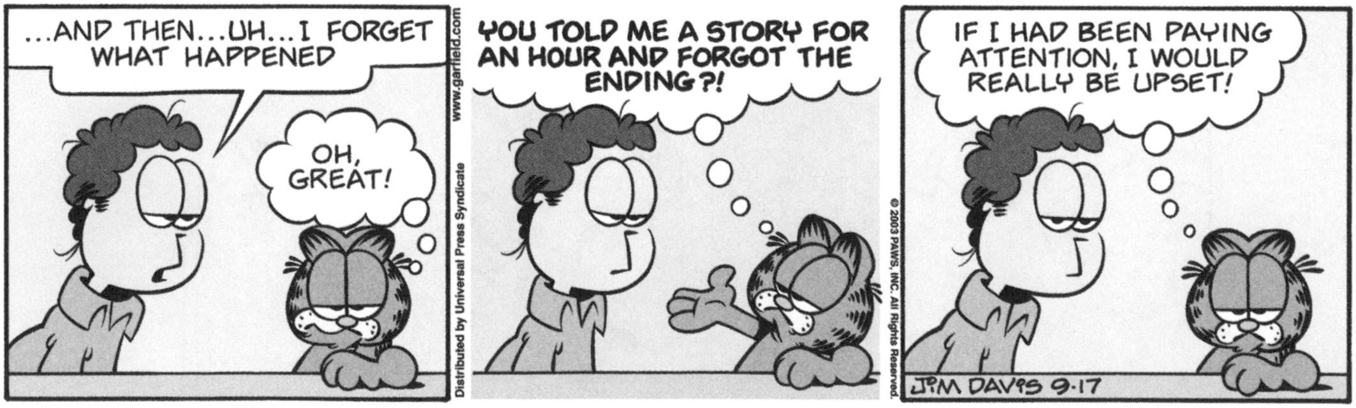
...AND THEN...UH...I FORGET WHAT HAPPENED
OH, GREAT!
www.garfield.com
Distributed by Universal Press Syndicate
YOU TOLD ME A STORY FOR AN HOUR AND FORGOT THE ENDING?!
IF I HAD BEEN PAYING ATTENTION, I WOULD REALLY BE UPSET!
© 2003 PAWS, INC. All Rights Reserved.
JIM DAVIS 9.17

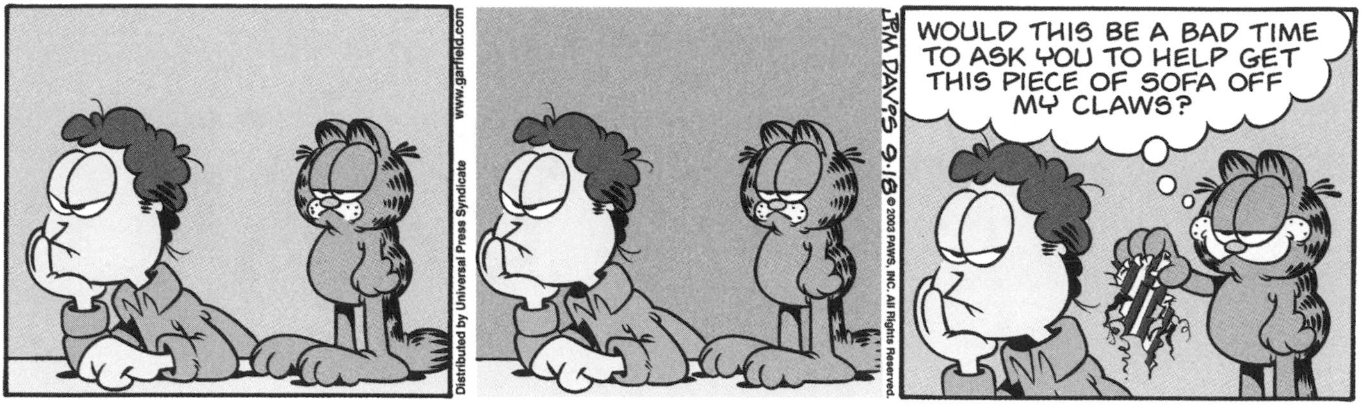
www.garfield.com
Distributed by Universal Press Syndicate
JIM DAVIS 9-18 © 2003 PAWS, INC. All Rights Reserved.
WOULD THIS BE A BAD TIME TO ASK YOU TO HELP GET THIS PIECE OF SOFA OFF MY CLAWS?

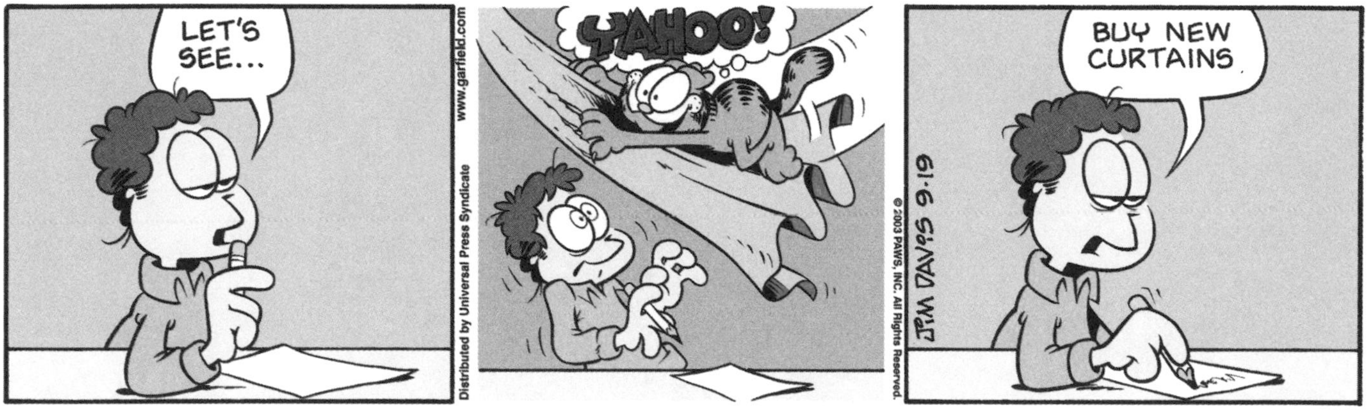
LET'S SEE...
www.garfield.com
Distributed by Universal Press Syndicate
YAHOO!
© 2003 PAWS, INC. All Rights Reserved.
JIM DAVIS 9-19
BUY NEW CURTAINS

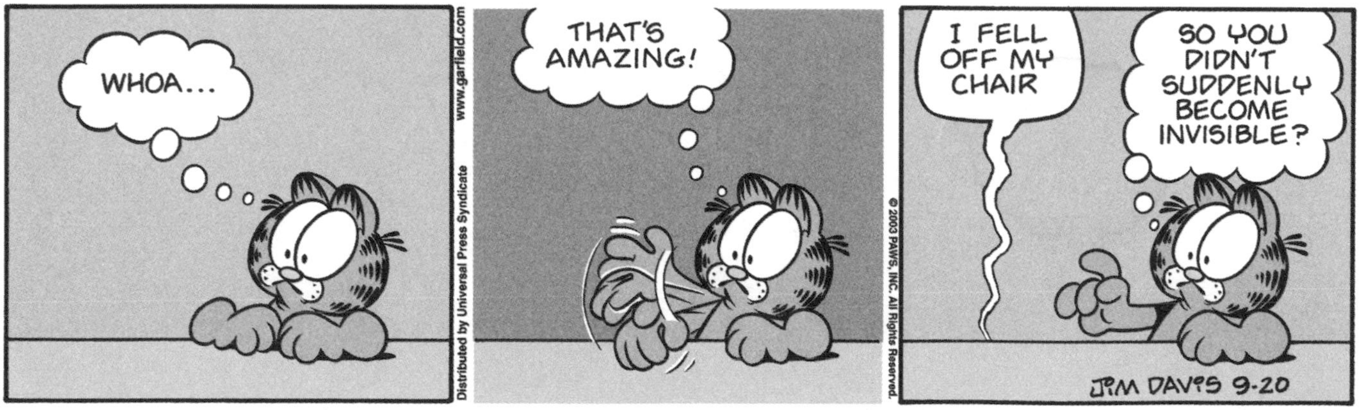
WHOA...
www.garfield.com
Distributed by Universal Press Syndicate
THAT'S AMAZING!
© 2003 PAWS, INC. All Rights Reserved.
I FELL OFF MY CHAIR
SO YOU DIDN'T SUDDENLY BECOME INVISIBLE?
JIM DAVIS 9-20

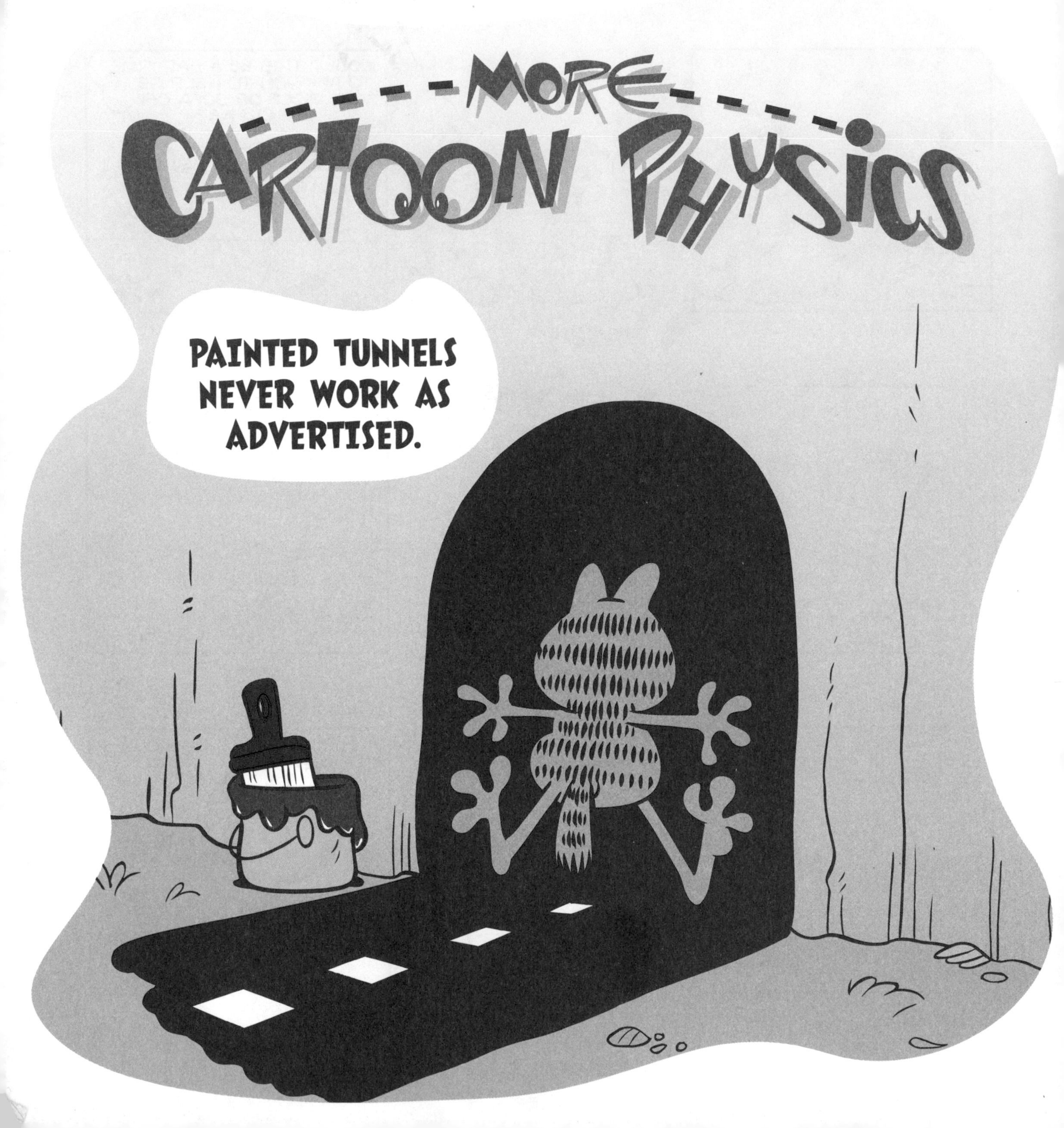
MORE
CARTOON PHYSICS
PAINTED TUNNELS NEVER WORK AS ADVERTISED.

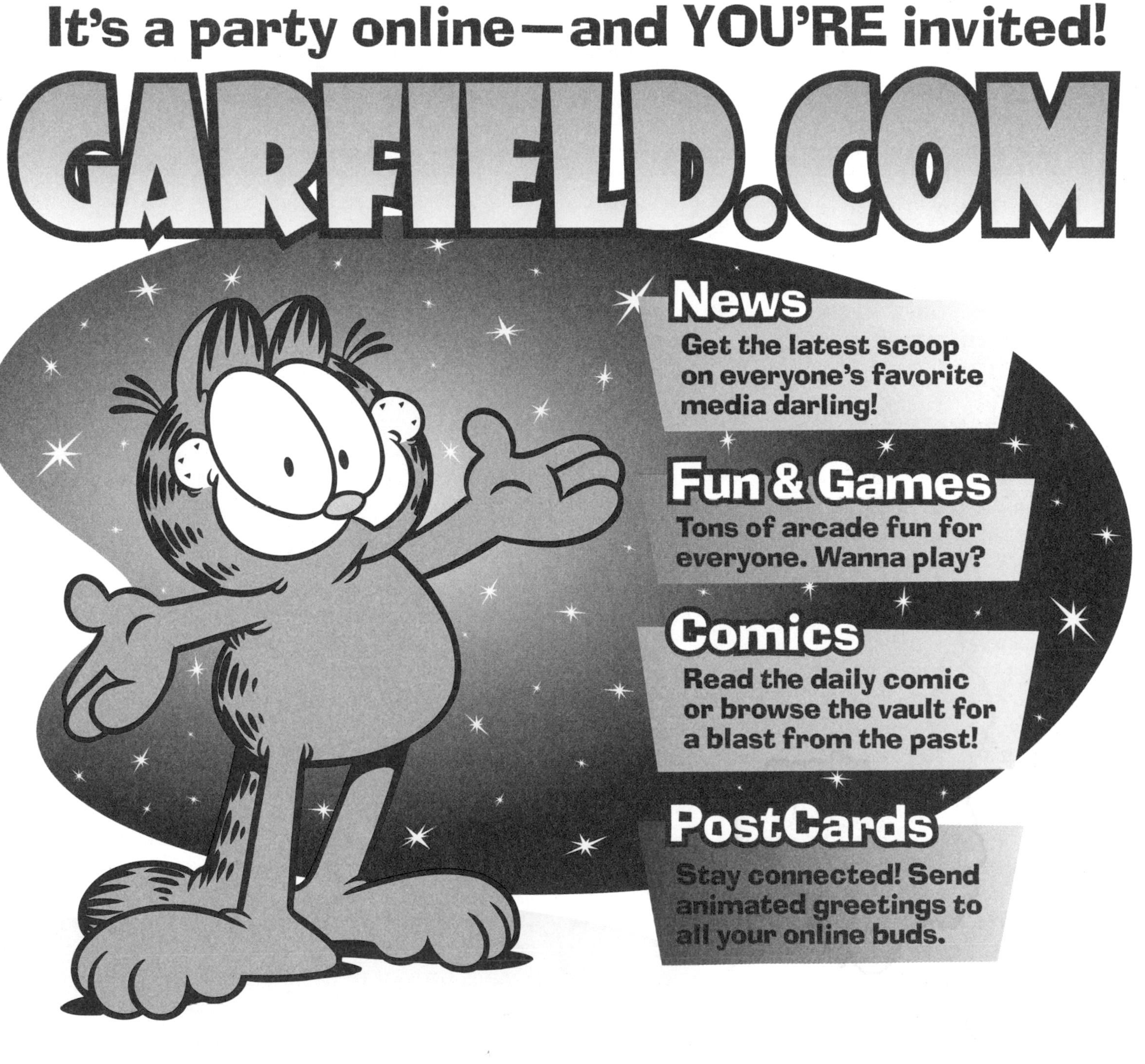
It's a party online—and YOU'RE invited!
GARFIELD.COM
News
Get the latest scoop on everyone's favorite media darling!
Fun & Games
Tons of arcade fun for everyone. Wanna play?
Comics
Read the daily comic or browse the vault for a blast from the past!
PostCards
Stay connected! Send animated greetings to all your online buds.

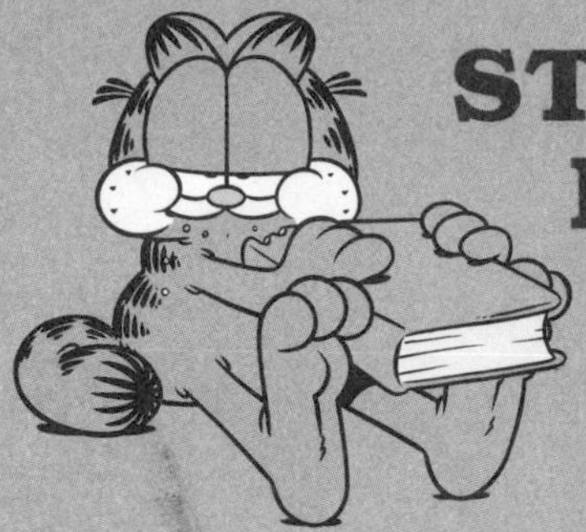

STRIPS, SPECIALS, OR BESTSELLING BOOKS . . . GARFIELD'S ON EVERYONE'S MENU.

Don't miss even one episode in the Tubby Tabby's hilarious series!

GARFIELD AT LARGE ....(#1) 978-0-345-44382-3
GARFIELD GAINS WEIGHT ....(#2) 978-0-345-44975-7
GARFIELD BIGGER THAN LIFE ....(#3) 978-0-345-45027-2
GARFIELD WEIGHS IN ....(#4) 978-0-345-45205-4
GARFIELD TAKES THE CAKE ....(#5) 978-0-345-44978-8
GARFIELD EATS HIS HEART OUT........(#6) 978-0-345-46459-0
GARFIELD SITS AROUND THE HOUSE..(#7) 978-0-345-46463-7
GARFIELD TIPS THE SCALES ....(#8) 978-0-345-46909-0
GARFIELD LOSES HIS FEET.................(#9) 978-0-345-46467-5
GARFIELD MAKES IT BIG....................(#10) 978-0-345-46468-2
GARFIELD ROLLS ON ....(#11) 978-0-345-47561-9
GARFIELD OUT TO LUNCH.................(#12) 978-0-345-47562-6
GARFIELD FOOD FOR THOUGHT......(#13) 978-0-345-47563-3
GARFIELD SWALLOWS HIS PRIDE....(#14) 978-0-345-34725-1
GARFIELD WORLDWIDE ....(#15) 978-0-345-35158-6
GARFIELD ROUNDS OUT....................(#16) 978-0-345-35388-7
GARFIELD CHEWS THE FAT...............(#17) 978-0-345-35956-8
GARFIELD GOES TO WAIST ....(#18) 978-0-345-36430-2
GARFIELD HANGS OUT.......................(#19) 978-0-345-36835-5
GARFIELD TAKES UP SPACE ....(#20) 978-0-345-37029-7
GARFIELD SAYS A MOUTHFUL ....(#21) 978-0-345-37368-7
GARFIELD BY THE POUND.................(#22) 978-0-345-37579-7
GARFIELD KEEPS HIS CHINS UP ......(#23) 978-0-345-37959-7
GARFIELD TAKES HIS LICKS..............(#24) 978-0-345-38170-5
GARFIELD HITS THE BIG TIME ....(#25) 978-0-345-38332-7
GARFIELD PULLS HIS WEIGHT..........(#26) 978-0-345-38666-3
GARFIELD DISHES IT OUT..................(#27) 978-0-345-39287-9
GARFIELD LIFE IN THE FAT LANE .....(#28) 978-0-345-39776-8
GARFIELD TONS OF FUN....................(#29) 978-0-345-40386-5
GARFIELD BIGGER AND BETTER......(#30) 978-0-345-40770-2
GARFIELD HAMS IT UP ....(#31) 978-0-345-41241-6
GARFIELD THINKS BIG........................(#32) 978-0-345-41671-1
GARFIELD THROWS HIS WEIGHT AROUND ....(#33) 978-0-345-42749-6
GARFIELD LIFE TO THE FULLEST .....(#34) 978-0-345-43239-1
GARFIELD FEEDS THE KITTY ....(#35) 978-0-345-43673-3
GARFIELD HOGS THE SPOTLIGHT ...(#36) 978-0-345-43922-2
GARFIELD BEEFS UP ....(#37) 978-0-345-44109-6
GARFIELD GETS COOKIN' ....(#38) 978-0-345-44582-7
GARFIELD EATS CROW ....(#39) 978-0-345-45201-6
GARFIELD SURVIVAL OF THE FATTEST ....(#40) 978-0-345-46458-3
GARFIELD OLDER AND WIDER..........(#41) 978-0-345-46462-0
GARFIELD PIGS OUT ....(#42) 978-0-345-46466-8

DVD TIE-INS

GARFIELD AS HIMSELF................................978-0-345-47805-4
GARFIELD HOLIDAY CELEBRATIONS.........978-0-345-47930-3
GARFIELD TRAVEL ADVENTURES 978-0-345-48087-3

AND DON'T MISS...

GARFIELD AT 25: IN DOG YEARS I'D BE DEAD 978-0-345-45204-7
GARFIELD'S JOKE ZONE/INSULTS.............978-0-345-46263-3
GARFIELD FAT CAT 3-PACK/ VOL. 1 978-0-345-46455-2
GARFIELD FAT CAT 3-PACK/ VOL. 2 978-0-345-46465-1
GARFIELD FAT CAT 3-PACK/ VOL. 13 978-0-345-46460-6
SEASON'S EATINGS: A VERY MERRY GARFIELD CHRISTMAS 978-0-345-47560-2
GARFIELD'S GUIDE TO EVERYTHING 978-0-345-46461-3
ODIE UNLEASHED! 978-0-345-46464-4
GARFIELD'S BOOK OF CAT NAMES............978-0-345-48516-8
THE GARFIELD JOURNAL............................978-0-345-46469-9
LIGHTS, CAMERA, HAIRBALLS!: GARFIELD AT THE MOVIES 978-0-345-49134-3

(#1–#13 marked with paw icon:) **New larger, full-color format!**